Digital Methodologies in the Sociology of Religion

Also available from Bloomsbury

Mediating Religion, Jolyon P. Mitchell

The Bloomsbury Companion to Religion and Film, edited by William L. Blizek

Media, Spiritualities and Social Change, edited by Stewart M. Hoover and
   Monica M. Emerich

Islamic Education in Britain, Alison Scott-Baumann and Sariya Cheruvallil-Contractor

Religion or Belief, Discrimination and Equality, Paul Weller, Kingsley Purdam, Nazila
   Ghanea and Sariya Cheruvallil-Contractor

Digital Methodologies in the Sociology of Religion

Edited by
Sariya Cheruvallil-Contractor
and Suha Shakkour

Bloomsbury Academic
An imprint of Bloomsbury Publishing Plc

B L O O M S B U R Y
LONDON • OXFORD • NEW YORK • NEW DELHI • SYDNEY

Bloomsbury Academic

An imprint of Bloomsbury Publishing Plc

50 Bedford Square	1385 Broadway
London	New York
WC1B 3DP	NY 10018
UK	USA

www.bloomsbury.com

BLOOMSBURY and the Diana logo are trademarks of Bloomsbury Publishing Plc

First published 2016

British Library Cataloguing-in-Publication Data
A catalogue record for this book is available from the British Library.

ISBN:	HB:	978-1-4725-7116-8
	PB:	978-1-4725-7115-1
	ePDF:	978-1-4725-7117-5
	ePub:	978-1-4725-7118-2

Library of Congress Cataloging-in-Publication Data
Digital methodologies in the sociology of religion / edited by
Sariya Cheruvallil-Contractor and Suha Shakkour. — 1 [edition].
pages cm
Includes bibliographical references and index.
ISBN 978-1-4725-7116-8 (hb) — ISBN 978-1-4725-7115-1 (pb) —
ISBN 978-1-4725-7117-5 (epdf) — ISBN 978-1-4725-7118-2 (epub)
1. Religion and sociology. 2. Social media—Religious aspects.
3. Digital media—Religious aspects. I. Cheruvallil-Contractor,
Sariya, editor.
BL60.D535 2015
306.60285—dc23
2015017888

Typeset by RefineCatch Limited, Bungay, Suffolk
Printed and bound in Great Britain

Contents

Figures

Contributors

Chris Allen is a Lecturer in the Institute of Applied Social Studies at the University of Birmingham having previously been Director of Research and Policy at a national equalities agency. For the past decade and a half, he has been undertaking research into Islamophobia and other discriminatory phenomena. This has included researching the experience of victims of Islamophobic hate crimes and the ideologies of the British far-right among others. As well as publishing widely and appearing in the media regularly, he was until recently an independent member of the Government's Anti-Muslim Hate Working Group.

Brian Altenhofen is a PhD candidate in Communication at Texas A&M University with a focus on media studies. His research interests include new media, digital culture and negotiations of authority within the Catholic Church. He has completed research in the areas of religious mobile apps and religious use of social media.

Daniel Arasa is currently Associate Professor of Digital Communications and Vice Dean of the Communications School at Santa Croce, having taught there since 2011. He has a Bachelor's Degree in Journalism from the Universitat Autònoma de Barcelona (UAB), Spain, an MA in Television and Radio from the Southern Methodist University (SMU), Dallas, TX, and a PhD in Social Institutional Communications by the Pontificia Università della Santa Croce, Rome, Italy. He worked from 1994 to 1997 as a journalist in Europa Press news agency (Spain). Moreover, he is a member of the Board of Directors of *Rome Reports TV*, a news agency specialized in the coverage of the Pope, the Vatican and the Catholic Church. He is author of *Church Communications Through Diocesan Websites. A Model of Analysis* (2008), and co-editor of *Religious Internet Communication. Facts, Experiences and Trends in the Catholic Church* (2010) and *Church Communication & the Culture of Controversy* (2010).

William Sims Bainbridge is a director of the Cyber-Human Systems Program at the National Science Foundation, and earned his doctorate in Sociology from Harvard University. He has published extensively in the sociology and history of religion, as well as many technology-related studies and computer software. With Rodney Stark, he published *The Future of Religion* (University of California Press, 1985), *A Theory of Religion* (Lang, 1987), and *Religion, Deviance and Social Control* (Routledge, 1996).

Other religion books include *Satan's Power* (University of California Press, 1978), *The Sociology of Religious Movements* (Routledge, 1997), *The Endtime Family* (State University of New York Press, 2002), *God from the Machine: Artificial Intelligence Models of Religious Belief* (AltaMira, 2006) and *Across the Secular Abyss* (Lexington, 2007). Recent related works are *The Warcraft Civilization* (MIT Press, 2010), *eGods: Faith Versus Fantasy in Computer Gaming* (Oxford University Press, 2013) and *An Information Technology Surrogate for Religion* (Palgrave-Macmillan, 2014).

Boris H. J. M. Brummans is an Associate Professor in the Département de Communication at the Université de Montréal in Canada. His research interests include the communicative constitution of organizations, mindful organizing, organizational conflict and organizational ethnography. He has contributed chapters to several edited books and his articles appear in international peer-reviewed journals such as *Communication Monographs*, *Human Relations*, *Information*, *Communication & Society*, *Journal of International and Intercultural Communication*, *Management Communication Quarterly* and *Qualitative Inquiry*.

Heidi A. Campbell is an Associate Professor of Communication at Texas A&M University where she teaches in media, religion and culture, and Director of the Network for New Media, Religion and Digital Culture Studies (http://digitalreligion.tamu.edu). She is author of *Exploring Religious Community Online* (Peter Lang, 2005) and *When Religion Meets New Media* (Routledge, 2010) and editor of *Digital Religion: Understanding Religious Practice in New Media World* (Routledge, 2013) and *Digital Judaism* (Routledge, 2015). She is widely published and has been quoted as an expert on religion and digital culture in such outlets as the *Chicago Tribune*, *Los Angeles Times*, *Wall Street Journal* and on the *BBC Radio World Service*.

Isamar Carrillo Masso has taught English, Literature, Linguistics and Media Studies since 1997 in Venezuela, Taiwan, the Czech Republic, Oman, and since 2009, in the UK. She has done research in Jewish Studies since 2001. Ms Carrillo Masso graduated with distinction in 2008 from Reading University, and is currently finishing a PhD at Bangor University, where she lectures in Media and Cultural Studies and functions as Copy-Editor to the *Journal of Gaming and Virtual Worlds*. Her research interests include transdisciplinary research methodologies, portrayals and performance of masculinities, mental illness, humour in discourse, and feminist critique of traditional and new media.

Pauline Hope Cheong is an Associate Professor at the Hugh Downs School of Human Communication, Arizona State University. She studies the complex interactions between communication technologies and different cultural communities around the world, including changing authority and community relations in spiritual organizing. Dr Cheong has published more than sixty articles and books, including articles in international peer reviewed journals such as *Journal of Computer Mediated Communication*, *Journal of Communication, Information, Communication & Society*, *The Information Society* and *New Media & Society*. She is the Lead Editor of *Digital Religion, Social Media and Culture: Perspectives, Practices, Futures* and *New Media and Intercultural Communication: Identity, Community and Politics*. She has received several research book and paper awards by the National and International Communication Associations.

Sariya Cheruvallil-Contractor is a Research Fellow at the Centre of Trust, Peace and Social Relations, Coventry University, UK. Prior to this, she worked at the universities of Derby and Gloucestershire. She specializes in the Sociology of Religion with particular emphasis on democratic research methodologies that seek to work *with* and *for* research participants. She is the author of *Muslim Women in Britain: Demystifying the Muslimah* (Routledge, 2012), co-author with Paul Weller, Nazila Ghanea and Kingsley Purdam of *Religion or Belief, Discrimination and Equality: Britain in Global Contexts* (Bloomsbury, 2013) and is co-author with Alison Scott-Baumann of *Islamic Education in Britain: New Pluralist Paradigms* (Bloomsbury, 2015).

Simone Heidbrink is a junior researcher and PhD candidate at the Institute of Religious Studies, University of Heidelberg, Germany. After majoring in Religious and Japanese Studies in Heidelberg and Nara (Japan), she received her Master's degree in 2005 and is now about to finish her doctoral thesis on a Christian liturgical reform movement called 'Emerging Church', which relies heavily on so-called 'Web 2.0' internet applications to distribute their views on Christianity, theology and the role of rituals. From 2005 to 2011 she was a member of the Collaborative Research Center 'Dynamics of Rituals' in the context of which she conducted research on websites, in social media and in the virtual 3D environment 'Second Life'. Simone's research focus is Rituals Studies, religion in museum contexts, (digital) Media Studies, the methods and theories of internet research as well as religion in digital games and gaming.

Tristram Hooley is a Professor in Career Education and Head of the International Centre for Guidance Studies at the University of Derby. He has research interests in the role of technology in education and research, career guidance policy and practice and the role of appearance and attractiveness in career. He has written extensively on the internet and online research methods and is the author of *What is Online Research?: Using the Internet for Social Science Research* (2012).

Tim Hutchings is a sociologist of digital religion. His PhD (Durham University, 2010) was an ethnographic study of five online Christian churches, exploring issues of authority, worship, community and the relationship between online and offline religion. He has subsequently completed postdoctoral research projects on digital storytelling and testimony (HUMlab, Umeå University, Sweden), digital Bible reading (CRESC, The Open University) and digital pilgrimage (CODEC, Durham University). Dr Hutchings' publications include articles in the *Nordic Journal of Religion & Society*, *Information, Communication & Society* and the *Australian Journal of Communication*, and book chapters in *Religion, Media and Social Change* (Routledge, 2015), *Digital Religion* (ed. Heidi Campbell, Routledge, 2013) and *Digital Religion, Social Media and Culture* (Peter Lang, 2012). Dr Hutchings is the Editor of the *Journal of Religion, Media and Digital Culture*.

Jennie M. Hwang is an Invited Researcher at the Département de Communication at Université de Montréal in Canada. Her research focuses on the effects of new technologies on individual well-being and learning, as well as children and media. She has contributed chapters to several edited books and her articles appear in international peer-reviewed journals such as *Information, Communication & Society*, *Journal of International and Intercultural Communication*, *Management Communication Quarterly* and *New Media & Society*.

Tobias Knoll is a junior researcher and PhD candidate at the Institute of Religious Studies, University of Heidelberg, Germany as well as an avid podcaster on all things related to gaming and geek culture. Having majored in Religious Studies and Political Science of South Asia, he received his Master's degree in 2012. Tobias is currently working on his doctoral thesis on religious implications and reception of moral decision-making systems in digital games like Mass Effect. His general focus of research is contemporary religion and player agency in video games as well as reception of, and discourse on, religion in popular geek and nerd culture.

Peter J. Martini is a doctoral candidate in the Interdisciplinary Social Psychology Program at the University of Nevada, Reno. His research interests include the intersection of health and identity, particularly within sexual orientation and religious minority groups. His methodological research focuses on the use of digital modes to reach hidden populations. His current research examines the impact of social network characteristics and minority identity on health and mental health, primarily using the minority stress model. He currently works at the Grant Sawyer Center for Justice Studies and serves as an instructor in applied statistics and consultant in the areas of quantitative and research methodology.

Juan Narbona is an Assistant Professor of Digital Communication at the School of Institutional Communications of the Pontifical University of the Holy Cross (Rome), and a journalist specializing in the internet and religion. Since 2000, he has also been the webmaster of Opus Dei, an institution of the Catholic Church (www.opusdei.org). He received his PhD in 2012, in which he focused on 'Online Communication of Humanitarian Nonprofit Institutions'.

Anna Piela is a lecturer in religious studies at Leeds Trinity University, teaching mostly sociology of religion and Islam-related modules. Her main research interests are gender, media and Islam. Her PhD, conducted at the Centre of Women's Studies at the University of York, was focused on women's contemporary readings of Islamic sources conducted in online discussion groups. In addition to the monograph *Muslim Women Online: Faith and Identity in Virtual Space* which was based on her PhD, she has published articles in *The Muslim World*, *Feminist Media Studies*, and other journals. She has also presented papers at major international conferences in religion and society, most recently at the British Association for the Study of Religion biannual conference. Currently she is working on her new research monograph *Wearing the Niqab: Fashioning Identity among Muslim Women in the UK*. She has also recently been commissioned to edit a four-volume collection of articles titled *Islam and Media* for the Routledge series *Critical Concepts in Islamic Studies*. Anna's last media engagement was participation in a debate about polygamy on the 'Forbidden Talk' programme on *Levant TV*.

Stephen Pihlaja is a Senior Lecturer in Stylistics at Newman University, Birmingham (UK). He holds a PhD in Applied Linguistics from the Open University. He researches language use in interaction online, particularly among people of different faiths and no faith on YouTube and social media. His first monograph, entitled *Antagonism on YouTube* describes an instance of 'drama' – or antagonistic debate – among Christians and atheists on YouTube. He is also a visiting research fellow at Heythrop College, University of London.

James T. Richardson, J.D., is a Professor of Sociology and Judicial Studies at the University of Nevada, Reno, where he is director of the Judicial Studies graduate degree program for trial judges, which is offered in conjunction with the National Judicial College and the National Council of Juvenile and Family Court Judges, both of which are headquartered on the university campus. He does research on new and other minority religious groups and how they are dealt with by governments and courts. His recent books include *Regulating Religion: Case Studies from around the Globe* (Kluwer, 2004), *Legal Cases* Involving *New Religions and Other Minority Faiths* (with Francois Bellanger, Ashgate, 2014), *Sociology of Sharia: Case Studies from around the World* (with Adam Possamai and Bryan Turner, Springer, 2014) and *Saints under Siege: The Texas State Raid on the Fundamentalist Latter Day Saints* (with Stuart Wright, New York University Press, 2011).

Heinz Scheifinger is an Assistant Professor of Sociology at King Fahd University of Petroleum and Minerals, Saudi Arabia. His research has largely focused on the intersection of Hinduism and digital media, and he has published a number of journal articles and book chapters which consider this from various angles. These include 'The *Jagannath* Temple and Online *Darshan*' in *Journal of Contemporary Religion* 24 (3): 233–49, 'Hindu Worship Online and Offline' in *Digital Religion – Understanding Religious Practice in New Media Worlds* (Routledge, 2013) and 'New Technology and

Change in the Hindu Tradition: The Internet in Historical Perspective' in *Asian Religions, Technology and Science* (Routledge, 2015).

Suha Shakkour is a Senior Lecturer in Sociology at the University of Derby. She received her BA and MA from the University of Western Ontario and her PhD from the University of St Andrews. Her research focuses on the integration and assimilation of Christian Palestinians in Britain, identity development among religious and ethnic minorities, and the experiences of Palestinian communities at home and in the diaspora.

Jasjit Singh is a research fellow at the University of Leeds based in the School of Philosophy, Religion and the History of Science. His research examines the religious lives of British South Asians with a particular focus on understanding processes of religious and cultural transmission and the different arenas in which this transmission occurs. To date he has examined the relationship between traditional arenas of religious learning (including the family environment and religious institutions) and newer arenas of transmission often organized by young people including camps, University faith societies and the internet. He has recently undertaken a project examining the role of the arts and music in religious learning and has a growing interest in the role of media.

Victoria A. Springer is a graduate of the interdisciplinary Social Psychology program at the University of Nevada, Reno. Her research interests include advancing the methodological techniques used to identify and access hidden or hard-to-reach populations, with a specific focus on understanding motivations, values, beliefs, and identity-related aspects of minority or marginalized groups. Her most recent methodological work in press (written with her chapter co-authors) compares the characteristics of crowdsourced online survey respondents obtained through Amazon's Mechanical Turk (MTurk) to nationally representative samples. She currently works in the private sector as an associate research manager for Adobe Systems, Inc. as part of a decision research team that specializes in new and emerging markets and innovative product development.

Paul Weller is a Professor of Inter-Religious Relations at the University of Derby where he is employed as University Research Excellence Framework and Research Student Academic Manager. He is also Visiting Fellow in the Oxford Centre for Christianity and Culture at Regent's Park College, University of Oxford. He was one of the founders; has been Vice Chair; and is currently a Trustee of the Multi-Faith Centre at the University of Derby. In the late 1990s, together with colleagues at the University of Derby he developed MultiFaithNet, an on-line resource for religions and inter-religious relations. He was academic lead on the 'Religion and Belief in Higher Education: Researching the Experiences of Staff and Students' research project commissioned by the Equality Challenge Unit and which features in his co-authored (with Tristram Hooley, with whom he also worked on this project) chapter in this volume. He was

Principal Investigator of the 'Religion and Belief, Discrimination and Equality in England and Wales: Theory, Policy and Practice, 2000–2010' research project that also features in Weller's co-authored chapter along with the 'Learning from Experience, Leading to Engagement: Belieforama Policy Brief Research for European Institutions and Civil Societies' research into Belieforama's anti-discrimination training around religion or belief and other equalities matters, of which Weller was academic lead, working with Sariya Cheruvallil-Contractor, the co-editor of this volume.

Jan Wysocki is currently working and teaching at the Institute of Religious Studies in the University of Heidelberg, Germany. He received his Master's Degree in Religious Studies in 2014 writing his thesis about the transformation of American religious symbols in *BioShock Infinite* and how religious actors are stereotyped in the game. For his doctoral thesis he is planning on exploring the notion of 'god' in digital games based on an article written in collaboration with Markus Wiemker. His main academic interest lies in the synthesis of Religious Studies and Game Studies. But he is also fond of topics like comparative theory, the religious history of America, as well as the great realm of popular culture. Together with Simone Heidbrink and Tobias Knoll he is working on *Online – Heidelberg Journal of Religions on the Internet*.

Acknowledgements

We begin by acknowledging the support of Economic and Social Research Council, UK (ESRC) for providing the initial seed funding for this project under its Digital Social Research (DSR) initiative. We would specifically like to thank Dr Megan Meredith-Lobay from DSR for her support.

This funding was used to bring together a cross-disciplinary group of sociologists working on online religion or belief to discuss their methodologies and the challenges they faced. We would like to thank all the delegates who attended this event and who shared their expertise and added momentum to this project. Special thanks are due to all the contributors to this volume who have spent time and energy to craft their initial discussions into full length chapters. This book would not have been possible without their efforts.

Colleagues at Bloomsbury have bought this book to life. We would like to thank Lalle Pursglove and Anna Macdiarmid for their commitment to this project and for their support throughout the publication process. Thanks are due to Kathy John for her excellent co-ordination of the pre-press stage of the book and for ensuring that everything stayed on schedule. Finally we would like to thank Sara Marchington for undertaking the copy-editing of this book, Suzy McGill, Giles Herman and other colleagues at Bloomsbury.

We also thank the University of Derby and the Centre for Society, Religion and Belief (SRB) for providing an academic home to this research, and we acknowledge in particular all the support received from Dr Kristin Aune (the then director of the SRB).

Finally, we thank our families for being patient with us when we were lost in editorial tasks and for their encouragement throughout this process.

Introduction: Digital Methodologies in the Sociology of Religion

Sariya Cheruvallil-Contractor and Suha Shakkour

As digital religious or belief communities and online identities become increasingly common, our approach to their study must necessarily adapt, and alongside this our understanding of the contexts, challenges, advantages and ethics of using digital methodologies. Drawing on a series of research examples, this book explores the epistemological underpinnings and rationale for the use of digital methodologies, and considers the ethical dilemmas and implementation difficulties faced by researchers in the Sociology of Religion. There is a burgeoning recognition of the significance of digital contexts, resources and methods in the Social Sciences and Humanities, and the rise in easy access to digital technologies has had a significant impact on how we represent ourselves, perceive our environment and interact with one another. As our online social interactions and digital selves become significant aspects of our lives, it is important that methods to study the digital are developed, prototyped, implemented and documented. Within the sociology of religion there is an urgent need for more theorizing and practical engagement with the opportunities that the 'digital' brings to this genre of study.

The sociology of religion: A (very) brief discussion

In this book, we conceptualize the sociology of religion as an interdisciplinary field that 'has as its subject the study of religion in its social context' (Furseth and Repstad 2006: 5). It deals with everyday lived religion as experienced in human interactions, communities and groups, which can often be different from scriptural or doctrinal religion. When working in the sociology of religion, interdisciplinarity is necessary as the intricacies of human life rarely fit into neat categories. So, for example, while on the one hand religious belief can lead to art and creative production, on the other hand it can necessitate the needs for laws and social policies that govern inter-faith and inter-community relations.

Therefore, in keeping with the tradition of interdisciplinary cooperation within the sociology of religion, this volume brings together scholars from a number of different disciplines and on a wide variety of subjects including feminism and women's studies, religious studies, social policy, sociology and theology – all of whom employ digital methodologies in their research. Given how new the field is, this book is intended both as a teaching tool and a reference guide that will help form the foundation of future research. It begins a process of 'joined-up', interdisciplinary, intellectual consideration of the role, and significance of, digital methods and contexts that begins to unpack some of the complexities associated with applying new methodologies.

Digital religion or belief

Religion or belief (including non-religious beliefs) can be understood as the philosophical worldviews that people live their lives by. Irrespective of whether these worldviews are derived from divine scripture or from rational human minds (or indeed from both), they must always respond to the contexts of believers, and in this sense they are in a constant state of flux. For a moment then, if we look at religious belief only, it may be described as a complex, ever-changing and contested confluence of divine revelation, prophetic guidance, scripture and ritual deriving from a theological standpoint. In the monotheistic religions at least, religious belief revolves around a constant centre – God – the certainty of whom is a source of solace for believers of all predilections (Cheruvallil-Contractor 2013). Non-religious belief may be defined by 'a relationship of difference to religion' (Lee 2012: 131) but also, and perhaps more significantly, as independent of religion and as the metaphysical positioning of a growing number of people, which is also similarly complex, ever-changing and contested. In this case, the focus of belief could be an overarching philosophical commitment to rational thinking.

From a sociological perspective, whether we are discussing religious or non-religious belief, the focus of research is the people who believe – people who determine the societal impact of religion or belief and who through their cultural milieus, habits and ways of believing have the capacity and agency to change religion. Religious and non-religious belief is constantly adapting to the social contexts, needs and eccentricities of religious and non-religiovs people. Thus, religion must adapt to diverse cultures, traditions, and now also to changing technologies.

The twentieth century saw the rise of religious television and radio programming, evangelical TV preachers and live broadcasts of sermons (Deacy and Arweck 2009). All of these necessarily affected the way that people experienced their faith. In the twenty-first century, the internet has gone further and changed both the way that people experience, as well as crucially, the way that they interact with and express their faith – moving social and spiritual lives from offline to online contexts. While these will possibly (and hopefully!) never be fully digitized, sociologists are observing an increasing reliance on digital technologies to express values, allegiances and multifaceted identities. If we are to fully understand how digital technology is changing social interactions, new research approaches that draw on digital methodologies become necessary, and sociologists of religion are both contributing to the field and learning as they go.

It is no longer unusual to find research projects and papers that explore online faith communities or particular aspects of faith communities' online practices (e.g. digital storytelling used to facilitate inter-faith dialogue in Cheruvallil-Contractor 2012; exploration of Muslim women's online religious identity in Piela 2011; cyber Islamic environments in Bunt 2009; Catholic congregations' use of internet communication in Cantoni and Zyga 2007). While researchers are in agreement about the growing social impact of digital religion or beliefs and the need to critically examine these, there is significantly less discussion of the methodologies that are being used to undertake these explorations. This volume addresses this gap in the literature by bringing together academics who are involved in researching different forms of belief to reflect on the 'digital' nature of the methodologies that they used and to encourage cross-fertilization of expertise, methodological innovation and collective learning. Yet alongside this, we recognize the need to reflect upon the impact this 'digitization' is having on religion. Campbell and Altenhofen, for instance, address this in Chapter 1 by considering the ways in which digital religion encompasses not only how religion is performed online, but also how religious communities have adapted, responded to and engaged with digital culture. Slightly paradoxically, as Springer et al. (Chapter 3) and Cheruvallil-Contractor (Chapter 6) point out, we also need to reflect upon the fact that not everyone will have access to the internet. This must be borne in mind when setting our terms of reference or objectives for research. Digital methods may only be used for groups and subgroups that have sufficient access to the internet to make the research findings meaningful. As previously noted, research in the field of digital religion is still in its relatively early stages, and this volume seeks to address the theoretical, practical and ethical dilemmas that have arisen. For instance, what are the epistemological underpinnings and rationale for the use of 'digital' methodologies? What ethical dilemmas do sociologists face while seeking to protect participants' interests in digital contexts that are often perceived as anonymized and therefore 'safe'? What measures should researchers take to ensure their own safety while conducting research online? Furthermore, implementing such 'digital' research also leads to practical challenges such as mismatched expectations of IT skills, limited access to specialized tools, project management, and remote management of research processes. By using research case studies, this book illustrates good practice, explores what is possible and what is not, and considers how complicated tensions and conflicting interests may be managed. In its coverage of what is happening in the 'field' it takes into account the needs of both students and young scholars who are seeking guidance in planning their first research projects, as well as established researchers who want awareness and knowledge of current research.

Reflecting on methods

The projects in this book are wide ranging in their approaches and include conceptual and theoretical discussions as well the practical challenges associated with utilizing a number of different technologies. In each chapter, the authors have analysed and reflected on research projects that focus on digital religion or belief. In Chapter 14, for example, Heidbrink, Knoll and Wysocki consider how best to approach research on religion in digital games; in Chapter 10 Piela discusses the use of Skype as a way to interview difficult to reach respondents; and in Chapter 9 Hutchings focuses on how YouVersion's 'Bible App' has changed how Christians interact with and explore their faith online.

The diverse range of digital methodologies used reflects the immense possibilities that the internet has produced for both users and researchers, and within this context, it is essential that we recognize the strengths and weaknesses associated with every methodological choice that we make, regardless of the field. As researchers, we choose specific research tools, negotiate access, reflect on our own positionality within the research and consider the ethical implications of all the choices that we make – all while bearing in mind that, ultimately, the methodology we choose should effectively and efficiently address the research questions to which we are seeking answers. As students, and even as seasoned researchers, it can be tempting to simply rely on methods that we are familiar with, ones that are 'tried and true'. To do so, however, would both hinder our progress as researchers and prevent us from exploring new social phenomena. Furthermore, as in the case of digital/online religion or belief, the 'familiar' methods are simply no longer sufficient, and even where we can use them, we need to tweak, adjust and amend them to be suited to the 'digital-ness' of the field.

The projects featured in this book, and the researchers that led them, are at the forefront of this movement towards developing new methods and methodologies that are appropriate and fit-for-purpose to engage with and analyse digital religion. These researchers have had to undergo the cycle of choosing methods and then adapting them to suit the digital contexts within which they were undertaking their research. They have had many successes that contributed to great achievements within their work. Yet, just as with every researcher, they have struggled and encountered hurdles, which meant that they had to go back to the drawing board. All the contributors in this volume reflect on their journey, setting out what worked and what did not work. They clarify why they chose the methods they used and their competence to deal with the issues they were exploring. In reflectively writing about their methodological choices, these researchers advance our understandings of digital methodologies and leave a conceptual and analytic 'trail' that other researchers may follow (Huberman and Miles 2002).

What about ethics?

In editing this book we realized that while undertaking digital research, particularly on a subject as sensitive as religion, ethical considerations require perhaps the greatest amount of reflection. First the dynamics of research are different. For example, although we are trained to put the safety and privacy of our respondents before the aims of our projects, how can we do so when the respondents themselves may be unknown, hidden behind online profiles – and in many cases difficult to identify or locate? Do we abandon our projects entirely? Do we take greater measures to ensure their privacy without compromising the integrity of our work or endangering ourselves in the process? And if so, then how?

Furthermore, while the real identities of research participants are not always known, the researcher is always known and has to be transparent about his or her identity. Indeed, in Chapter 8, Singh comments on the need for researchers to have an established 'staff profile' on their university webpages, which they can use to introduce themselves to research participants. According to him, being publicly visible and transparent about one's identity can encourage participation in the research because participants feel they know and can trust the researcher. On the other hand, however, this can create an additional dilemma for researchers. In digital research, the researcher is always known (or at least, should be, ethically speaking), whereas usually only the digital identities of research participants are known. In such contexts, in her chapter (Chapter 6) Cheruvallil-Contractor suggests that it is important to reflect upon and consider frameworks to ensure protection of the researcher's privacy and security.

Second, there is the problem of the 'fuzziness' between the public and the private on the internet. Although the internet is largely a public space, there nevertheless remains an (albeit frequently unspoken) expectation of privacy – or at least an expectation that the information that people share will generally be sought only by individuals who are interested in similar ideas, and certainly not by researchers seeking to analyse their contributions. In addition to this, there is the issue that people do not always recognize how public the internet is and that, often, what they post is accessible to individuals beyond their immediate families, friends and professional networks. And third, while research participants may believe that online they can be anonymous, technology that can track down internet users does exist. What implications does this have on assuring the anonymity and confidentiality of the research participants? As Allen rightly notes in Chapter 4, people say things online that they would not say offline, and as researchers we must be aware that the narratives we receive may be influenced by the perception of anonymity as well as the pressure to conform to online peer pressure.

Another important element to consider is positionality, and this is considered in many of the chapters in this book. The internet has necessarily changed the dynamics of conducting research, and the 'fuzziness' between the public and the private can have implications for how researchers represent themselves online, and crucially how they are perceived. First, in order to undertake research on a particular religious group in the online world, the researcher must have knowledge of its activities in the offline world. Second, traditional insider–outsider boundaries and researcher–researched hierarchies, as understood and experienced in the offline world, do not always remain the same in the online world, though naturally some similarities exist. Often, to be able to analyse a particular online community, the researcher must embed himself or herself in that community, becoming a part of it. This has the practical benefit of allowing the researcher to become aware of the culture, language and social norms within that group, thus allowing him or her to better collect, and then analyse the data. Yet, this also presents a number of ethical dilemmas: should the researcher participate within the group or should he or she be a mute spectator? What influence will the researcher's presence (including a silent presence) have on the group? What about objectivity and subjectivity – do these debates even matter anymore? A number of chapters in this volume discuss positionality, the issues authors faced and how they dealt with these issues.

The digitization of religion, and the need to research a sensitive subject online, has led to researchers being confronted by situations in which current ethical guidelines are no longer sufficient. There is an urgent need to develop new thinking and new ethical guidelines to underpin all research that is being conducted online – particularly for a subject area such as religion or belief, which is already highly sensitive. Through consolidating the experiences and expertise of a number of researchers, this volume initiates this process and seeks to extend our understanding of how to conduct ethically sound research within a constantly changing virtual field.

Structure of the book

This volume is divided into four parts: (1) Digitizing Research in the Sociology of Religion; (2) Social Networking Sites and Digital Ethnography; (3) Digital Communication; and (4) Virtual Reality and Religion. Each is aimed at providing insight into a different arena of digital religion and recommendations for how the reader may best approach his or her research project.

The first chapter in this book, by Campbell and Altenhofen, introduces readers to digital religion and charts the evolution of methodologies to study digital religion. Each subsequent chapter represents a specific research project or stream of research focusing on different religious or belief groups. Included within this volume are chapters on Hinduism, Sikhism, Christianity, Islam, Judaism and non-religion. Each chapter also discusses a number of different digital tools including Skype, YouTube, and online surveys, and considers religion or belief in a number of different contexts, including video games, online forums and virtual worlds.

This volume is intended as a theoretical and practical guide to readers, aimed at sharing good practice and encouraging researchers to explore this new field. Each section is, therefore, structured so that the reader can peek into the research journey as experienced by the author of that particular chapter. In so doing, the reader can gain insight into the research strategies used and analyse what worked and what did not. Included within each chapter is also a summary of the findings – the purpose of which is only to provide a context within which the methodology can be understood and studied. Methodology remains at the heart of each chapter, with a thorough discussion of the specific tools used and reflections on the practicalities, nuances, and of course, ethics and ethical considerations of the research. We believe that this is where advancements in digital methods are going to have to move fastest and furthest. Finally, each chapter includes two or three 'tips' that readers may use when undertaking their own research projects.

Chapter summaries

Part 1, Digitizing Research in the Sociology of Religion, begins in **Chapter 1** with a consideration of the evolution of digital methodologies that are used for the study of the sociology of religion. In this chapter, Campbell and Altenhofen present an overview of the evolution of digital methods used to study religion. More specifically, they focus on the unique methodological approaches and ethical challenges that scholars have had to consider within this unique area of scholarly inquiry over four waves of research. Campbell and Altenhofen reflect on the current and future challenges, and assert the urgency for an interdisciplinary common ground where scholars studying digital religion can come together to discuss methodology.

In **Chapter 2**, Hooley and Weller consider the benefits and challenges of utilizing online surveys both alone and as part of a mixed method project that also incorporated traditional postal surveys. Focusing on three different experiences, they guide the reader through the practical aspects of choosing the right online and offline tools (including the use of online surveys and framing questions appropriately for online and offline surveys), the difficulties associated with sampling an online and offline population (for instance, who is included/excluded with each approach and whether it is possible to incorporate online surveys into a pre-existing longitudinal study), and the ethical dilemmas faced (online surveys can, in some ways, distance the researcher from the researched – how do we ensure respondents' safety in an online space?). Throughout their work, Hooley and Weller encourage readers to carefully consider, and reconsider, their understanding of the digital religious world and its changing population, and in so doing design effective and ethically sound research projects.

In **Chapter 3** Springer et al. discuss the methodological considerations for using online crowdsourcing to reach special groups – they demonstrate how this tool can be used to reach mainstream and minority religious groups. They also consider the usefulness of this tool with regard to 'hidden' or 'hard-to-reach' groups such as those who may be marginalized or who face discrimination in society due to their beliefs, cultural background or behaviours. They discuss a 'replicable multi-stage survey approach' that they developed, to reduce homogeneity within samples and to access diverse views and opinions, not just the most dominant ones. They also present a consideration of the limitations of this approach in that not all social groups may be accessed through this method – for example religious groups that do not engage with modern technology will not be accessible through this method.

Part 2 is about digital ethnography and the study of religious and non-religious communities online. In the first chapter (**Chapter 4**) of this section, Allen highlights the growing incidence of public opposition towards the building and development of mosques in the West Midlands region in the United Kingdom and the use of social networking and new media – especially Facebook – to disseminate and garner support for such opposition. This chapter considers the challenges and pitfalls faced both as researcher and researched in relation to positioning, legitimacy and validity. It presents an incisive discussion about the blurring of the private and public in virtual spaces and the impact of this on social and research interactions online.

YouTube has become a key hub of content creation and consumption. The site attracts a variety of diverse users from divergent sociopolitical, geographic, and faith backgrounds. In **Chapter 5**, Pihlaja describes the research methods he employed to investigate the interaction between atheists and Christians on YouTube, looking particularly at how specific interactions led to antagonism and, what he calls, 'drama' among users. He uses a discourse-centred online ethnography to analyse language use in its context, thus enabling him to take into account ongoing narratives and storylines in particular communities.

In **Chapter 6**, Cheruvallil-Contractor presents a considered approach to conducting research within online Sufi discussion forums. Alongside a discussion of the practical challenges faced (for instance, which forum to choose, and when and how to participate in discussion threads), she also presents a consideration of the ethical dilemmas faced (including how to develop and maintain trust online and protect the identity of participants), and the need to ensure the safety of both the researched and the researcher (particularly in anonymous online forums, how do respondents understand the public and the private? And what are the implications of being 'known' to 'unknown' respondents?). Cheruvallil-Contractor frames her work within a Feminist-Pragmatist epistemological stance that encourages participants to be active members and leaders of the research project, thus creating an online space that is collaboratively developed.

In **Chapter 7**, Scheifinger discusses his research of digital Hinduism and considers how the internet has altered the religious experience with special reference to online *pujas*. He notes that, in addition to creating a more egalitarian space where previously inaccessible religious rituals can be performed, the internet has also provided a digital religious marketplace of sorts where different organizations must compete for followers. Drawing on both offline and online research strategies, Scheifinger considers how Rational Choice Theory may be applied to a digital religious marketplace to help broaden our understanding of how religions can develop within an already crowded online space. He further presents a thoughtful discussion of the ethics of conducting research within a digital religious sphere that encourages the reader to not think exclusively in terms of the 'online' and 'offline' field.

Chapter 8 presents a consideration of the ways in which young British Sikhs engage with their faith in an online context. Drawing on both online surveys and face-to-face interviews, Singh discusses the benefits and challenges of conducting mixed method research, and reflects on the practical as well as ethical implications associated with each approach. Throughout this work, he considers how the different reasons that young British Sikhs use digital spaces in the first place (for religious knowledge or for religious engagement) influence their online interactions. He further discusses the importance of continuously reflecting on one's positionality throughout the research process and the importance of being 'known' to respondents while ensuring their anonymity. By adapting his research methods to suit the needs of his participants, Singh emphasizes the need to think carefully about the population being studied and ensure that the methods used are tailored to each project.

Part 3 considers the effectiveness of digital communications. It begins with **Chapter 9**, in which Hutchings discusses approaches to studying religious software using YouVersion's 'Bible App' as a case study. Throughout this chapter, he considers both the impact of the software on users (for instance, does engaging with a digital, as opposed to more traditional, text impact the user's religious experience?) and the design of the software itself (including the arena in which the software was developed). In addressing these issues, Hutchings employs a mixed method approach utilizing both interviews and digital ethnography. Focusing primarily on the latter for this chapter, he discusses the practical and ethical challenges associated with digital ethnography in both an online (e.g. engaging with social media forums) and offline (e.g. working with religious app designers) space. In so doing, he encourages the reader both to consider how existing methods may be adapted for an online context and to think more broadly about methodological innovations necessary for a digital research era.

The niqab, or face veil, that some Muslim women wear has become a politically loaded symbol of Islam, denoting the Otherness of women who wear it. **Chapter 10** begins with a recognition that although many voices speak about the niqab, the women who wear it are seldom asked their opinion. In this chapter, Piela reflects on her use of videoconference interviews to engage with Muslim women who wear the niqab. She presents an in-depth discussion about the nuances of this tool, providing readers with detailed practical guidelines and ethical considerations that need to be borne in mind while using Skype.

In **Chapter 11** Arasa and Narbona consider the effectiveness of religious institutions' online presence. By developing an Online Communication Model (OCM), which analyses both their corporate (i.e. official websites) and public (i.e. social media) messages, the authors are able to consider how religious institutions can improve and maintain their relationship with their audiences. Drawing on the Catholic Relief Services as a case study, they discuss how by measuring the level and type of interaction by users, the OCM can be used to help to ensure an organization's online presence is continuously effective and suited to an ever-changing digital environment. They further present a thoughtful reflection of the challenges that religious institutions face online (including the ethical dilemmas) and consider what aspect of religion can, and crucially cannot, be transmitted online.

In **Chapter 12**, Cheong et al. draw upon their study of a Taiwanese Buddhist organization to examine how top-down and bottom-up communicative processes are used to construct religious authority. They trace the interpretative processes by which we come to understand the (re)construction of religious authority through multimedia productions and branding, as well as through lay invocation of a religious leader's mantras and aphorisms across social media communication platforms. In doing so, they outline a mixed methods communicative approach that they used to uncover how religious leaders are scripting their roles to perform under changing information flows and rising forms of global religiosity, as well as how believers are utilizing digital and social media to build a sense of global belonging.

Part 4 is about undertaking research about religion or belief in virtual reality contexts. It begins with **Chapter 13** in which Bainbridge considers the benefits and challenges of digital ethnography. Drawing on the popular multi-player online game, *World of Warcraft*, he considers the aspects of religious elements from the 'real world' that have been secularized within it. By presenting a thoughtful and practical consideration of conducting research in a virtual world, he encourages the reader to immerse him/herself in the field while continuously being aware of the ethical implications associated with this. Throughout this chapter, Bainbridge reflects on the wider context in which gameworlds exist, and discusses the importance of adapting one's methodologies within the sociology of religion to suit a changing field.

In **Chapter 14**, Heidbrink et al. present a practical and compelling guide to conducting research on religion in/and digital games, incorporating two different approaches. The first is aimed at researchers seeking to study religious elements within the games themselves, and the second focuses on researchers considering a player-centred approach that examines interactions within the game (as well as in reference, and in relation, to it). Throughout their chapter, the authors discuss the implications of undertaking each form of research and direct the reader through the various challenges they may face. This practical approach is complemented by a thoughtful discussion of the ethical considerations that must be taken into account, and concludes with a set of helpful points that encourage the reader to step beyond the known aspects of the digital field and begin to develop to their own methodologies.

In **Chapter 15**, Carrillo Masso combines critical and multimodal discourse analysis with corpus linguistics to develop a qualitative and quantitative method with which to undertake research on video games. Focusing on the game, *The Shivah: A Rabbinical Adventure* as a case study, she illustrates her methodology, specifically focusing on portrayals of Jewishness. Within this chapter, Carrillo Masso recommends the use of software such as FRAPS to record gameplay and Transana to manage and navigate data. She provides a useful discussion of the practicalities of undertaking such research, including a useful reminder to check copyrights and the legalities of accessing video games.

Concluding thoughts

This volume considers the digital methodologies and tools that are used to research online experiences and articulations of religion or belief (including non-religious belief). As elements of an individual's life that are often expressed both personally and publicly, conducting research on religion or belief necessarily requires us to be aware of cultural sensitivities, social etiquette, historical precedence, and contemporary political situations within and around the religion or belief group that we are studying. As with any project, we must be keenly aware of the implications of our research both on the individuals we are studying as well as the wider community of which they are a part. For instance, are we representing the individuals and groups honestly – and is this even possible? Have we taken adequate measures to ensure the safety of our respondents? Have the benefits of conducting this research outweighed the costs? And how do we begin to measure this? All of these considerations must also apply to research about religion or belief that is undertaken online, and as argued by the researchers in this book, even greater care must be taken when the respondents are unknown even to the researcher.

The internet has allowed a wide range of groups and individuals to come together, including those who traditionally did not – and in some cases, could not – interact. This meeting of diversity has had both a positive and negative impact. On the one hand, they have allowed individuals to connect with one another through their dedication to common causes or values. On the other hand, however, they have also enabled tense interactions to occur with greater frequency and ease. One no longer needs to be in physical proximity to known and unknown persons to direct attacks at them. Thus, for scholars engaged in the study of religion and belief, the internet has afforded us a great many advantages; however, these have come at the cost of making an already elaborate and potentially controversial field of research even more complicated. In this web of diversity and complexity, the authors of this volume leave a trail that future researchers can follow and develop.

Part 1 Digitizing Research in the Sociology of Religion

1 Methodological Challenges, Innovations and Growing Pains in Digital Religion Research

HEIDI A. CAMPBELL AND BRIAN ALTENHOFEN

The study of religion and new media is a unique area of scholarly inquiry, which is often referred to as the study of digital religion. Digital religion explores not just how religion is performed online, but how religious communities have adapted, responded to, and engaged with the digital culture. Digital religion is defined as,

> Religion that is constituted in new ways through digital media and cultures . . . this recognizes that the reformulation of existing religious practices have both online and offline implications. It also means digital culture negotiates our understandings of religious practice in ways that can lead to new experiences, authenticity and spiritual reflexivity.
>
> Campbell 2013: 3

This new sphere of religious engagement has also given rise to new methods of investigation in order to carefully observe and analyse the religious practices and meanings that have evolved in this new arena. When approaching the study of digital religion, especially as it relates to employing digital methods, several key contextual elements must be kept in mind.

First, the study of digital religion is situated in a broader methodological and intellectual framework. Research into digital culture and technology has taken place since the late 1970s and early 1980s (i.e. Kiesler et al. 1984; Turkle 1985), and many of the tools that draw on the sociological study of religion online are based on methods that emerged from early approaches developed in computer science, computer-mediation communications and human computer interactions (HCI) approaches. These disciplines sought to understand how computer users in organizations responded and developed certain patterns of interactions within computer supported work environments (i.e. Wellman 1997). Since methods like online ethnography and discourse analysis first emerged, they were often informed by different sets of values and logics of the technological frameworks (Markham 1998; Hakken 1999). When we consider what methodologies we employ in the study of digital religion, it is important to realize that many of our methods have emerged from different disciplines and can influence the process of analysis and interpretation.

Second, internet studies, in general, and digital religion studies specifically, have been interdisciplinary projects from their beginning. They involve not only scholars from religious studies, theology and sociology of religion, but people in fields such as area studies, media studies, political science and psychology. Each of these different disciplines have their own way of approaching the study of religion within digital media, and their own presupposition about how methods such as ethnography or survey data collection should be completed (i.e. Baym 2005). This means open dialogue is required in order to understand how our disciplinary roots may flavour our research methods and willingness to share and learn from other scholars using different approaches to study similar phenomena. This interdisciplinarity can be a challenge, but it can also widen the breadth of our work as we learn how different methodologies can be adopted and adapted in our work.

Third, when considering the study of digital religion, researchers need to remember that they are studying a unique aspect of digital culture. They are not looking only at the psychological environment of the digital realm or studying the issues of power and gender, but researchers are doing these things in relation to the frame of religion and religious cultures. This requires fluency and sensitivity to the different offline religious traditions and how their truth claims and worldviews are translated and negotiated in online spaces (Campbell 2010). Therefore, it is important to keep in mind that researchers are studying multiple contexts and cultures simultaneously when conducting online research of religion, which makes scholarship unique and complex. In short, when studying digital religion, researchers need to consider how the systems of knowledge within particular disciplines shape perspectives of research and how participants and environments may require unique methodologies.

TIP 1

Due to the interdisciplinary nature of the study of religion and the internet, which has been ongoing since the early 1990s, it is essential to do a broad and comprehensive literature review of any area of research before beginning your investigation in order to see how your various research themes may have already been approached both within digital religion and internet studies. A good starting point is the searchable bibliographic database provided by the Network for New Media, Religion and Digital Culture, found at: http://digitalreligion.tamu.edu/biblio.

With these issues in mind, this chapter seeks to outline the dominant research foci, methodological approaches and ethical challenges faced by scholars in the study of digital religion. This can be described as four waves of online research that have occurred since the mid-1990s to the present. The framework comes from the work of Hojsgaard and Warburg (2005) in their collection on *Religion and Cyberspace*, which came out of the first international conference on religion and the internet held in Copenhagen in 2001. In the introduction of their book, they laid out three different waves of research related to internet studies, which collates with the general development of the field. These three waves are identified as: (1) descriptive documentation; (2) methodological categorization; and (3) the theoretical turn. Here, we also add a fourth wave, which is described as (4) embedded implications to capture current trends in research. This framework helps highlight how the field of digital religion has developed in the last two decades, the range of methodological approaches employed, and ethical issues that emerged during those time periods. The aim is to provide an overview of the current challenges researchers are facing, especially within the current context of digital religious studies.

Four waves of research on digital religion

This overview of the four waves of research on digital religion highlights observations in three key areas: (a) primary scholarly focus and questions pursued during a given wave of scholarship; (b) the common methodological approaches and innovations engaged; and (c) the ethical challenges this form or approach of research poses.

Wave 1: The descriptive

Hojsgaard and Warburg (2005), in their description of the first wave of research, focused on the new and extraordinary aspects of cyberspace in which religion 'could (and probably would) do almost anything' (p. 8). Internet scholars sought to document and describe these new phenomena of online events, while trying to weigh utopian and dystopian discourse about how the internet would save or ruin the world. Early studies of religion and the internet tended to offer a general survey of religious experimentation with the internet and suggested observations on the potential religious and cultural implications (i.e. Zaleski 1997; Brasher 2001), positive reflections on how the internet may reconnect people with spirituality in postmodern society (i.e. Cobb 1998; Wertheim 1999), or critical analysis on the ethical challenges posed by digital technology (i.e. Houston 1998; Wolf 2003a). While many of these texts have now become dated due to the quickly evolving nature of technology, they provided important early documentation of the rise of different forms of religion online, as well as highlighted key initial observations about the nature of how religious rituals and community was practised online.

In the initial wave of research, scholars often focused on documenting how different religious groups were performing and practising religion online, with interest in how the internet might point towards new innovations in religion and religiosity. Researchers and users were often caught up in the newness of internet technology, which yielded strong responses that were either very utopian, claiming the internet was going to revolutionize our world for good, or dystopian, predicting the internet would destroy all social structures and weaken interpersonal interactions (i.e. Benedikt 1992; Hafner and Lyon 1996). In the mid-1990s, online communities were popular areas of study, as people were using email, Bulletin Board Systems (BBSs) and newsgroups to create new space for social engagement.

Many scholars looked at religious websites and sought to understand how people were engaging with them (Zaleski 1997). In this first phase people were merely trying to understand the capabilities of the internet and digital culture (i.e. O'Leary 1996). Hence, there was a lot of participation in online ethnography. Researchers immersed themselves into online environments to observe or engage these new forms of interaction in order to document and describe what was happening in these contexts. Most of the research studies in this first wave were case study oriented, looking intensely into the rich and thick description of one incident and attempting to unpack its meaning and implications. In the 1990s, religious communities began to emerge in many different text-based environments from early chat forums, like internet relay chat to faith-based discussion forums in newsgroups and on BBSs (Ciolek 2004). Research on online prayer and church-like forums in the late 1990s demonstrated how religious internet users explored new ways of building community and congregations in what was often popularly described as a 'disembodied' space (Campbell 2003). People were engaging in text-based forums and building communities and forming relationships. Also during this era, there were a lot of different religious groups either from official institutions or individuals trying to move religious activities to the internet. For example, Islamonline.net provided Fatwas that became very popular during this era. In this first wave, there were many interesting in-depth studies – from O'Leary's (1996) work predicting how new religious movements may benefit from networked interactions, to Fernback's (2002) study on Wicca bulletin board–based communities, many scholars provided substantial studies to help lay the groundwork for future research.

The access scholars had to religious environments was a unique aspect of this era. Researchers could observe and study many groups and religious activities in ways that had never been possible. For example, a researcher could never simply have walked into a Wiccan Coven to record and investigate sacred and private rituals, but online a researcher could easily join and observe both of the religious and social components. This led to many tensions for early scholars. One crucial tension centred on framing of the nature of 'reality' versus 'the virtual'. Popular understanding often assumed that what was found offline was real, and the online was simply virtual, or a digitized representation of reality. In other words, researchers experienced challenges in conceptualizing and comparing online gathering spaces and the information and experience supposedly offered in offline environments. Simply, there was something not as real, or even false, in the online environments. Scholars understood these environments as a new kind of social space and interaction, but struggled to understand how to frame these digital contexts in relation to larger social processes. Early ethnographies also articulated tensions about the extent to which researchers could simultaneously serve in the role of critical observer and community participant in online environments. How much participation is required to obtain an insider's view and be seen as a member of a group? To what extent may online participation influence or bias one's critical evaluation of a given community or context? Many tensions arose due to the novelty of the research and scholars learning how to use the technology at the same time.

Third, as seen in Fernback's study (2002), a researcher could go into an online environment, easily observe what was going on, and not disclose to participants the nature of the study. Scholars had to wrestle with what kind of self-disclosure was required. Was it enough to simply ask permission of the person who owned the email list or the web master of the site? Or must a researcher continually reveal to participants the nature of the researcher's participation within the group? Many interesting tensions emerged around such issues during this era and led to clearer parameters in research to come.

Wave 2: The categorical

Hojsgaard and Warburg (2005) noted that the second wave of research focused on a 'more realistic perspective' in which scholarly emphasis was placed on people who were generating these new forms of religious expression online and not just the technology. They observed how scholars attempted to provide categorizations and typologies to understand common trends within internet practice. This type of work is easily seen in the three most cited scholarly books on religion and internet studies, all representing edited collections with studies drawn from different conferences highlighting various studies on religion online. *Religion on the Internet: Research Prospects and Promises* (Hadden and Cowan 2000) was important, as it was the first collection seeking to identify early issues being explored by scholars. These scholars examined the impact of the internet on religious groups and culture, though many often seemed to be influenced by utopian or dystopian outlooks regarding the internet, which was characteristic of many early studies about the internet. Dawson and Cowan's *Religion Online* (2004) represented a more diverse and sophisticated collection of studies offering insights into a diversity of religious traditions and more detailed analysis on issues related to religious identity, affiliation and ritual negotiations online. Finally, Hojsgaard and Warburg's *Religion and Cyberspace* (2005) represented papers from the 2001 international conference, 'Religious Encounters with Digital Networks Conference'. These volumes sought to identify common questioning and forms of methodology scholars were employing in this area of study. While all three are valuable collections, they represent disparate collections of studies seeking to identify key scholarship and findings, rather than cohesive commentaries on how religious groups and practices, as a whole, are being shaped by the internet, technology and culture. Here, questions of religious identity and authenticity of religious practice online began to surface as key concerns for researchers.

In this era, we see the emergence of more types of online worship spaces, virtual temples and cyberchurches. The first blogs also began to appear at this time. We see a movement towards a different understanding of space and engagements online. In order to study these kinds of processes, researchers had to try to provide a methodology categorization. Many scholars depended on grounded theory. Coming from fields such as psychology or sociology and media studies, where theoretical perspectives and methods emerge primarily from close observation and ethnographic work and then lead to critical reflection on trends observed and comparisons with other studies (i.e. Jones 1997). Scholars also began to recognize that observations from a single case study were often not sufficient to make large-scale claims about religious practice online and comparative case studies became popular.

There was also a systematizing of online methods as researchers developed more standardized methods in which online surveys were conducted and developed online interview protocols. In this era, much research was conducted on cyberchurches. These ranged from simple text-based websites where a user could simply navigate through hyperlinks and digital text, to full interaction in a virtual chapel or chat rooms that used typing and audio technology to provide a more real-time worship experience (Dawson and Cowan 2004). For example, the *Church of Fools* was one of the first virtual reality worship environments where people entered a digital cathedral environment as an avatar and engaged with others in a worship service of prayers, hymn signing and listening to guest preachers offer sermons. Within these kinds of environments, scholars tried not just to describe the different features of these cyberchurches, but also to uncover the different levels of participant engagement and their intentions. Scholars were attempting to answer questions such as: What motivates people to go online? What are the different ranges of responses to how people engage and conceptualize the online environment? During this period, Helland (2000) introduced the influential framework of 'religion online' versus 'online religion'. This was one of the first theoretical devices used to distinguish how people participated online and the extent to which religion online was imported from offline religious practices or originated purely online. Helland sought to identify discernible characteristics between religion and religious activity that was created for the sole purpose of an online community and the importation of traditional structures and theologies of the religious structures to the online realm.

Within this wave several ethical tensions arose. First, researchers reflected on how to treat digital texts in relation to their producers. The text became understood as the embodiment of the person online. But how does a researcher encapsulate that text in the analysis? What is the connection between the text and the people that produce that text? How do scholars treat and analyse a text that is seen as the representation of a person's identity and body online? This led to a second tension, centred on how to deal with internet users' anonymity. How should researchers quote people who use handles as identifiers? The handle is associated with the person, so to what extent does this identifier disclose the identity of the individual in potentially problematic ways? Researchers were still trying to understand what was public and what was private online. To what extent are conversations private and should researchers be treating them as such? Should scholars cloak people's identity if they are already shielded by an online identification of a handle? How should researchers document and cite these nuances of online research? These were a few of the many questions that researchers had to negotiate in their research design and presentation of findings during the second wave of research of religion online.

Wave 3: The theoretical

According to Hojsgaard and Warburg (2005), the third wave was only beginning to surface in the mid-2000s as a 'bricolage of scholarship coming from different backgrounds' (p. 9). Third wave research was characterized by a turn towards theoretical and interpretative inquiry, where scholars sought to identify methods and tools for analysing data and assessing findings in light of larger theoretical frameworks. In this era the study of online ritual, community and identity were explored in more detail and looked at in light of how the embeddedness of the internet in everyday life was influencing religious digital practice. Scholars drew conclusions about how examples of religion online, such as religious rituals (i.e. Helland 2007; Kruger 2005), community (i.e. Cheong and Poon 2009; Campbell 2010) and identity (i.e. Lövheim 2005; Cowan 2005), were impacting religious communities and organizations as well as mirrored practices in broader offline contexts. New dominant research themes like authority also emerged, such as considering how the internet challenges established religious authorities (i.e. Barker, E. 2005), empowers new religious leaders (i.e. Campbell and Golan 2011) and provides new opportunities for traditional leaders to reassert influence online (i.e. Barzilai-Nahon and Barzilai 2005). New theoretical and methodological frameworks were also taking shape. Some scholars sought to provide systematic interpretive tools for analysing offline religious communities' negotiation patterns with new media (Campbell 2010) and nuanced understanding of authority negotiations online (Campbell 2007).

During the third wave of scholarship a concerted effort was made to answer the interpretive question, 'so what?' There was a need to explain and contextualize research efforts to see how studies of religion online illuminated not just trends in digital culture, but pointed to larger shifts in religious culture in general. Scholars also saw a growth in religious groups and organizations online, indicating an increased recognition among religious institutions in the importance of having a presence online and using the web in more concrete ways for religious dissemination of information and mission. The negotiation between offline entities and their online counterparts became an important issue to consider. In order to accomplish this type of analysis, scholars began to implement more large-scale comparative work. Researchers were starting to see comparisons not just between individual case studies, but also across broader religious traditions. The theoretical perspectives became more complex as the methodology expanded to greater data sets. Researchers moved more towards detailed content analysis. Therefore, as the web became more visual and oral, expansion of earlier research on text-based data was completed. It became important to develop methods that included visual cultural studies and translated that into the online contexts.

With the blending of offline and online expressions of religion, there was also a culturing of technology in unique ways. For example, Jewish groups created internet filters to protect religious community members from problematic internet content. Thus, some religious community leaders attempted to create kosher websites to protect and prevent community members from falling prey to immoral content (i.e. Campbell 2010; Campbell and Golan 2011). Other religious organizations and individuals also created religious versions of popular technologies, such as GodTube. com and Millatfacebook.com, representing Christian and Muslim versions of YouTube and Facebook. These tried to duplicate the similar services of popular social media platforms, but offer them in a religiously safe environment. Also during this era researchers turned their attention to the study of the rise of virtual worlds like *Second Life*, and the proliferation of religious activities via the use of avatars became a point of interest for digital religion researchers (i.e. Miczek 2008). Many scholars became interested in the study of religious implications, in areas like *Second Life*, where many virtual Buddhist temples, Jewish synagogues, churches, and even a digital version of the Sistine Chapel became present. This wave of research grappled with the question of how to study the visual representations of people in avatars, as well as the digital duplicates of worship environments that are created in the virtual world. During this theoretical turn, researchers further investigated religious internet studies of groups in order to understand how digital spaces replicated or helped facilitate new religious trends in a broader cultural context. The Heidelberg Ritual Dynamics Group, at the University of Heidelberg, did a great deal of research on *Second Life* trying to develop theoretical methods to study the virtual worlds in religion. Cheong and Poon (2009) studied the new media use of Buddhist and Christian religious leaders in Singapore to better understand how they attempted to bridge religious rituals in online and offline contexts. Campbell (2010) compared Muslim, Jewish and Christian groups' negotiations with the internet to not merely document, but really understand how the internet affects religious offline culture.

Like the other waves, several unique ethical and research-oriented tensions emerged. The Internal Review Boards (IRBs), institutional research boards at American universities that monitor the ethical practice of scholars, began to take seriously and monitor the unique challenges posed by doing online research. By this time there was a growing recognition for the need to develop and adopt clear protocols for online research. IRBs had determined what kinds of permissions were necessary and how to properly disclose and document particular types of information such as informed consent and protection of the research subject's identity. Codes of ethics developed groups such as the Association of Internet Researchers to serve as vital, initial protocols when seeking to create research standards in international contexts. The IRB remains an important vetting process to secure the proper treatment of the human subject online. Indubitably, an important question centred on how researchers synthesize this process in online research and how they treated research participants differently in a virtual world context. The potential legal and ethical ramifications became immensely important. The blending of offline and online realms meant that often-private groups were made public, which in some ways is positive for researchers, but may expose a group to more public scrutiny than an organization was aware or agreed to. This could be problematic, especially if they represented a closed religious group with normally rigid social boundaries seeking to protect their information and members from public scrutiny. The researcher had to take such complexities into account.

Wave 4: The integrated/convergent

These three waves – the descriptive, the categorical and the theoretical – have become an important descriptive typology used by various researchers, including those in this book, to describe the progression and development of research in religion and internet studies. The metaphor of the different waves of research is often used to describe how research methods and approaches to various research questions have emerged and matured over time, as our knowledge of the implications of internet technologies on various social and cultural processes has progressed. Some scholars have also suggested that a fourth wave of research on religion online is emerging, offering further refinement and development of methodological approaches, as well as the creation of typologies for categorization and interpretation purposes (Campbell and Lövheim 2011). This is seen in new methodological models being offered to assist scholars in more fine-tuned analysis of religious internet contexts, such as those offered in the study of religious ritual in virtual world environments (Grieve 2010). This current wave of research also seeks to stress the need for more longitudinal studies on the relationship between religious groups' adoption and adaptation of online contexts. Such work requires a careful study of 'the social and institutional implications of practicing religion online; and what impact, if any, this will have on the construction of identity, community, authority and authenticity in wider culture' (Campbell and Lövheim 2011: 1085). It is here, in this current wave of research, that this volume seeks to make an important contribution.

Presently, the internet serves as an integral sphere of everyday life. It is embedded to some degree in many people's existence and daily routines. Researchers must move towards a nuanced consideration of how these technologies and spaces have also become embedded in religious culture. The internet is not a completely separate space; it is integrated by its proximity in many religious behaviours and rituals. As part of everyday social life, it is also a central part of religious existence as well. While social media has been around for several years, only within the past few years have religious scholars given considerable attention to how the internet affects religion in these spaces. Studies on Facebook and Twitter have been difficult because permission from users to study such spaces and behaviours does not come easily, and neither does the development of tools and methods to study such platforms. Mobile media and applications represent other underexplored digital religious contexts. Considerably more attention needs to be paid to the integration of the offline context to the online, as well as a better understanding of how embedded the internet has become in the digital ecosystems of religious organizations and communities. More critical reflection is needed to consider how researchers should approach these areas of study methodologically. Some scholars have had success in adapting approaches that had been developed in other disciplines to study religious digital contexts, especially as they relate to big data. Hence, within the past five years there has been a strong emphasis on moving towards the use of more quantitative methods in the study of digital religion.

Much of the research in the first ten to twenty years related to religion online was primarily qualitative. Many scholars started to understand that if large claims are going to be made, they needed to draw on larger and broader data sets to make these claims. Because digital tools have been developed for gathering user profile information on Twitter and Facebook, such big data sets are now becoming available. There needs to be much more research on religious use of Facebook, Twitter, YouTube, Instagram and religious apps to understand how these innovations have developed and impacted religious practices and understanding. Ethical questions arise, however, as to how we deal with these data sets without violating confidentiality.

Some important studies taking a more quantitative and large-scale approach have emerged. For example, Vis, van Zoonen and Mihelj (2011) studied the rise of the *Fitna* video in order to understand how Muslims negotiate with cosmopolitanism of Islam represented through YouTube videos. Hutchings (2012) researched an online movement called 'I Am Second'. It produced a number of videos telling a story about religious identity. Hutchings then looked at the circulation of that identity as well as the spread of the message through the internet. Haughey and Campbell (2013) looked at Facebook forums to understand how online memorialization develops. Campbell and DeLashmutt's (2013) research looked at what is called multi-site churches (churches that function as a network of sites overseen by a parent congregation and have a strong online presence) to look at ecclesiological and rhetorical patterns of how members make cognitive links between their online participation and religious identity. These studies illustrate the important blending of online/offline contexts but also posed serious challenges. They also often draw on vast amounts of online data that require digital tools to help categorize, sort and analyse the findings and correlations such research offered. These raise important questions about the benefits as well as shortcomings of using large data sets, and the benefits and challenges such work poses to researchers. How can scholars maintain the integrity of their treatment of research participants when they are reduced to large data sets drawn from social media outlets, making private information a vital public commodity for online researchers?

Also, issues of privacy and copyright of information continue to be a challenge for researchers. Many questions remain about what is or should be considered private versus public, when scholars can create programs that search out, and collate and reveal personal content about informants in ways that expose them as never before. Furthermore, scholars must consider how their content online, as well as print content, presents a public profile that could be seen as a breach of confidentiality of their subject. How do researchers deal with the outcomes and findings of research? Often times, especially because research online can be widely and quickly disseminated in ways not previously possible, it may get co-opted into purposes that authors may not be comfortable with. Are there boundaries that scholars can put around their work in order to have a little more control over how their research is used or not used?

Conclusion

In conclusion, there is still much to learn about religion and digital culture. While noteworthy findings have surfaced and many discoveries have been made, there still are many areas of inquiry unanswered regarding technology's intersecting and impacting religion. For instance, questions related to how the internet shapes religious violence, activism and the long-term impact of technological appropriation on religious communities and social infrastructures are all areas that must be researched further. New techniques are needed to study these areas of research and standardization of methods will help aid in our understanding of religion's relationship to the digital realm. It is immensely important to teach the next generation of scholars of sociology of religion that a continued effort of interdisciplinary cohesion is needed in order to develop common ground for conversation among scholars seeking to study digital religion.

TIP 2

While digital methods have become a popular way to discuss methodologies related to online research, it is important to recognize that there is no one clear or unified definition for this term. Digital methodologies can refer to the use of 'digital tools' or software (i.e. using iPads or programs like NVivo) that are used to gather traditional ethnographic data, research that is conducted in a 'digital environment' (i.e. in the virtual world of Second life or web-based online community) or employing a 'digital technique' (i.e. data scraping Facebook profiles for specific information) (see Tsuria et al. 2015). For a good overview of the different approaches and understanding of Digital Method consult: Markham, A. and Baym, N. (2008) Internet Inquiry: Conversations About Method, CA: Sage; and Miller, D. and Horst, H. (2012) *Digital Anthropology*, London: Bloomsbury Academic.

This chapter has laid out the short history of digital religion scholarship. It has provided an overview of four major waves of research that have developed through the last twenty years. The first wave of scholarship described and documented the many ways in which the internet was going to enhance or destroy religion, as utopian and dystopian views of the internet often shaped the researcher's focus. The second wave became a bit more precise by recognizing that the technology alone was not shaping religion. The individual users and religious organizations using the technology also played a part in the development of digital tools for religious purposes. This provided a more nuanced understanding of digital religion. This then led to the third wave, where a broadening of theoretical frames was developed to better describe the phenomenon of digital religion beyond mere categorization and typological mapping. Through these waves a deeper understanding of the intersecting areas of religion and digital technologies is taking place. The field now seems placed within a fourth wave of research where a more refined methodological approach and theoretical reflection can emerge to even better describe and interpret the ways in which religion is being performed and is shaping the internet.

2 Surveying the Religious and Non-Religious Online

TRISTRAM HOOLEY AND PAUL WELLER

Introduction

The internet provides a powerful tool for researchers interested in religion and belief. The ability to transcend space and to undertake research quickly and efficiently via the internet offers opportunities for researching both online and onsite phenomena. As early as 1996, a piece in *Time Magazine* (Chama 1996: 52–9) gave notice of the arrival of an era in which the internet was increasingly intersecting with both the development of religion and belief, and with its study.

In the mid to late 1990s, one of the co-authors of this chapter was involved in the development of *MultiFaithNet* (see Weller 1998a and 1998b) an online resource for study and research in relation to religious and inter-faith initiatives.[1] Since then, the internet been used as a tool in researching religion and belief, and a number of wholly online religious communities have developed and become the focus of research (Dawson and Hennebry 1999; Hojsgaard and Warburg 2005) while the internet has penetrated into nearly all aspects of religious life (Campbell 2012). Research has also begun to explore the way in which religion and belief intersects with the use of social technologies (Armfield and Holbert 2003; Bobkowski 2008; Campbell and La Pastina 2010; and Spence 2014).

Researchers who wish to examine these issues should proceed carefully and recognize that both religion and belief, and the technologies used to research them, are shaping each other in a host of different ways. While there is value in investigating what Bell (2006) refers to as the 'techno-spiritual', technology is also utilized by people with religion and belief perspectives for more mundane and logistical purposes. It is becoming increasingly difficult to escape the internet, which inevitably seeps into the perspectives and practices of both religious people and of those who live by other ethical and philosophical orientations. Researchers may legitimately be interested in all of these intersections.

For researchers who are interested in the intersection between religion and technology, online research methods seem a natural fit. However, it is possible to investigate online phenomena through the use of entirely onsite research methods. For example, research can be undertaken into how people use the internet for religion and belief or any other purpose by interviewing them or asking them to complete a paper-based survey. One example is the Pew Research Center's (2013) survey on *The World's Muslims: Religion, Politics and Society*, which was based on face-to-face interviews of over 38,000 Muslims and included questions on the use of the internet and social networking. Conversely, it is also possible to use online methods to explore wholly onsite phenomena.

This chapter focuses on online surveys, arguing that they offer major opportunities for researchers of religion and belief. The discussion draws on the authors' experience of undertaking three online surveys that explored different aspects of religion and belief. These projects included a mixed postal and online survey of religious organizations within a project exploring religion, belief, discrimination and equality in England and Wales; an entirely online survey of the religion or belief experience in UK higher education; and a cross-European online survey of participants and trainers who had participated in the religion and belief diversity and anti-discrimination training offered by the Belieforama community of practice.

Research contexts

The Religion and Belief, Discrimination and Equality in England and Wales: Theory, Policy and Practice (2000–2010) project[2] was funded by the UK's Arts and Humanities Research Council and the Economic and Social Research Council.[3] It built on an earlier project commissioned by the Home Office conducted between 1999 and 2001 (Weller, Feldman and Purdam 2001). Together with a systematic review of 130 legal cases; a review of other relevant bibliographical evidence; fieldwork interviews; and focus groups, the research also included a postal and online survey of religious and inter-faith organizations.

The online version of the questionnaire survey was developed using the open source survey software, Lime Survey.[4] Following a pilot of both postal and online modes, the survey was conducted during 2010 and 2011 on a stratified sample of 1,754 national and local religious and inter-faith organizations in England and Wales. This resulted in 499 responses (a response rate of almost 29 per cent), with the vast majority (439) of those responding to the postal survey. The online survey was primarily used as a means to follow up non-respondents to the postal survey, or to elicit responses from those organizations for which initial postal addresses proved to be incorrect.

To enable longitudinal comparison of the results, the majority of the questions asked by the survey completed in 2001 were also asked in 2011, and 201 organizations (almost 12 per cent of the total sample) responded to both surveys. The survey results were exported from Lime Survey to the SPSS[5] statistical analysis software package within which they were analysed. The detailed findings of the project, including the survey, are published in Weller et al. (2013a, 2013b).

The Religion and Belief in Higher Education: Researching the Experiences of Staff and Students[6] project was commissioned by the Equality Challenge Unit to support the development of an evidence base for understanding the experience of staff and students in higher education who identify with a religion or belief. The study was a mixed methods project, including a literature review, stakeholder consultation, institutional case studies, and two online surveys – one aimed at staff and the other at students.

The questionnaires were administered online to enable the survey to have as wide a national reach as possible and to maximize the number of possible respondents. The surveys used SNAP software[7] and were open from 28 October 2010 until 3 January 2011. Respondents were recruited through a range of sources. The surveys were marketed through gatekeepers including religion and belief groups, higher education institutions, trade unions, professional associations, and social media. They were also openly available on the internet.

The surveys collected responses from individuals working or studying in HEIs located in all four countries of the UK, resulting in responses from 3,077 staff from 131 institutions and 3,935 students from 101 institutions. Following the closure of the survey, data was downloaded, cleaned and analysed using SPSS. The findings of the project were published by the Equality Challenge Unit (Weller, Hooley and Moore 2011).

The Belieforama[8] community of practice has grown out of a series of European Union funded projects to develop trainings focused on religion and belief diversity and anti-discrimination. Since 2004, over 2,000 people have engaged with these trainings. Consultants were appointed to gather feedback and draw wider conclusions from the Belieforama projects. The research was informed by a range of historic documentation and reports; a consultation with representatives of European level religion or belief organizations and NGOs concerned with religion or belief; an online survey of previous training participants; and Skype[9] interviews with participants who had also acted as trainers.

Because the research needed to be undertaken with participants located in many European countries, an online survey of over 360 training participants for whom Belieforama held current email contact details was developed in English, French, German and Spanish language versions. A pilot was conducted with the project's partner organizations in early February 2012, while the finalized survey was carried out from February to April 2012 and 110 responses were received. As with the Religion and Belief, Discrimination and Equality project in the UK, Lime Survey was used. Because of the relatively low numbers of respondents, Lime Survey was also used to analyse the data. The results were published Belieforama reports (Weller and Contractor 2012a, 2012b).

Methodologies

Online surveys: The overall field

Online surveys have been used extensively to investigate religion and belief issues (e.g. Connor, Davidson and Lee 2003; Kellems et al. 2010; and Van Laar, Derks and Ellemers 2013). The three projects discussed in this chapter therefore stand among a range of other studies that have developed practice. Such research practice has not been extensively discussed in methodological terms that engage with the intersection between technical and substantive issues within the use of online methods to research religion and belief.

Online research methods have developed rapidly across a range of disciplines (Hooley, Marriott and Wellens 2012). Researchers in the projects introduced above drew on general methodological thinking in relation to online surveys in the design, recruitment and analysis (e.g. Couper 2008; Evans and Mathur 2005; and Dillman, Tortora and Bowker 1998) and on literature addressing specific methodological issues concerned with online surveys that address religion and belief (Bader, Mencken and Froese 2007; and Royle and Shellhammer 2007).

Madge et al. (2006) highlight a range of general advantages for researchers in using online surveys. These include speed of data collection, volume of data, savings in cost, flexibility, increases in data accuracy due to the loss of recording and data entry errors, access to diverse research populations, and the potential for increased anonymity. Madge et al. also discuss a number of areas of concern including the potential for sample bias (whether the population accessible to an online survey is different to that which can be reached using other survey approaches); measurement error (whether respondents behave in a different way because they are participating online compared to another survey method); non-response bias; high levels of survey drop-out; technical problems; and a range of ethical issues which are shaped by the nature of the online environment.

Ethical considerations

All social research has the potential to raise ethical issues. In recent years social research has been increasingly subject to formal ethical regulation (ESRC 2010). Much of this framework draws on medical ethics models and particularly enshrines the laudable principles of beneficence and non-maleficence. Such an approach emphasizes certain processes including the gaining of informed consent, clarity about confidentiality and anonymity and attention to issues of data storage and archiving that continue to be important in the online environment. This is not the place for a general discussion on the ethics of social science research. However, it is useful to briefly consider whether there are any particular ethical considerations that are associated with doing online survey research on religion and belief.

The Association of Internet Researchers (AOIR) Ethics Working Committee has produced detailed guidance on ethical research on the internet (2012). These guidelines emphasize a pluralistic and contextually situated approach to research ethics. Unsurprisingly, therefore, given the differing contexts of the three projects discussed in this chapter, the ethical approaches taken in each of the projects differed in terms of their approach to matters of participant engagement, anonymity and the engagement of wider stakeholders in the research. However, all three projects did produce detailed justifications for the ethical approach taken that were then reviewed and approved by ethics committees operating within the context of the University of

Derby Research Ethics Code of Practice[10] and this meant that there was a common framework within which these diverse approaches were considered and approved.

A key element of the AOIR guidelines is the reminder that the distance between the research and the research participant that is created by the mediating environment of the internet should not allow us to forget that this remains research with individuals who have the right to be treated respectfully. AOIR also suggest that internet researchers should carefully attend to the context within which research takes place, thinking about how the online spaces and gatekeepers that are used to recruit to surveys may frame an individual's responses and encourage them to behave in certain ways. For example, using a religious leader as a gatekeeper to survey participants may frame the likelihood of participants' engagement as well as the nature of their engagement with a particular survey.

Online survey research typically gathers large amounts of data about individuals. One new ethical challenge that is posed by the increasingly data rich environment of the internet is the possibility of linking survey data with existing data. The existence of online versions of the electoral register, lists of attendees at religious events, court records and so on mean that it is potentially possible to link survey data to the wider contexts of individuals' lives. This could then potentially be used to scrutinize and validate (or otherwise) the information that people provide in surveys (e.g. is what an individual tells you about their church attendance supported by an analysis of their Facebook account?). Clearly this kind of data triangulation raises major ethical issues that need to be handled carefully. It also opens up some fascinating possibilities for researchers if these issues can be squared. There are also broader ethical issues associated with recruitment, categorization and interpretation that are addressed further in this chapter. However, it is important for researchers to attend to the particular contexts of the internet and to recognize that they frame thinking about what constitutes ethical research.

The selection of survey tools

As set out previously, the case studies employed two different tools to administer the surveys described: Lime Survey and SNAP. In other projects the researchers have also used tools such as SurveyMonkey[11] and Google Forms.[12] A common question relates to the relative strengths and weaknesses of these different tools and whether it is possible to identify which is best for which purpose. It is difficult to provide definitive answers to this – not least because the functionality of the tools as well as the range of tools available changes very rapidly. However, Hooley, Marriott and Wellens (2012) set out a range of questions that researchers should ask when choosing a tool. These include attending to the usability of the tool for both researchers and respondents; the range of question types; the amount of questions and responses it can handle; and the cost of the tool.

An important ethical question also relates to the data security and confidentiality offered. This is particularly true for cloud-based survey tools where data security and confidentiality will be governed both by the policies of the company that provides the tools and by the laws of the country in which they are based. Researchers should investigate this as part of the selection of the tool. Concern about the data security of various providers was influential in the selection of the tool utilized for the surveys in all of the case study projects. An additional consideration is whether the tool offers any analytical functionality. This can be particularly useful in monitoring survey results while surveys are ongoing. It is also important that tools support researchers to export data into formats that are compatible with common analytical tools such as Excel or SPSS.

The quality of online survey tools continues to increase. All of the tools mentioned, and many others besides, can support high-quality professional research. However, it remains important for researchers to carefully investigate the tools they plan to use, particularly where they might be researching sensitive subjects in relation to which confidentiality and anonymity are paramount.

Sampling and recruitment

TIP 1

Many of the issues relating to online surveys are simply reframings of issues that exist in all survey research.

Many of the issues relating to online surveys are simply reframings of issues that exist in all survey research. Much of the reframing is due to differing levels of digital literacy (skill in using the digital environment) and digital access (opportunity to use the digital environment) across the population. The fact that not everyone has equal access to the internet and that not everyone is able to use it equally well raises a number of issues for sampling and recruitment. Researchers have to address the question of whether their online surveys are seeking to sample from the entire population (including those who cannot or do not use the internet) or only the segment of the population which is active online.

Researchers in Britain have some good data, which provides insights to the way in which an online survey might skew the sample (ONS 2014). This, for example, shows that while three-quarters of adults in Britain use the internet every day, around 13 per cent of the population report that they have never used it. The data also provides insights into how this differentiation might manifest in relation to other demographic factors. In particular, it suggests that younger people are more likely to use the internet than older people, and that the reasons that people give for not having access to the internet include those related to income, disability and rurality/remoteness. The relative clarity that is afforded by Office of National Statistics (ONS) work on the British population may not be available in other countries or for those seeking to research sub-populations of various kinds – for example, Christians.

An awareness of internet penetration may influence sampling strategies and considerations about the appropriateness of online surveys or the use of mixed mode data collection strategies.

TIP 2

An awareness of internet penetration may influence sampling strategies and considerations about the appropriateness of online surveys or the use of mixed mode data collection strategies.

Unpacking some of these issues with reference to the three projects introduced above illustrates some of the issues. For example, in relation to digital literacy, the 1999–2001 predecessor of the Religion and Belief, Discrimination and Equality project decided that internet penetration at that time was not sufficient to use an online survey. The organizational samples and contact details identified for that project were derived from the database underlying the 1997 edition of *Religions in the UK: A Multi-Faith Directory* (Weller 1997), from which it was evident that a large number of religious and inter-faith organizations had not yet developed online contact possibilities. Thus, while email contact was used in the 1999–2001 project, it was only as a means to try to establish follow-up contact with non-responding organizations.

By the time of the 2010–12 project, this had changed, as was evident from the database underlying the *Religions in the UK: Directory, 2007–2010* (Weller, ed., 2007). Even so, at the proposal stage for the 2010–12 project there was insufficient confidence to conduct a fully online survey. In addition, given the project's aim to have a longitudinal comparison of the results, there was some concern about the possible measurement error in terms of the comparability of survey results conducted in two entirely different modes. The literature on this issue is complex, with Sax, Gilmartin and Bryant (2003) and Dillman et al. (2009) arguing that there are differences in the way people respond to different modes of survey, while several other studies have found there are few differences in the way people respond to different survey modes (Arnau, Thompson and Cook 2001; Gosling et al. 2004; and Fleming and Bowden 2009). In the end, this latter view seemed to be borne out by analysis of the survey data gathered by the Religion and Belief, Discrimination and Equality project where there was no significant evidence of a different pattern to the 60 online responses compared with the 339 postal questionnaires.

Within the Religion and Belief, Discrimination and Equality project the online form of the questionnaire was designed to play only a supplementary role to the postal survey, the aim of the former being primarily to boost the likely number of responses. Converse et al.'s (2008) mixed postal/web-based survey reported increased response rates, and this was confirmed by Dillman et al. (2009), who combined together a wider range of different survey methods. However, while mixed-mode surveys may increase response rates, online surveys have often been found to have lower response rates (Shih and Fan 2008), although they arguably deliver less missing data (Dolnicar, Laesser and Matus 2009).

The other two case studies (Religion and Belief in Higher Education and Belieforama) opted to deploy their surveys solely online. These decisions were largely motivated by the advantages that online surveys offer in extending reach across geographically dispersed populations in an efficient and accurate way. In the Belieforama project, the population was Belieforama's training participants, drawn from various countries across Europe, the vast majority of whom had provided email addresses via their original participation in the Belieforama training, and so could be sent invitations to respond to the survey. In the Religion and Belief in Higher Education project, the project aimed to gather a substantial volume of survey responses (around 6,000). Both in terms of eliciting such numbers from an open invitation survey to staff and students spread across a large number of institutions, and for handling and analysing the volume of data arising, an online survey offered substantial advantages. Given the nature of the higher education sector it was possible to assume near universal penetration of the internet to staff and students. Although there was discussion about whether such an assumption would exclude ancillary staff who may not have computer accounts as part of their roles, consultation with some higher education institutions suggested that it was common for all directly employed staff to be issued with computer accounts. While recognizing that the use of an online survey mode remains imperfect, it was judged that those who would be excluded would be no more likely to be better represented through postal or telephone surveys. An assumption was also made about the level of digital literacy in the higher education sector given that higher education offers a relatively unusual case in which it is possible to assume high levels of digital literacy.

The relative confidence about digital literacy and access does not mean that the use of an online survey in the HE context raised no sampling issues. Chief among these was the question of how the use of an open online survey might influence the representation of different religion and belief positions as well as other demographic and organizational issues relevant to the research. Online engagement and online religious engagement are not necessarily the same thing. For example, a Sikh may be an active member of the sikhsonline community[13] or a regular user of the goSikh[14] online store. However, it is also possible that Sikhs who are both devout and observant members of the religion and fully digitally literate, choose not to announce that religious belief online or access online information relating to their religion.

Such differences in online behaviour also alter the usefulness of online gatekeepers, such as the owners of sikhsonline or goSikh, and consequently influence the sample. How religion and belief and the use of technology intersect is under-researched, but Royle and Shellhammer (2007) found some patterns in the ways in which religion and belief intersected with the use of technology and willingness to complete online surveys. They found that different levels of engagement with online surveys were secured across different types of churches and demographic populations. Nevertheless, many individuals do use the internet to find out about, and participate in, their religion or belief. Such individuals can sometimes be described as being members of online communities, although such online communities frequently overlap with face-to-face communities. The existence of such communities and foci for online manifestations of religion and belief (such as popular websites) also raises the important role that online gatekeepers have in the recruitment of respondents to online surveys. A webmaster, blogger or manager of a social networking site has the power to give or deny access, as well as the power to profile and promote the research in ways that enhance or diminish the likelihood of good response rates.

Murray and Sixsmith (1998) have argued that the involvement of such gatekeepers is essential for ensuring online research engagement. Online gatekeepers, like their onsite equivalents, are not value free and may have their own opinions on the nature of the research being undertaken. The ownership of websites featuring religion or belief may mean that researchers are seeking to access the population through a variety of state, religious, charitable, third sector and commercial organizations, as well as via committed individuals. The level of interest in the research and the wish of the researchers to access a representative population is likely to differ across all of these different groups and relate to the aims of the research project in question.

In the Religion and Belief in Higher Education project, gatekeepers were actively courted and utilized to disseminate the survey. Key gatekeepers included the Higher Education Equal Opportunities Network, the National Union of Students, a range of students' religion and belief groups (for example, the Union of Jewish Students, Federation of Student Islamic Societies and the National Federation of Atheist, Humanist and Secular Student Societies) as well as individual equality and diversity practitioners and human resources staff. Many of these were both onsite and online gatekeepers who maintained a network of contacts through face-to-face meetings and a range of online tools including email lists, organizational websites and social technologies such as Facebook and Twitter.

The use of gatekeepers can be effective in ensuring recruitment to surveys. Gatekeepers have both access to, and credibility with, the survey population that is likely to exceed that of the researchers. However, the use of such gatekeepers also raises concerns about non-response bias, and in particular the danger that the survey only accesses those whose religion and belief identities are associated with organizations and networks. The internet has generally lowered the threshold for participation in organizations and networks (Shirky 2009), meaning that even very thinly spread positions have the opportunity to organize and develop networks online. However, a reliance on gatekeepers will still tend to favour more digitally active, better resourced and larger groups as well as those that are actively campaigning for a particular outcome to the research. This is especially the case where open recruitment strategies are used.

Concerns about the sample bias associated with the use of gatekeepers highlight particular concerns about reaching individuals whose religion or belief position is antithetical to the development of organizations or even networks. This may be either because of a philosophical or theological belief in the primacy of personal conscience or because they have what Voas (2009) describes as 'fuzzy fidelity'. In the Religion and Belief in HE project we sought to address this by actively recruiting as diverse a range of gatekeepers as possible and ensuring that they included both gatekeepers who were responsible for religion and belief focused networks as well as those who were concerned with institutional roles in HE and other cross-cutting identities.

There are a range of other sampling issues which are strongly related to the research questions that the researcher seeks to answer. Is the research concerned with the whole population and, if so, across which geographical areas? Is it concerned with a particular sector (such as in the higher education project discussed above)? Is it concerned with particular ethnicities? Or with those who identify with a particular range of religion and/or belief positions (as with the Religion and Belief, Discrimination and Equality project noted above)? Or with those who identify with any religion or belief position at all? Or with those who have had a particular experience (such as participating in Belieforama)? Or some other sub-population? Such decisions in turn raise a number of issues regardless of the approach that is taken to administering the survey. So, for example, the identification of religious populations and sub-populations raises definitional questions about what is meant by belief (see Cheruvallil-Contractor et al. 2013).

Furthermore, when analysing populations by religion and belief, we have to recognize serious limitations in what is known about the general population. As with the previous discussion of levels of digital access and digital literacy, some information about religious affiliations may be available at the national level,[15] but frequently there is very little relating to sub-populations. Such concerns about the overall quality and availability of data can make the confident stratification of samples challenging. So, for example, there was at the time of the project no baseline data on which to base assumptions about the religion and belief composition of higher education.[16] Consequently the HE research had to provide indicative rather than statistically representative results and this in turn influenced survey design. However, the survey data was triangulated with what was known about the demographic composition of the sector and with what was known about the national demographics of religion and belief. This triangulation provided some confidence that, while results may not be technically representative, they are at least strongly indicative. However, it also raised some interesting differences for example, about why HE seemed to have less Christians and more people who professed 'no religion' than the general population, on which it was possible to speculate, but not fully to answer.

TIP 3

When analysing populations by religion and belief, we have to recognize serious limitations in what is known about the general population. Such concerns about the overall quality and availability of data can make the confident stratification of samples challenging.

Recruitment to surveys is a process that takes place over a period of time. In the Religion and Belief in HE project, and in the Religion and Belief, Discrimination and Equality project, responses to the surveys were regularly monitored. In the former project this was on a weekly basis to examine the breakdown of responses in terms of numbers: of religion or belief groups, of types of HEI, and of national and regional location. Where the research team felt that there were insufficient responses in relation to any of these factors, approaches were made to institutions and organizations to engage their support in raising the profile of the project and surveys. However, such monitoring and targeting approaches again raise issues about the quality of information that is available as a whole. Where this is weak, there is a danger of trying to make the sample fit into pre-conceived and potentially incorrect assumptions.

This discussion of sampling and recruitment issues highlights some of the challenges when planning and conducting online research on religion and belief issues. At the core of these challenges is our limited knowledge about the level of digital access and digital literacy in any given sub-population combined with our limited knowledge about the distribution of religion and belief positions. The Religion and Belief in Higher Education project's process of open recruitment combined with triangulation and careful monitoring of the response rates offers one way to proceed. It also highlights the importance of gatekeepers in supporting recruitment to online surveys as well as the potential limitations of such approaches for the statistical representativeness of the research.

Framing effective questions

How to frame questions is also an important consideration in developing online surveys to explore religion and belief issues. Religion and belief identities are subtle and there is potential for misunderstanding and even offence. Surveys that are conducted face-to-face can use a researcher to mediate the questions and to provide participants with clarification. Like postal surveys, online surveys have to stand for themselves, which requires a focus on clarity and usability, and means that brevity is often a virtue. Many of the issues around effective question construction are generic and not specific either to online surveys, or to religion and belief. Further discussion of issues relating to survey question design is set in many generic discussions of survey design (e.g. Fowler 1995; Bradburn, Sudman and Wansink 2004).

More specifically related to religion and belief, there are a number of issues that prove challenging due to the breadth of experience encompassed within the 'religion and belief' envelope. For example, the higher education project asked the question 'Do you use a place of worship or religious assembly outside of your university/college?' With hindsight such a question may be seen to exclude particular types of activity that we would ideally have included. For example, it is doubtful that respondents would have cited 'sceptics clubs'[17] as a possible answer to this question. It is perhaps also unlikely that an individual who described themselves as 'spiritual' would see this question as providing an appropriate vehicle for discussing the various ways and venues within which they manifest this spirituality. Such concerns return us to complex definitional and ontological questions that it may be possible to explore in an extended piece of writing, but to which it can be difficult to do justice in a survey question.

The 'religion and belief' formulation is very wide, and it is often difficult to include those who are religious and anti-religious, monotheistic and pantheistic, participants in organized religion, or those who are more loosely affiliated and so on. Online surveys offer one potential way to address this through the use of what are often largely invisible routings to specific questions sets, but this in turn raises both questions about survey design and analysis. For example, how far is it possible to analyse a question about 'where do you worship' alongside one about 'where do you feel most spiritual' and another about 'where do you express your humanism'? Such analysis runs the risk of losing the specificity of the way in which people answer these subtly different questions. A further challenge is offered by the fact that religion and belief identities are not hermetically sealed, but rather overlap and interact.

A related issue is the previously mentioned 'fuzzy fidelity' (Voas 2009) and the fact that people's belief may be partial or undefined. Still further complexity is added by the relationship between religion and belief, community, identity and politics. In the context of creating effective questions for a survey, all of these issues raise challenges. Thus, it is possible to answer 'Christian' to all of the following questions:

- What is your religion or belief?
- What religion or belief do you most associate with?
- What religion or belief do you practise?

Each of these asks a different question, yet within the context of an online survey it is not likely to be possible to ask all of these. In an online survey such definitional and ontological issues have to be translated into a series of technical questions. These include making decisions about the level of pre-coding; the use of question type (for example, can the answer to 'what is your religion or belief?' be a multiple answer question or does it have to be a multiple choice question); and the use of routing and the amount of explanatory text that it is necessary or advisable to use.

Concluding reflections

The use of online surveys brought considerable benefits to the case study research projects. However, as our reflection on these case studies shows, their use also raised a number of issues that had to be worked through methodologically. Thus, recruitment and sampling present a number of specific challenges for researchers of religion and belief using online surveys. Where populations are clearly online and identifiable by their religion and belief positions, it is possible to utilize stratified sampling strategies and to understand the representativeness of data in very precise ways. Where this is not the case, as is normal, sampling and data analysis inevitably becomes less precise and more subjective. The identification of prior knowledge about the sample, data triangulation and the use of a wide range of gatekeepers and recruitment approaches may all help to address these issues, but none offer a magic bullet.

The discussion about the framing of questions has raised more issues than it has solved. As with many issues there is no perfect answer, but the challenge of addressing questions quantitatively without forcing people into pre-coded boxes that do not describe their realities is a very real one. Careful consideration of the implications of particular question formulations, of pre-coded responses and of the types of questions used is essential if researchers are to avoid reductive descriptions of complex matters.

In summary, online methods are a valuable part of the toolkit of the researcher of religion or belief. While they offer many advantages and are becoming ever more popular, it is important that they continue to be used carefully, and in a way that is formed by both critical and ethical awareness. A willingness to interrogate what we know about the demographics of both online participation and religion and belief must remain at the heart of such endeavours.

3 Online Crowdsourcing Methods for Identifying and Studying Religious Groups as Special Populations

VICTORIA A. SPRINGER, PETER J. MARTINI AND JAMES T. RICHARDSON

Introduction

Studying special groups can present a number of methodological challenges to even the most experienced scholar. Researchers must often deal with limited resources, such as time, funding and access to members of the groups they wish to study. Of each of these concerns, access to members of special, rare or hidden groups is by far the most essential challenge as no expenditure of time, money or other resources can make up for the inability to reach them. The difficulty in pursuing this type of research has been discussed in the research literature for several decades (e.g., see Sudman, Sirken and Cowan 1988). The study of religious groups is no exception.

The difficulties with special population studies are not limited to the struggles faced by researchers. The people who belong to special religious groups (or any unique population) may themselves face constraints, such as an inability to meet with researchers or unwillingness to participate through direct contact methods. For example, receiving a copy of a survey in the mail may inadvertently reveal participation in a research study, which may have unintended consequences for the researchers as well as the participant. In any study, the protection of participant identity and minimal disruption to their daily lives is essential to ensure that the highest ethical standards of research are upheld.

Adopting digital methods in the study of special groups has the potential to help researchers overcome these types of barriers and concerns. This chapter describes methodological considerations for using online crowdsourcing to reach special groups. Specifically, this chapter emphasizes the utility of this approach for reaching mainstream and minority religious groups, including the results of a 2013 study of religious groups in the United States based on this technique.

Hidden population research in the digital age

Hidden populations share a common foundation: the trait, characteristic or other feature that defines them is typically rare, often stigmatized, and not easily observable by researchers. Accordingly, it is usually not possible to know the size of the population, establish a comprehensive contact list or employ traditional sampling methods when working with these groups. Some members of hidden populations may not wish to be identified, approached or contacted, which poses additional challenges for researchers (Heckathorn 1997; Duncan, White and Nicholson 2003). This is particularly true for groups that are marginalized or face discrimination in society due to their beliefs, cultural background or behaviours, such as risky or illegal activities.

The popularity and prevalence of the internet presents an opportunity to reach hidden populations. According to the United States Census Bureau, the percentage of households with internet access at home increased from 18 per cent in 1984 to 74.8 per cent in 2012. As of 2012, 78.9 per cent of American households have a computer at home and 94.8 per cent of those households use it to connect to the internet – often through multiple digital devices. There is still some evidence of the 'digital divide' between younger and older segments of the population, with over 85 per cent of 25- to 44-year-olds using the internet, compared to 78 per cent of 45- to 65-year-olds and only 53 per cent of those over the age of 65. For those who did not use the internet at home, 12 per cent report that they do not want it and only 7 per cent indicate that they cannot afford it.

Taken together, these trends suggest that the internet is prevalent and accessible for studying respondents in the United States. However, international assessment of internet use suggests that internet use is not as prevalent in other geographic regions. As of 2011, the International Telecommunications Union estimates that one third of the world's population is online – and that number continues to grow. Accordingly, the appropriateness of using online survey methods for reaching hidden populations will vary according to the specific type and location of the group of interest.

Using online surveys for the study of hidden populations has been most often reported in the public health literature in the study of risky behaviours. Duncan, White and Nicholson (2003) found that this method produced the largest sample of successful illicit drug users ever surveyed and consequently recommended using online surveys to reach hidden populations. Koch and Emrey (2001) found that using the internet to survey marginalized populations did not result in a sample that was biased due to self-selection. In other words, the researchers found that people who chose to participate in an online survey were not systematically different from those who did not. Indeed, the characteristics of gay and lesbian participants (their sample of interest) who participated in the online surveys matched national data on the characteristic of this group in the general population. Research continues to grow and attest to the advantageous use of technology to improve research with hidden populations (Matthews and Cramer 2008; Shaghaghi, Bhopal and Sheikh 2011).

The use of online surveys to reach hidden populations may be particularly well suited to minority groups that are known to use the internet. Though this is by no means a necessary requirement to use online surveys to attempt to reach hidden populations, it is reasonable to assume that the odds of successfully accessing these populations increases if those populations are present online. One example is the growing study of Muslims in the United States as a minority religious population.

Research has suggested that Muslims have a meaningful and growing online presence. Their use of the internet is a topic of study in and of itself, including work on how the fundamental tenets of Islam are interpreted through the use of the internet and online discussions (Akou 2010). Research shows that Muslims are also turning to the internet to connect with their identity and community (Hendricks 2006), and participate in religious activities (Ho, Lee and Hameed 2008). For Muslims who choose to go online, the internet provides a virtual community and sense of connectedness, which is particularly important when Muslims are a minority in diverse societies (Rantakallio 2011).

This same logic can be extended to any hidden population that is known to have a presence on the internet. Recent research by Martini, Springer and Richardson (2014) suggests that a variety of special populations are accessible through online approaches. One of the most recent innovations in online research is the use of crowdsourcing – a topic to which we now turn.

Crowdsourcing through online labour markets

Crowdsourcing originated in practical applications involving the distribution of labour or effort across a group. The term 'crowdsourcing' was coined in 2005 as combination of 'crowd' and 'outsourcing', which accurately conveys its form and function (Brabham 2008). Crowdsourcing is typically characterized by the use of online communities as labour markets to complete work for pay or other compensation (e.g. credits, sweepstake entries).

To date, the most popular crowdsourcing option to emerge from the crowdsourcing phenomenon is Amazon's Mechanical Turk (MTurk). MTurk was established in 2005 as a worldwide online labour market and has since become a rich resource of social science research subjects. According to Amazon, there are over 500,000 'Workers' in the MTurk labour market, half of which are located in the United States. The majority of the remaining 'Workers' are located in India, but it is possible to access people from around the world – though they are present in far fewer numbers.

The market aspect of MTurk is simple. 'Workers' that are registered with Amazon search for, select and complete assignments. Each assignment earns the worker a specified amount of monetary compensation. The exchange of assignments, completed work and compensation are handled through the online infrastructure provided by Amazon. The MTurk online interface is accessed entirely through web browsers (e.g. Google Chrome, Mozilla Firefox, Internet Explorer) and does not require that software be downloaded or installed.

According to MTurk, this labour market is based on the premise that there are still many things that human beings can do more efficiently than computers. Indeed, the assignments that workers complete are called 'human intelligence tasks' or HITs, in reference to the unique qualities that people bring to tasks that cannot be fully automated or carried out by machines. HITs are created by 'Requesters' (such as social scientists) who seek fast and efficient means of completing a variety of assignments. This includes the traditional crowdsourcing-based distribution of labour to the workers as well as the more recent social scientific use of workers as survey respondents and experimental subjects.

The most common types of HITs (assignments) include finding information (e.g. on a website), image tagging/categorization/filtering, writing tasks (re-write/edit, review), audio transcription, website feedback or usability testing and surveys, polls and questionnaires. Surveys may be built using simple point-and-click tools through MTurk or external links may be provided to surveys created and hosted through other online tools (e.g. SurveyMonkey, Qualtrics). There is a wide range of compensation levels offered depending on the time required and complexity of the task. In general, the longer the assignment, the more the Requester should expect to pay the worker for their time.

TIP 2

Choose research compensation based on what is fair to the research participant and within the budgetary constraints of your study. The temptation for 'cheap' data through online crowdsourcing options should not lead researchers to short-change participants.

MTurk keeps track of the performance of workers, including the number of HITs they have successfully completed and the number of times that they have had their work rejected. Requesters may reject work for any number of reasons. For example, the accuracy rate may fall below a certain minimum threshold (e.g. categorizing images incorrectly) or the assignment may have been completed too quickly, leading the requester to question the validity of the data (e.g. a ten-minute survey completed in one minute). The requester – or researcher – has the final say regarding which work will be accepted and rejected to ensure data quality.

For social scientists, the human quality of MTurk is one of its greatest strengths. The popularity of MTurk as a source of participants has continued to grow in the social sciences as sociologists, psychologists, behavioural economists and consumer behaviour researchers have begun to recruit online. As a testament to its potential, there is some informal evidence that sixteen of the top thirty US universities collect behavioural data via MTurk (Goodman, Cryder and Cheema 2012). The study of MTurk itself has become a topic of interest to population researchers, methodologists and other scholars who wish to understand its limitations as well as its potential.

MTurk appears to be a high-quality source of research participants. Early research indicated that workers were similar demographically to other internet-based research panels (Ipeirotis 2008 and 2010) and efforts to replicate classic research findings have been successful using MTurk. This includes studies in the fields of decision-making (Paolacci, Chandler and Ipeirotis 2010), behavioural economics (Horton, Rand and Zeckhauser 2011; Suri and Watts 2011) and political science (Berinsky, Huber and Lenz 2012). This paints an optimistic picture for the continued use of MTurk for research in the social sciences.

A question that typically arises when considering the use of MTurk workers as research subjects is exactly what type of people are the workers? That is, can researchers believe the information reported by the workers and how do they compare to the general population? Research has shown that the demographic information reported by MTurk workers is both reliable and accurate (Buhrmest, Kwang and Gosling 2011; Rand 2012). In their extensive evaluation of the representativeness of MTurk compared to local convenience samples, internet-based panel surveys and elite national probability samples for political science research, Berinsky et al. (2012) concluded that MTurk does not perfectly coincide with the demographic and attitudinal characteristics of the United States population. However, the MTurk population is not wildly distorted either.

For those seeking hidden groups, MTurk appears to be a strong resource for reaching special populations, including underrepresented gender and sexual identities (i.e. LGBT), minority religious groups and rare health-related populations (i.e. intravenous drug users). Martini, Springer and Richardson (2014) found that each of these groups was more common in the US MTurk sample than in US-based, nationally representative comparison surveys (World Values Survey, National Survey for Family Growth). Based on its ease of use, access to US and worldwide participants and availability to any researcher with internet access, MTurk appears to be a promising tool for the study of mainstream and minority religious groups. Research results regarding the presence of specific denominations and religious groups in the United States to which MTurk Workers belonged will be discussed later in this chapter.

Methods for identifying special populations online

One of the chief goals when conducting research is generalizability. In survey research this is often accomplished through random sampling. Random sampling is a method of collecting respondents that represent the variability in the population one is researching. Random sampling, as well as stratified sampling methods, preserves the heterogeneity within a population, allowing researchers to collect samples that are representative of the diversity in the target group (Groves et al. 2009). However, not every population can be randomly sampled with ease. Salganik and Heckathorn (2004) refer to populations that cannot be studied using standard sampling and estimation techniques as 'hidden populations'. As discussed in previous sections, these hidden populations have various attributes, but due to size, geographic dispersion, or prejudice and stigmatization, rare and hidden populations are difficult to obtain. This is particular true when using random sampling, thus individuals interested in researching issues that impact these hard-to-reach folks often turn to the use of a non-random sampling methodology.

A fairly common methodology for finding hard-to-reach populations relies on respondent-driven sampling (RDS) approaches, in which individuals in the target population provide researchers with additional contacts within the population and those contacts provide yet more names. Therefore, the sample is populated by individuals *known* to belong to the target population by virtue of their connection to at least one other member of the sample. This method results in a sample that tends to be homogeneous on certain characteristics, as social networks tend to be comprised of individuals who are like one another (see McPherson, Smith-Lovin and Cook 2001). Due to this homogeneity and the lack of probability sampling, research conducted using RDS methods does not generalize to the hidden population being researched. This homogeneity can be particularly problematic when the target population is known to have diverse subcultures or groupings that may be entirely excluded due to the homogeneity of the sample.

For example, much of the research conducted on Muslims in the United States uses mosque-driven samples in which researchers work with participants from a particular mosque. Because respondents are drawn from and interact via a particular mosque they tend to be similar on characteristics important to social science and religion scholars. All respondents are most likely from the same denomination within Islam (e.g. all Sunni, all Shia); they are also more likely to be from similar socioeconomic statuses and countries of origin. If one plans to study the social or psychological behaviours of Americans of Muslim faith the homogeneity within the sample puts limitations on the generalizability of results. So, a mosque-driven sample can capture the behaviours of a specific portion of American Muslim society, but not all American Muslims.

With the purpose of obtaining a more heterogeneous sample, we have developed a replicable multi-stage survey approach for reaching target populations using US MTurk Workers. This process consists of two surveys – a screening survey and a primary survey. Initially, MTurk Workers are invited to participate in a screening survey that assesses numerous demographic characteristics of interest to the researchers. The HIT is listed on MTurk using a generic title that has nothing to do with the target population (e.g. 'We want to know more about you!'). The screening survey is used to identify workers who are members of the population of interest and is structured to take around five minutes and workers are paid for this HIT regardless of their qualification for the primary survey. The screening survey should be short and cover a variety of topics in addition to simply identifying members of the target population and should follow MTurk community standards for worker pay (~$6 to $8 per hour). The purpose of the screening survey is to quickly assess a large number of individuals without alerting them to either the population of interest, or the focus of the research within the population of interest. For example, in our work on American and Muslim identity within US Muslims, the screening survey used in our study asked workers a series of questions on religious denomination and beliefs (wherein we identified our target population), but also completed sections on political beliefs, health, mental health and drug use.

Once the screening survey is completed, workers who self-identify as members of the population of interest are then offered the opportunity to participate in the primary in-depth survey (typically ranging from twenty to thirty minutes), for which they receive additional, increased compensation (again, in line with MTurk community standards of ~$6 to $8 per hour). Thus, all workers receive a nominal amount for the screening survey, while only self-identified members of the population of interest are offered an opportunity to participate in an *additional* survey at the completion of the screener. The multi-tier approach to identifying hidden populations was constructed to compensate for two possible problems with crowdsourcing applications. The first is overt selection bias and misrepresentation of the target characteristics, and the second is the worry that workers are 'experts' at taking surveys and thus represent a different population than the general public.

TIP 3

Take the time to think through the most important characteristics of the people you would like to study in your research. The multi-stage approach to identifying and surveying special groups works best when the group you want to reach is clearly defined.

Selection and misrepresentation

When using crowdsourcing services to find minority populations, misrepresentation and selection bias are key concerns. A survey that transparently asks for members of a particular community may draw the attention of some community members, but it may also attract respondents who feign membership in the hidden population. We have intentionally tried to avoid selection bias and misrepresentation by not explicitly stating our target population in the language of the MTurk HIT for the screening survey. Additionally, the screening survey contains questions beyond simply identifying a target population. Once identified, members of the target population are told that researchers are interested in their community. This method of essentially blind screening and recruitment is intended to minimize overt lying or misrepresentation to qualify for the higher paying primary survey. However, there is an added benefit in that such a generic screener and HIT are unlikely to draw a specific segment of the population of interest. Thus selection bias for the primary survey is decreased – but cannot be outright eliminated.

Homogeneity of masters-only samples

Amazon allows researchers to restrict their HITs to individuals who have high survey completion rates and favourable reviews from other requesters. In fact, there is an added layer of proficiency in which requesters may limit their HIT to 'master workers' who satisfactorily complete the same type of HIT across a broad range of requesters. From a statistical perspective, employing systematic constraints by requiring workers to be masters or have a certain HIT completion rate may artificially decrease the variability present in a population. For tasks requiring high precision (e.g. image categorization) for which 'master' workers are selected, this is likely a desirable outcome. For social science researchers, the potential increase of homogeneity in restricting such samples may unintentionally impact results and fail to represent the attitudes, behaviours, or other outcomes of the worker population as a whole (compromising its generalizability to the general public). This is a particular worry in survey research in which this task proficiency results in workers who are experts at taking surveys quickly. To solve this problem we removed all qualifications from our worker selection. In other words, our survey is open to *any* worker regardless of tenure or prior HIT completion rate. The absence of restrictions results in a sample in which many participants are new to MTurk. We are currently planning additional survey research to explore differences in social science surveys completed by masters (only) vs. general worker samples to assess the extent of these potential differences. It should be noted, that MTurk allows requesters to utilize other methods of finding specific populations – chief among them is the use of qualification tests.

Specificity of screening criteria and rewarding workers

To date, we have not utilized the 'qualifications test' options available in the programming tools for two reasons. First and foremost, the complexity of target population identification and screening for our research has required the use of advanced survey software to properly segment workers (beyond the current capabilities of the 'qualifications' tools). Additionally, we have taken the approach to reward the worker community commensarate with the time they have spent participating in our research – including being screened. The expense of screening workers to identify highly specialized target markets in conjunction with the increased compensation for those who qualify has proven to be a cost-effective alternative to other commercially available options (e.g. Ask Your Target Market and SurveyMonkey

Audience). Future work may examine time-to-completion and data quality for multi-stage surveys vs. single survey with required 'qualification test' to explore the benefits and challenges of each approach.

Application to the study of US Muslims

In the wake of the negative national and international events, Muslims in Western societies have endured discrimination and stigmatization, raising questions about the effects of such treatment on self-identity. For Muslims living in the United States, one possible outcome is an internal conflict that makes it difficult to reconcile having both an American and Muslim identity. With this idea in mind we set out to understand how a Muslim and American identity impacts the lives of Muslims living in the United States. To accomplish this goal we applied the multi-tier survey approach discussed in this chapter. Our findings are from a US sample of MTurk Workers, with no other restrictions on worker participation. Data collection occurred from June 2013 to January 2014 (seven months). The HIT for the screening survey was published multiple times (called 'batches'), with each batch screening approximately 300 MTurk Workers. Batches took between six and twenty-three days to completely fill, with each batch screening 300 workers in an average of seventeen days. During that time, 3,189 MTurk Workers in the US accessed the screening survey, 150 of whom indicated they were Muslim (4.7 per cent). As discussed above, after completing the screening survey, all 150 Muslims were given an opportunity to participate in the primary survey. Each participant who self-identified as a Muslim was given a unique code that would grant access to the primary survey, thus individuals could not gain admittance to the primary survey without first passing through the screening survey to obtain an access code. A total of 116 respondents (76.7 per cent[1]) went on to complete the primary survey, which contained questions about their experiences in the US, their encounters with prejudice and discrimination and their identity as both Muslims and Americans.

The sample of Muslims we collected looks very similar to other online samples when you look at basic demographics. Males make up approximately 56 per cent of the sample. Respondents ranged from 18 to 72 years in age, with an average age of 28 years. The sample was relatively well educated – 42 per cent of respondents had a college degree and an additional 37 per cent reported some education beyond high school. About one-third of respondents were married (35.8 per cent) or had children (31.8 per cent). Based on these characteristics our sample of Muslims was similar to non-Muslim samples obtained using other online methodologies. However, one of our chief goals in conducting this research was to create a sample that represented the unique diversity within the American Muslims.

Of those who responded to our survey, an overwhelming majority were US citizens (89 per cent), and 71 per cent of respondents were born in the United States. Of those respondents who were US citizens, 57 per cent were first generation, 15 per cent were second generation and 28 per cent were third generation American citizens. Denominationally, the sample was very diverse. The majority of respondents were Sunni (60.2 per cent), followed by Shi'a (13.3 per cent), Sufi (6.2 per cent) and Nation of Islam (4.4 per cent). These numbers are very similar to the numbers reported by Pew in the 2011 report of Muslim Americans. Thus, the multi-tier approach was able to produce a sample that was demographically similar to other online samples in terms of age, gender, education, marriage and presence of children. And it was also able to produce a sample that mirrored the denominational diversity in a national sample of American Muslims collected using a standard random-digit dialling approach to reach survey participants.[2]

Strengths of this approach

The greatest benefits of using online crowdsourcing to reach religious groups are its convenience for the researchers and participants, and the relatively low cost – compared to other methods. To conduct this type of research, only a computer with internet access and enough technical knowledge to use a simple website are required. Likewise, the participants who complete research studies through online labour markets need no additional training or technology to engage in the study. The ability to remain anonymous to the researchers through this method helps protect their identity and conceal their participation from others, unless they choose to reveal it. The results of the research presented in this chapter suggest that Amazon's Mechanical Turk is a strong source of participants from a variety of religious groups in the United States. However, the applicability of this method for researching religious groups outside of the US is currently unknown.

Challenges of this approach

The limitations associated with this method of studying religious groups can be addressed through the use of multiple method approaches to present a full and robust set of findings. For example, it may be more appropriate to approach religious elders in community-based samples through face-to-face interview methods, rather than attempting to find them through digital technologies. The need to leverage other methods depends on the goals of the researchers and the scope of the study. As previously mentioned, a thorough assessment of the fit between the type of sample produced by this approach and the goals of the research should be undertaken before choosing to employ this method. The convenience of this approach should not outweigh the choice of another approach if alternative methods are a more appropriate choice for the population of interest or the purpose of the study.

There are also ethical considerations that should be mentioned in the use of any digital method of reaching special populations. First and foremost, participant identity must be safeguarded for the protection of the individual participant as well as the group that he or she represents. We have mentioned the anonymity of reaching research participants through MTurk. There are limits to the identity protection in place through the MTurk interface. For example, any MTurk Worker who chooses to contact their Requester through MTurk must do so at the expense of revealing their personal e-mail address. Accordingly, these communications must be kept strictly confidential in order to assure participants are fully protected. Participant compensation should also be carefully considered when conducting research through online crowdsourced methods. Though online crowdsourcing is praised for both its convenience and cost effectiveness, the allure of inexpensive data collection should never outweigh the participant right to fair compensation. At risk or disadvantaged groups who are accessible through methods such as this may be particularly vulnerable.

Other considerations

The choice to use crowdsourcing to reach religious groups must first and foremost reasonably allow the researchers to access their population of interest. For example, it would be unreasonable to assume that religious groups who do not engage with modern technology would be accessible through this method. Researchers should also consider whether or not any systematic differences might make the individuals who participate through an online labour market somehow different from those who might have been reached through another method. For example, online samples may adequately capture young and educated members of religious groups, more so than older or less educated members of the same group. Caution should be exercised in interpreting results of this type of research. If, in the example, the sample was disproportionately young, the results may not reflect the attitudes, beliefs or behaviours of older members of the group. The strength of any study lies in its design, and online crowdsourcing can be an excellent and effective tool for researching religious groups.

Part 2 Social Networking Sites and Digital Ethnography

4 Facebook as Anti-social Media: Using Facebook Groups to Engage Opponents to the Building of Dudley Mosque

CHRIS ALLEN

In 2010, research undertaken on behalf of the European Muslim Research Centre (EMRC) at the University of Exeter highlighted how the expression of Islamophobia in the West Midlands region of England, in particular the 'Black Country' – a colloquial name given to the former industrialized area to the north of the city of Birmingham comprising the towns of Dudley, Walsall and Wolverhampton – was taking two particularly interesting forms (Allen 2010a). First, this was through the relatively widespread opposition being shown towards the building and development of mosques in the area. To illustrate this, three mosques were firebombed in 2009 alone, two of which were completely destroyed (Allen 2010a). Second, was how the internet, especially social media and networking sites such as Facebook, was being used to voice and disseminate information about that opposition. Many of these sites were also disseminating highly explicit and highly inciting Islamophobic content. From the research undertaken, both had been catalysed by the unfolding situation in Dudley where since the late 1990s some of the town's Muslim communities had been engaged in an ongoing campaign to build what detractors sought to describe as a 'super-mosque'. For a full exposition of the Dudley mosque 'story' see Allen's 'Between Critical and Uncritical Understandings: A Case Study Analyzing the Claims of Islamophobia Made in the Context of the Proposed "Super-Mosque" in Dudley, England' (2013a).

Unlike opposition to mosques seen elsewhere, the use of social media in the West Midlands appeared – at the time at least – somewhat unique. Noting the ease with which new alliances, groups and networks are contemporarily able to be established online (Shirky 2009), the West Midlands research highlighted how a good number of those exploiting these new online spaces were aligned to, or active within, far-right and neo-Nazi movements. Two of the most prominent were the British National Party (BNP) and English Defence League (EDL) (Allen 2010a). One of the first examples of this was evident in the Facebook group, *Say No to Solihull Mosque*, created and maintained by supporters of the BNP. With the group attracting more than 1,600 members, more than 1,000 messages were posted on the group's wall in a fortnight (Allen 2014). Soon after, other Facebook groups also began to emerge that similarly sought to oppose mosques: many opposing the proposed Dudley mosque the largest of which – at 1 January 2012 – had more than 19,000 members. Some of the new online spaces and groups were given deliberately confrontational and offensive names, for instance one Facebook group was named *Fuk* [sic] *the Dudley Mosque, Let's Build a Big Fat Pig There Instead*.

Facebook: anti-social media

While Facebook has recently changed its policy and closed most of the groups referred to here, at the time of the research being undertaken each of the groups had publicly accessible walls that carried highly offensive and explicit Islamophobic posts and content. Somewhat surprising was how much of this content was accompanied by the names and photos of individuals; surprising because Islamophobic discourses – like other discriminatory phenomena and discourses – are rarely so overt and attributable in public spaces (Allen 2010b). This is even more surprising when, as Back et al. (2010) note, research has shown that the majority of Facebook users are genuine and have profiles that match their true identities. Consequently, these Islamophobic discourses were easily attributable. Noting Markham and Baym's (2009) findings, this could be because of the shifting nature of the private and public spaces that is occurring online, where private citizens are increasingly willing to share even the most personal and private aspects of their lives to mass and increasingly indiscriminate audiences. Nonetheless, this appeared to be something quite new and distinct in relation to opposing the building of mosques as indeed the public discourses of Islamophobia as well.

As noted previously, however, since mid-2012 Facebook has closed all of the groups referred to here as indeed many others also. While some have transferred to other social networking platforms, some have disappeared completely. This is not to suggest that the problem of Islamophobia online has disappeared. The government-funded third party monitoring organization *Tell MAMA* (MAMA being an acronym for 'measuring anti-Muslim attacks') suggests that levels of Islamophobic discourses online are not just ongoing but are exponentially growing, especially through Twitter. A team from the University of Teeside has recently independently verified MAMA's data, suggesting that in its first year of operation 74 per cent of incidents took place online; 69 per cent of which were linked with those affiliated to far-right organizations (Copsey et al. 2013). While the contemporary situation is therefore different, a lineage exists in terms of how the internet is becoming increasingly popular for disseminating Islamophobic content, how social media is the preferred approach to do so, and how many of those doing so are either active within or have direct links to the far-right.

With this in mind, the findings from the initial West Midlands research highlighted two potential research opportunities. First, to explore the opposition being expressed towards mosques – in particular Dudley mosque – taking place online via Facebook groups; second, to explore social media as both a site and a method of research. In response to this, a pilot study was initiated in late 2011 that sought to explore both of these opportunities. At the time, a pilot study was preferred as it was unknown that Facebook would subsequently change its policies and thereby close all of the groups soon after the pilot finished. As such, the aim of the study – which ran from late-2011 to mid-2012 – was to explore the causes and drivers of opposition to the mosque through Facebook groups while using those same Facebook groups as a site for research and inquiry. The findings from the first part of the pilot's aim has recently been published elsewhere (Allen 2014); the second is focused upon here. In doing so, this chapter starts by exploring the online methods and approaches employed, paying particular attention to the methodological challenges encountered. From here, some consideration is given to the ethics of undertaking this type of research before concluding on the pilot study's findings and a contextualization in terms of digital methodologies.

Approaches to using Facebook groups

As before, far-right groups had not only been using social media to oppose mosques and campaign against Muslims and Islam in Dudley. As research shows, the BNP had orchestrated a particularly polemical Islamophobic campaign via Facebook against the proposed Solihull mosque a number of years previous (Allen 2010a). An indicative post is shown below:

> These bastards [Muslims] will not go away and until we kick them all out and send them back to their own countries we will have to continue fighting this war. But every time a Muslim blows himself up or abuses a white person or tries to take over a neighbourhood we gain more supporters. Time is actually on our side and all of Europe is itching to kick these useless perverts out of Europe. I do not know one person who wants Muslims in Europe . . . If Hitler hadn't gone and messed things up for nationalism we would never have let them in. Well the tables are turning and these guys are toast.
>
> cited in Allen 2010a

As Lee explains, online spaces appear to afford individuals a greater sense of security: 'the less involved face-to-face contact, the more likely respondents were to admit to socially undesirable behaviour' (2000: 3). Consequently, it would seem that this 'sense of security' gave space for some to be far more overt and explicit in voicing their discriminatory and prejudicial views than they maybe would have been in a face-to-face setting. Likewise, Elm et al. (2009) who explain how online spaces continually invert and blur the boundaries between the private and the public where that which might typically be restricted to the privatized spaces have nowadays begun to permeate the public also, albeit public spaces that exist online. Online spaces therefore create environments where social disruption occurs: where the demarcation between what is and what is not acceptable and unacceptable, private and public, legitimate and illegitimate and so on become increasingly blurred. As Markham and Baym note in relation to this, the result is an ever-increasing 'willingness of private citizens to bare the most personal and private elements of their lives to mass audiences' (2009: xi). Given that prejudices and discriminations are typically restricted to the private, therefore, it is maybe unsurprising that given the social disruption that is occurring through the proliferation of social media that discriminatory and hate-fuelled sentiments and expressions are beginning to become evident in what might be something resembling social media's public spaces.

The site for the pilot research was the Facebook group opposing the mosque that had the greatest number of followers. Identified as, *Stop Dudley Super Mosque and Islamic Village* (membership circa 21,000 as at 1 January 2012), it was necessary to then join the group. To do so, a personal Facebook profile was preferred (the rationale for this is considered in the following section). Shortly after joining the group, an initial introduction was posted on the group wall. At this stage, the idea was that the pilot would reflect or at least seek to explore, something of an online ethnographic approach. In doing so, it was necessary to presume that standard offline ethnographic techniques and approaches could be meaningfully applied to online spaces and that the role of the researcher would be one of participation as opposed to observation alone. As Hine (2012) notes, however, finding somewhere online that allows for online ethnography to be a success can be something of a matter of luck. And this was the case with the Facebook group identified. While members of the group were regularly posting content and wall posts, it became apparent quite soon after joining the group that the ethnographic approach was not going to bear fruit; not in the shorter term at least. It was also morally problematic for the researcher to actively participate in the opposition process thereby raising a number of ethical concerns as regards positionality within such spaces.

Navigating 'social disruption'

Increasingly, the role became one of mere observer and so an alternative approach was required that went beyond that of 'specialist lurker' (Kozinets 2006). In response, a further statement inviting members to engage in research was posted onto the public wall expressing an interest in why members felt it necessary to oppose the Dudley mosque. Given a mere handful of members responded, it was decided that another, more direct approach was required. In preference of sending blanket messages to all the group's members – noting how blanket wall messages had been largely ignored – direct messages were sent to the most prolific posters to the group's wall, identified using manual monitoring and recording methods. Again though, while a few responses were received, most seemed wholly reluctant to participate in the research. This was particularly confusing given many continued to post personally attributable and highly explicit Islamophobic messages on the group's wall. One way of trying to explain this might be to consider Lee's (2000) theories relating to unobtrusive research methods. In the context of Facebook therefore, to what extent might direct messages and other forms of one-to-one contact be perceived as face-to-face contact? Might direct contact online be perceived as being similar to, if not necessarily the same as, face-to-face contact offline?

In order to try and overcome this latest barrier, a new approach was adopted that drew upon Back et al.'s (2010) observations about the need to close the gap between the actual and self-idealized individual on Facebook. In trying to ensure group members felt that a critical distance was maintained throughout, it was decided that the offer of anonymity might encourage greater participation and engagement. Recalling Lee (2000) once more, anonymity did indeed prove to be successful. Clearly seen by members as affording them greater individual protection – possibly maintaining a greater sense of distance between group member, Facebook group and online public statements and expressions – it seemed that expressing something to a known and attributable individual was still quite different – whether online or offline – from expressing much the same to a mass, unknown and entirely indiscriminate audience. Developing this approach duly required the creation of an anonymous online questionnaire. In doing so, the observations of Hine (2012) were noted: that while there are distinct advantages of collecting social research data using the internet, there are some disadvantages also, especially if questionnaires and other similar methods are complex and confusing. In response to this, the questionnaire was conceived to be as simple as possible comprising three multiple choice type quantitative questions – relating to age, gender and location – and six open, qualitative type questions. A question relating to consent was incorporated at the start of the questionnaire.

Links to the questionnaire were sent via a direct message to the fifty most prolific wall posters. The message included a clear statement about anonymity should they choose to participate. Noting Hewson et al. (2003), such a non-probabilistic sampling method was not without problem. Most pertinent of these were the fact that respondents would be far from representative of the general population at large, thereby meaning that any findings would lack generalizability. While recognising this, such an approach remained valid given the sample did not need to be representative of any wider population. Instead, the research was focused on the views of a very specific group of individuals for whom opposing the mosque through the use of Facebook was their common cause. Such an approach is not without precedent away from the virtual and online also. As Hewson et al. (2003) rightly note, social and behavioural science research routinely employs selective approaches to sampling when investigating special interests and so some equity was apparent between the methodologies being used online with those that have been used traditionally offline. In this way, the pilot reflected a non-probability approach to sampling.

TIP 1

Online questionnaires seem to be a good way of engaging people about sensitive subjects.

The offer and reassurance of anonymity prompted unprecedented results in light of obstacles encountered previously. Having sent fifty requests, the outcome was the completion of sixty-five online questionnaires. The somewhat overwhelming response seemed to reflect the findings of those such as Illingworth (2001) who found that online questionnaires were a good way of engaging people about sensitive subjects. The recognition of sensitivity would therefore appear to be an extremely important issue and one that any future research would need to take into account. From the completion of sixty-five questionnaires from fifty invitations to participate, some snowballing took place with members seemingly forwarding the link onto others. While not entirely problematic the snowballing did prompt some methodological reflection not least because it was impossible to differentiate between those invited and those gained through snowballing. Equally problematic was that because snowballing was unexpected, it was also unclear as to whether those who were brought in during the process of snowballing were members of the Facebook group or not. Clearly any future research would require the incorporation of some necessary safeguards, to confirm the membership of respondents in order to constrain the sample. This might merely be the inclusion of a further quantitative question confirming membership of the group.

TIP 2

Future research will require the incorporation of some necessary safeguards to confirm that respondents meet the eligibility criteria for the research sample – in the case of Facebook this could be membership of the group/s being researched.

Ethics and engagement

While Hine (2012) balances the fact that online questionnaires have the potential to result in relatively high levels of non-response against a tendency of them being poorly or sparsely completed, here the outcome was quite the opposite. In terms of quality of completion, the vast majority were completed to a good standard.

Throughout the questionnaires, arguments and ideas were reasonably well articulated and were seen to include a wide range of different reasons for opposing Dudley mosque. While the full findings can be found in Allen (2014), themes that emerged out of the detailed analyses undertaken included planning permission and the legislation associated with this, the 'fear' of Muslims and Islam, anxieties about the building of mosques more specifically, and notions about 'Islamification' not least of the Dudley landscape. While some respondents did indeed express overtly racist and Islamophobic ideas, the majority interestingly did not. Similarly, the majority did not explicitly convey any links or affiliations with far-right groups and movements. One thing that was somewhat unexpected was the amount of respondents who completed the questionnaire using a form of what might be best described as 'text-speak'. A significant number also completed their questionnaires using a very strong Black Country dialect: some combining 'text-speak' with Black Country dialects. With this in mind, if answers were to be used verbatim such might be difficult for some readers to fully understand.

Unsurprisingly, the emergence of digital methodologies and online research has prompted significant debate about the ethics of doing so. As Hine (2012) warns, the accessibility of data available online has led some to fear that the online spaces – whether public or private – would become something of a 'research playground' where researchers would be inclined to gather as much information and data as possible without due concern for the people involved. In particular, this has been focused on the way in which consent can and indeed is sought from research participants, as also how consent applies to the use of collected data and information. As Hine adds, the emergent position is one that is far from clear cut. While there has been a code of practice published by the Association of Internet Researchers (Ess & AoIR Ethics Working Committee 2002), the problem lies in the fact that the code of practice basically replicates the ethics applicable to offline research for that which is being undertaken online.

There are of course those scenarios where informed consent might not be entirely appropriate. Take for instance the fact that this pilot was initially focused on information and comments that were posted on a publicly visible Facebook group wall. If this is public, then to what extent might informed consent always be necessary? If similar information was taken from a physical noticeboard in the 'real' offline world, then it is highly unlikely that any similar informed consent would be required. But as before, the online spaces are continually inverting and blurring the boundaries between the private and the public (Elm et al. 2009). Consequently, not only do traditional offline methods and approaches – as also ethics and consent especially – need to be recognized and acknowledged but so too they might need to be reinvented and renegotiated in order to try and maintain some equity between the online and offline. Likewise, the social disruption that occurs raises questions that, as yet, remain comprehensively and adequately unanswered: about what is and indeed, what is not acceptable, private and public, legitimate and illegitimate and so on. As before, this is made ever more problematic and contentious given the willingness of people to share even the most personal and private elements of their lives to widely indiscriminate audiences (Markham and Baym 2009).

Beyond the findings

As a pilot, this research sought to engage members of a Facebook group opposing the proposed Dudley mosque to explore the causes and drivers underpinning their opposition. Additionally, the pilot sought to highlight preliminary findings about how social and political opposition functions in the virtual spaces. As before, however, it is necessary to reiterate the limitations of the pilot not least given the constraints of the methodologies adopted and that this was a somewhat opportunistic study. As many of these groups referred to here have since been closed down by Facebook, these findings might need to be seen to be largely indicative. Nonetheless, the study generated significant qualitative data and used in conjunction with the research undertaken on behalf of the EMRC, it is possible that the findings will have a wider appeal and impact. Evidence of this can be seen in how the pilot provided new opportunities to re-consider and re-contextualize existing scholarly literature while also providing a timely insight into the opposition expressed towards the building of mosques. Likewise, the pilot provides findings worthy of consideration – and further questioning – as regards the relevance of social media, social networking and online tools as both a method and site for research.

From the findings alone, the opposition shown towards Dudley mosque clearly resonates with opposition shown towards the building of mosques elsewhere. Drawing on a wide range of different arguments and justifications, these reflected previously identified themes for opposition, in particular those identified by Gale (2005): of Islam being 'alien' to English heritage and Christian identity, and fears of an expansion of Islam and Muslims in the surrounding area. Reframing these within a contemporary context, it could be argued that the findings from the pilot went further than Gale's study, highlighting a number of more pressing, contemporarily contextualized arguments. This included opposing the mosque through challenging the decision-making of the planning authority, something that the existing literature only tentatively touches upon. More substantially though, the pilot highlighted how the mosque – and by consequence, Islam and Muslims – was perceived to be exclusive, a drain on limited public money and resources, as also being deemed unnecessary and far from 'needed' by anyone in the town, Muslim or non-. The findings also touched upon the growing public antipathy being shown towards all forms of public religion and religiosity in today's Britain, not just that shown towards Islam and Muslims alone.

Consequently, to what extent is it legitimate therefore to suggest that any opposition that accentuates difference might not necessarily be Islamophobic but might have the potential to be interpreted as such and thereby fuel the discrimination perpetuated by others? What the findings from this study suggest is that even where there is some evidence of an 'us' and 'them' dichotomy existing, it would be extremely difficult and rather simplistic to suggest that all those voicing such views were Islamophobic: discriminatory probably, but Islamophobic not necessarily. Which creates a series of very real dilemmas. For instance, where do the boundaries of Islamophobia begin and end? Similarly, when are the lines between valid and invalid, legitimate and illegitimate opposition crossed? Likewise, how can one know when justified opposition transgresses into unjustified opposition?

Facebook groups as outlets

What the study in Dudley shows is that a good number of people – even those who are prepared to express their opposition in the blurred reality/unreality of the private/public online spaces – have many different oppositional viewpoints that they perceive to be legitimate, valid or justified. The vast majority are not, one might suggest, Islamophobic, anti-Muslim or anti-Islamic per se; nor are they even likely to be explicitly prejudicial or discriminatory as indeed the findings would suggest. Yet when those individuals fail to acquire a voice – where they feel excluded, ignored and marginalized – it is possible for their views to harden requiring them to seek outlets – or conversely, 'outlets' such as the far-right to seek them – in order to find valorization. Any ensuing Islamophobia therefore may be the consequence of a transitional process of seeking valorization and not necessarily a start point for many, whether focusing on those joining Facebook groups or those voicing opposition elsewhere. The reasons for joining and being a member of an online Facebook group that opposes the building of a mosque therefore may not be as simple as one might expect. Instead, the reasons might be far more complex and multifaceted and driven by social and political conditions as much as anything else.

Which is where the irony becomes apparent: connecting all those engaged through the Facebook group was their sense of disconnect. This sense of disconnect maybe provides some insight into why Facebook groups, social networks and other online spaces are not only being used to oppose mosques but more importantly to encourage others to do so. As Gurak and Logie (2003: 31) put it:

> the highly specialised virtual spaces on the internet make it easy to join a community and quickly understand and assume this community ethos . . . often, participants do not have to spend time making introductory remarks or defending the premises of their statements. This 'instant ethos' makes it easy to reach many individuals of similar values.

In conjunction with the lack – or at least the perceived lack – of opportunities to engage and find a voice in the offline 'real' spaces, it would seem that social media will increasingly provide those immediate opportunities to not only find a voice but so too to have that voice duly valorized. This will, as Facebook has found since this research was completed, require a constant process of scrutiny and revision in order to try and ensure that those 'individuals of similar values' have fewer opportunities to form communities which have the potential to foster and promote prejudice, discrimination, bigotry and hate. And it is here that notions of opposition become relevant once more. As Shirky notes: 'when it becomes simple to form groups, we get both the good and the bad ones. This is going to force society from simply preventing groups from forming to actively deciding which existing ones to try to oppose' (2009: 21). It is therefore likely that groups opposing others that oppose will be undoubtedly necessary and that greater emphasis on digital methodologies that allow access to these groups will become ever more commonplace.

5 Analysing YouTube Interaction: A Discourse-centred Approach

STEPHEN PIHLAJA

Introduction

For researchers interested in social interaction, online experience and community on the internet and social media, YouTube offers seemingly endless possibilities. With millions of users worldwide, interacting with one another on any topic imaginable, YouTube provides access to a variety of communities and discourses, presented in diverse ways from a variety of perspectives. With this access, however, comes a great number of challenges and obstacles that must also be overcome, from deciding where to start in one's analysis, to what data to analyse and how to do analysis. With so many possibilities, researchers must make difficult, but important decisions on how to focus and develop their research questions and aims to offer useful and narrow insights. In this chapter, I will detail my own discourse-centred approach to analysis of YouTube interaction (Pihlaja 2014), describing to the reader how I isolated videos for analysis, how I chose my analytic methods, and what my analysis allowed me to say about the videos that I chose to analyse.

Doing research on YouTube

On any given day, YouTube's front page is populated with a range of videos serving as windows to societies all over the world. YouTube provides not only a service for users to upload and publish digital video online, but also a 'web 2.0' environment where users both consume content and interact socially with others. The video is only the beginning of the interaction: the ability to comment on and share the video across the web allows it to become a hub for interaction, both online on a variety of sites (on Facebook pages, Twitter feeds, blogs, etc.) and in offline interaction as users view videos together and comment on the content to one another.

YouTube's interactive features provide many opportunities for user text production and interaction, including usernames linked to YouTube channels; video-hosting; text attached to videos, including titles, video descriptions, and 'tags' (keywords); and comments on videos. Users can upload videos of themselves speaking to the camera (called 'vlogs') about any topic or issue that interests them. Others can then make text comments on the video or record their own videos in response, creating a video or comment 'thread' in which videos and responses follow a common topic of interaction over an extended period. All of these opportunities provide data for research, showing how users present themselves on the site, how they interact with others, and how communities of users develop and evolve over time.

How to think about and research online communication has been a long-standing question for discourse analysts and researchers interested in social interaction. Historically, Herring states that two underlying assumptions have framed computer-mediated communication (CMC) research: 'first, that "new" CMC technologies are really new; and second, that CMC technologies shape communication, and through it social behaviour' (2004: 26). As technology continues to advance, however, CMC has become increasingly diversified, with a multiplicity of platforms users can and do utilize for interaction. Moreover, with mobile technology, a clear distinction between offline and online worlds can be difficult to make, with users viewing YouTube videos in a variety of settings. The question in internet research is not only how the affordances of particular platforms shape the interaction that takes place within them, researchers must consider how interactions on a given platform affect and influence interactions in and on other sites, both offline and online. YouTube videos and reception of the videos in comments can offer key insights then in how users understand others and how communities of users develop, serving as a kind of historical record of a group of users.

However, like many social media sites, users control the visibility of content they produce. YouTube users can post videos, but then remove them after a time. Users can control who posts on their page, serving as censors for content. These controls lead to significant difficulty in tracing social interaction, because key moments in interaction among users might be lost as users delete videos or accounts that they feel reflect poorly on them and the public image they hope to cultivate. In tracing the development of a community then, key arguments or moments of antagonistic interaction can be lost from the public record, with the present interaction among users being shaped by a series of videos or interactions that are no longer publicly visible, but which may have played pivotal roles in how the community developed. Moreover, the interaction of users offline around an online text is also lost, with no public record of conversations offline.

Given the rich set of opportunities for social interaction available on the YouTube page and the importance of seeing how communities develop over time, adapting a set of analytic tools to account for all video page elements is a necessity for analysing interaction on the site. Rather than being a static, textual artefact that can be extracted and analysed, YouTube video pages change over time. Users can post and take down videos whenever they choose, often resulting in different videos being available for analysis at different times. Analysis of YouTube drama must then take into account not only the videos that are available for analysis, but other videos that may have appeared and been subsequently removed. In an attempt to provide a framework for doing discourse analysis in dynamic online environments, Androutsopoulos (2008) has developed 'discourse-centred online ethnography' to describe and analyse online communities, treating online discourse as emergent.

Essentially, Androutsopoulos argues that the researcher must also engage online texts and environments as dynamic flows, suggesting systematic observation and direct contact with participants coupled with analysis of user discourse to provide a comprehensive description of online data. Observing the videos of a group or community over time allows the researcher to protect against holes in the data that might emerge as users post and delete messages. Contacting users also allows for some coverage of disappearance of data, as you can ask users about past interaction and videos they may have seen or posted that subsequently have been removed. At the same time, by focusing analysis on the discourse occurring on video pages, the actual interaction of users is foregrounded, serving as an empirical record of social interaction and allowing the researcher to look carefully at how users actually interacted, rather than their recollection. It also solves a key ethical problem frequent in other forms of research because YouTube videos are not participants in a study – they are copyrighted materials, which must be treated as such. They are the self-published works of creators, but they are not the creators themselves.

TIP 1

YouTube videos are copyrighted materials – always respect the copyright owners and cite their work.

With these tools, discourse activity can be compared and contrasted over time, and analysis can move between local and global phenomena (Androutsopoulos 2010). The method provides the researcher, through observation, with the ability to situate analysed videos in a local-historical (or history of interaction within a community) context. The researcher is then aware of the history of interaction between users, giving a perspective on why certain issues may arise within a community. When, for example, an argument appears in a community of users, the researcher can draw on their own observations of previous videos and note any previous interaction between users that may have served as a catalyst for the current disagreement. Second, it foregrounds the importance of situated discourse analysis which treats discourse activity as embedded in a particular interactional context that is also changing over time.

Of course, ethnographic approaches always carry with them complex issues of reflexivity for the analyst, as observation produces more subjective data than, for example, logs of chats from internet message boards. Moreover, particularly with observation, the analyst must first choose a site for analysis, which is problematic in its own right (Schofield 2002), and in doing so focus exclusively on a very narrow group of video creators, potentially limiting the generalizability of any findings. Although the setting of specific research is important, given the reflexive nature of observation, research processes cannot follow clear linear paths or positivist, quantitative paradigms that place value on formulating and testing hypotheses. Rather, settings for research evolve with research questions, methods and participants (Hammersley and Atkinson 2007), and the researcher must be willing to adapt to dynamism in the research setting. This adaptability is, however, a key asset to analysing YouTube interaction. Instead of being tied to a particular quantitative approach that requires a representative sample of YouTube videos, methods can be adapted to respond to the particular interaction observed in public videos, finding the best tools to describe the videos being observed.

Data collection and analytic methods

For my research, I chose to focus on the ways in which YouTube 'drama' (or antagonistic debate) developed. I was not only interested in one-off antagonistic comments or videos made by users, but how antagonistic interaction affected the development of a community over time. In previous research I had done this by looking at the antagonistic interaction between a Christian on YouTube (who called himself jezuzfreek777) and an atheist (fakesagan) (Pihlaja 2011), I had learned some important things about 'drama' interaction. First, I realized that 'drama' often cannot be identified until after it has occurred. Drama can develop between two users in isolated single video threads or in comments sections in which two individuals have a disagreement, but it can also occur on a larger scale among groups of affiliated users when individual comments and/or video responses become broader disagreements. Second, I realized that drama is not always clearly linear: it does not often have clear beginnings and endings, with past interactions, friendships and new disagreements affecting how users interact with one another and how they position themselves either in opposition to or affiliation with others.

TIP 2

Situate analysis of online discourse within the community it occurs and observe the community over time.

To identify drama for analysis, I therefore first needed to identify a community. Using systematic observation from October 2008 to August 2010, I identified a group of users who regularly interacted through a recursive process of observing individual user interactions, identifying users who frequently interacted, and subscribing to and following users over the course of the observation period. I observed approximately twenty users, with individual users making videos and engaging at different levels of involvement over time. Throughout the period of observation, I used the YouTube function of 'favouriting' (or bookmarking for later viewing) videos that related to different drama topics, attempting to identify videos for analysis as they were posted.

I observed quite a bit of YouTube drama in this time, but users frequently removed videos. This became a key problem for me in collecting data because every time I identified some drama for analysis, the absence of many of the videos of one or more central figures in the drama made analysis impossible as one side of the 'antagonistic debate' was missing. Although it appeared unlikely that all videos from a drama event could be recovered, having videos showing all sides of the central arguments, as well as response videos from others was needed to describe how and why drama developed in discourse activity. The importance of having observed the drama while it was occurring was also evident as the reconstruction of past events by users often included omissions of key facts and descriptions of the circumstances in which an initial drama event had occurred.

The drama I chose to analyse, like the earlier work that I did, began with an argument between an atheist (called Crosisborg) and a Christian (Yokeup) in which insults were exchanged. There was a long history of drama between Crosisborg and Yokeup, which developed from Yokeup's condemnation of Christians who were friendly with Crosisborg and his argument that Christians should not be friends with atheists. At one point in their interaction in late-2008/early-2009, Crosisborg made a video that included joking about Yokeup's wife, Caroline, calling her a 'lesbian' and making negative comments about her sexuality. This was offensive to Yokeup and Caroline because Caroline's story of conversion to Christianity included a claim that she had changed her sexuality, having previously been involved in a relationship with a woman before converting. By calling her a 'lesbian', Crosisborg rejected Caroline's own description of herself and insulted Yokeup by appearing to challenge both the validity of their relationship and Yokeup's own masculinity.

In response, Yokeup called Crosisborg 'human garbage', and after great outrage from other viewers, Yokeup argued that he had only called Crosisborg 'human garbage' because all non-Christians were 'human garbage', using the parable of the vine and the branches from John 15 to support his argument. In John 15, Jesus speaks to his disciples using a parable, and uses metaphors to tell the story of God, as a gardener, caring for a vine. On the vine, there are some branches that produce fruit, and some branches that wither and die. The branches that wither and die are thrown into a fire and burned. Yokeup used this story to justify his insult of Crosisborg, saying that the word 'garbage' was equivalent to the 'withered branches' in the parable and it was therefore acceptable to call unbelievers 'human garbage'.

As mentioned above, the problem of videos being removed was a key issue in my analysis. The initial videos that both Crosisborg and Yokeup made were subsequently removed and were not online at the time of data collection, although two atheist users did download Yokeup's videos and reuse elements of these (including video and images) in their own videos. Yokeup made several videos after the initial insult describing what he had done, but never re-uploaded his initial insult of Crosisborg. With what remained online, I was able to reconstruct some of what Yokeup had said in the initial interaction with Crosisborg, but the removal of the video served as an important problem that led to the development of the drama: what *had* Yokeup said exactly? Even the people who had seen the original disagreed.

Both Christians and atheists responded to Yokeup, and videos made around the topic of 'human garbage' focused on the offensive nature of Yokeup's words and his reading of the Bible to justify it, which several Christians argued was incorrect. Disagreement over how to respond to Yokeup as well as over Yokeup's appeal to the moral authority of the Bible to justify his use of 'human garbage' led to new arguments. The atheist users Crosisborg and philhellenes responded angrily towards Yokeup and insulted him, while another atheist PaulsEgo, in contrast, argued that Yokeup was representing the true form of Christianity in his offensive talk and should be encouraged to continue to make videos that highlighted the hateful nature of religion in general, and Christianity in particular. Others, specifically Crosisborg, who was friends with other Christians, felt that Yokeup should be denounced by both Christians and atheists.

Among the Christians, significant debate occurred around Yokeup's reading of the Bible. When Yokeup argued that John 15 supported calling all non-Christians 'human garbage', some self-proclaimed 'believers' questioned Yokeup's interpretation of John 15, claiming that the use of the term was inappropriate because of the context of the parable. These denouncements came, however, with caveats about the need for Christians to 'preach the truth' about hell and judgement. Although the initial videos were posted primarily from January to May 2009, disagreements about the term 'human garbage' could be seen throughout 2010 as Yokeup continued to use the term and to make the same defence rooted in his interpretation of John 15.

The 'human garbage' drama centred around Yokeup's channel which I had been subscribed to since the beginning of the observation period, and I had observed the 'human garbage' drama as it occurred, viewing many of the videos that were subsequently taken down. This provided me background knowledge of the events that led up to the drama. After having observed the 'human garbage' drama as it occurred between January and June 2009, in the summer of 2010, I initially identified forty videos which appeared to be both related to the 'human garbage' drama and remained posted on the site. Starting with a search for the term 'human garbage', potential videos related to the topic were identified from appearing in the search and from examining responses to these videos and videos made around the time of the controversy.

After the forty videos were identified as potentially having some relation to the 'human garbage' drama, I initially watched all the videos and read all the comments. I then focused on videos made in relation to the initial controversy (i.e. Yokeup's first uses of 'human garbage', the initial responses, and his subsequent defence of the term) and discarded videos that did not ultimately relate to the drama. Twenty videos posted either near the time of the initial controversy or reposted later were therefore identified for analysis. Within the twenty videos, three specific exchanges between users (i.e. videos and responses) were further identified for close discourse analysis. The three drama exchanges represented three different kinds of interaction: Christian and atheist; atheist and atheist; and Christian and Christian. Collecting a large corpus of data and identifying specific videos within the corpus for close discourse analysis allowed both for a macro-level description of discourse activity throughout the whole of the 'human garbage' drama, and for a micro-level description and analysis of actual instances of interaction.

Privacy concerns of the users were balanced with the position taken by YouTube in terms of copyright. On YouTube, users can post a video privately or publish it publicly on the site. YouTube states explicitly in their user policy, 'Any videos that you submit to the YouTube Sites may be redistributed through the internet and other media channels, and may be viewed by the general public' (YouTube 2008). YouTube also explicitly states copyright policy: 'When you create something original, you own the copyright for it. Likewise, when other people create content, they may have a copyright to it. As a creative community, its essential that everyone on YouTube respect the copyrights of others' (YouTube 2008). According to YouTube policy, YouTube videos are therefore protected and subject to the laws and rules surrounding the use of copyrighted materials.

Still, with regard to the potential for harm to the users that might occur from analysis of their videos, I confirmed that the videos analysed in this project were all made by adult users who appeared to be aware of YouTube policy about the publicly accessible nature of their work. Although their public position does not guarantee that users would not suffer harm from analysis of their videos, it does appear unlikely. Care was taken in the analysis not to favour any position in the 'human garbage' drama and to present all users with respect and deference. Given the nature of drama interaction, particularly the hateful descriptions of others, I also considered whether or not my analysis might give further voice to the antagonistic language contained in videos. Although I recognize the potential for hateful language to be spread with the dissemination of this research, its value in elucidating how disagreement and misunderstanding occurs between people of different beliefs and faith backgrounds outweighs the potential harm from repeating and reproducing the discourse activity.

After identifying the videos for analysis, I then needed to settle on a method of discourse analysis. Discourse-centred online ethnography does not prescribe a certain approach to discourse analysis because different environments and different interactions would benefit from different methods. Given my goals and research focus of providing a full description of the drama that I was analysing, my choice of discourse analytic methods was tied in many ways to the particular drama that I observed. The drama, as I observed it, was focused on a couple of main things, related to Yokeup's act of calling Crosisborg 'human garbage' and how the drama emerged: first, was it ever okay for one person to call another person 'human garbage'? Second, what did it mean to be a Christian and what should the role of Biblical interpretation be in the development of drama? And third, how did drama develop around the different stories and narratives that users told about themselves and others?

As these issues emerged, I chose to analyse the discourse using the following concepts and methods:

- Metaphor analysis (Cameron and Maslen 2010).
- Categorization analysis (Housley and Fitzgerald 2002).

- Impoliteness (Culpeper 2011).
- Positioning (Harré and van Langenhove 1998).

Broadly speaking, these approaches to discourse analysis worked on different scales, moving from a very close word-to-word method (in metaphor analysis) to a macro analysis of narratives (in positioning analysis). This allowed me to move between scales and compare and contrast findings among different approaches. I will briefly describe these four methods and what their findings showed below.

Metaphor analysis was used to investigate how the users talked about the word 'garbage' and whether or not it was acceptable to use the parable of John 15 to defend it. Looking at how metaphor was developed in the interactions, I could see how different words were used to mean different things, depending on the user. Metaphor analysis allowed me to look at how users read the Bible and what they believed about it, and how atheists were able to take Yokeup's use of 'human garbage' to link him with metaphorical language to other negative evaluations, such as comparing him to Hitler. Using this analysis, I found that users regularly employed metaphor to explain and describe the actions and character of themselves and others in terms of Biblical language, often disagreeing with others about how the Bible should be applied to the YouTube context. Disagreements around this were key to how drama developed.

Categorization analysis allowed me to look at how self-proclaimed atheists described self-proclaimed Christians and could use the actions of one person (in most cases, Yokeup) to speak more broadly about the whole category. Analysing the use of categories in discourse also allowed me to see how Christians differentiated among one another, often using categories that were also metaphorical. For example, Yokeup made a video warning of 'wolves' among the 'sheep', categorizing some users as sheep and others as wolves, depending how he evaluated them and their actions. Using this analysis, I found that users employed the categories dynamically, with the categories having different meanings at different times, depending on who was categorizing whom.

Impoliteness gave me a theoretical basis and vocabulary for talking about the actions of users in the drama, particularly differentiating among the different expectations that users had for social interaction. Yokeup, for example, argued that calling others 'human garbage' was acceptable because it was taken from the Bible and the 'word of God' and therefore, should not be offensive to, in particular, other Christians. Using this analysis, I found that users considered different words and actions to be offensive, and that users often tried to offer justification for what they said.

Positioning was used to describe patterns of reasoning that are evident in the positions that people take from themselves (and give to others) in social interaction, and what those positions show about 'storylines' that user talk follows. This analysis allowed me to look at the drama from a higher scale, looking at how categories and actions in the drama allowed users to tell stories about themselves and others and gave a moral reasoning for particular positions that were taken. Using this analysis, I found that users positioned themselves in conflicting ways and this led to drama. For example, while Yokeup positioned himself as a 'loving preacher' when he called others 'human garbage', claiming to be showing them love by 'preaching the gospel', others positioned him as a 'bully'. In contrast and describing the exact same action, the atheist user positioned Yokeup as a 'psychopath' doing violence to others.

Drawing on my observation and the analysis of language outlined above, I concluded that inflammatory language led to 'drama' because:

- users had diverse expectations about social interaction and organization;
- users drew upon the Bible's moral authority to support opposing actions; and
- YouTube's technical features afforded immediate reactions to non-present others.

The 'drama' developed when users' responses to one another created both additional topics for antagonistic debate and more disagreement about which words and actions were acceptable. These findings were built on a robust description of the community that took into account the interaction leading up to the disagreement and the discourse following from it. The analysis allowed me to take into account the dynamic nature of interaction on the site, positioning my analysis in light of the changes to the community over time.

Reflections

Although this approach to analysis of YouTube was ultimately successful, it was not without its difficulties. Throughout this chapter, I have mentioned the difficulty of users removing videos, and how this can serve as an impediment to doing good research on YouTube. Indeed, in my own project this was a significant problem, as I was not able to recover what was initially said in the drama. That said, my own attempt to recover the initial interaction between Yokeup and Crosisborg mirrored what the users were attempting to do in the drama interaction, trying not only to recover what was actually said, but also manipulate the words of others for their own purposes. The absence of videos rather than being a detriment to interaction was actually an affordance that users exploited for their own purposes. As a researcher, I then made it my goal not to understand what exactly was said in the data that I could not access, but to rather look at reception of the videos and see how the reaction led to different developments in the community.

TIP 3

Adapt methods as the situation changes.

In adapting discourse-centred online ethnography, I ultimately left out a key element: direct contact with users. I initially attempted to contact users to conduct interviews, but was largely unsuccessful. Most users did not respond to the request, while others responded but declined to be interviewed. Given the difficulty in gaining access to the community, and particularly to the central figures in the drama, I chose to focus primarily on observation of the community and of the public interaction among users on video pages. Although this necessarily limited the perspective of the research to the outsider perspective (and arguably invalidates it as an 'ethnography'), descriptions of contextualized discourse did, I believe, still provide insight about user experience, as well as reports of intention and how hearers interpret the intentions of others.

My methodology also limited my analysis to the interaction of users on the YouTube page. At the time of my research in 2009, although use of mobile technology was growing, the interaction among the users in my dataset was largely limited to YouTube. As technology develops, researchers must take into account the diversity of use of social media and must consider whether or not other sites of interaction need to be considered in addition to YouTube data. Where to look for interaction and what is necessary to include or exclude will be dependent largely on the research aims and focus of a particular project. Different challenges will emerge depending on what questions a researcher is attempting to answer, and methods must be adapted as communities and technologies develop.

As a framework, a discourse-centred approach to YouTube interaction allows researchers to look at individual instances of interaction on video pages and place them in larger contexts of community interaction. By situating interaction in this way, the researcher can move between scales, understanding individual videos and comments in light of a larger emerging community. By being able to both look back at the historical circumstances leading up to an interaction, as well as forward to see the consequences of the interaction, the researcher then places themselves in a unique position to talk with authority about the conditions and consequences of interaction and offer insight about how and why communities emerge and develop in the ways that they do.

6   Online Sufism: Methodological Thoughts on Researching Esoteric Islam in an Online Context

SARIYA CHERUVALLIL-CONTRACTOR

Online Sufism: A complicated research field

Sufism is a widely accepted term, usually understood as the 'mystical' or 'spiritual' branch of Islam that is often represented as the emotional side of the Muslim faith. In 2012–13, I explored how young people were taking this esoteric practice to the online world. On forums and blogs they were discussing their Sufi beliefs. In doing so they were enacting their faith and experiencing it digitally. The findings of this project are summarized here; the detailed findings are published separately (please see Cheruvallil-Contractor 2013). In line with the purpose of this volume, this chapter focuses on the methodology that was used to work with these young Sufis – key areas that we shall look at are positionality, research practicalities and ethics.

'Online Sufism' – a conundrum of sorts

According to Werbner and Basu (1998) Sufism is the realm of emotional discourse as opposed to theologians' discussions. As a 'practice' it is often said that this term cannot be definitively defined or even understood except perhaps in the hearts and minds of those who practise and hence *experience* this esoteric route to Islamic spiritual accomplishment (Cheruvallil-Contractor 2013). The origins of the term are debated with Shah arguing that it is nothing but authentic Islamic practice (1980). Across Muslim communities there is a range of opinion. At one end are those who agree with Shah – that this is how 'everyday Islam' has been practised over the centuries and at the other are those who dismiss it as a heretical innovation that has no place in Islam at all. It is against this messy backdrop, of a difficult to define esoteric 'ism', that my research sought to further complicate matters by examining how and why young Muslims have taken their Sufi practice online, what shape this 'online Sufism' is taking, and what impact this is having on Sufism as a whole. As this was a *sociological*, rather than a *theological*, exploration this research did not dwell too much on the esoteric or spiritual aspects of Sufism, but rather examined how young Muslims express and enunciate their particular Sufi beliefs on various internet forums.

The young people with whom I worked were attempting to experience their Sufi practice online, where they felt they had the freedom to interrogate and critically engage with their faith. The online space, they felt, was relatively non-hierarchical and not dominated by community elders who may hold more traditional views. In this online world, the spoken word was replaced by the written word, 'emoticons' replaced expressions and 'online-social-network prattle' was interspersed with philosophical theology. Within this virtual space of faith, emotions, belief and technology, young people articulate religious understandings and positions which are uniquely their own and, as far as they are concerned, these religious positions were inherently real. It is within this context of 'virtuality', reality and 'virtual realities' that I explored young people's articulations of their Sufi beliefs. The online discussions of these young Sufis were often simplistic yet they also made strong verbal and non-verbal statements about their faith, beliefs and religious dogmas.

Religion and religious belief tend to have aspects that are undertaken in private – that determine a believer's personal relationship with a divine, higher being. There are also aspects that are communal – activities that are undertaken in a community. For Sufism, the traditional spaces where such activities take place are the *zawiyas* (or Sufi lodges), *dargahs* and *darbars* (mausoleums of Sufi saints) and also, to a lesser extent, in mosques. In these spaces, activities include religious learning, *dhikr* (or contemplation and worship). Despite the above communal aspects of Sufism, the Sufi path is essentially experienced as an intimate and personal journey that a *mureed* (an initiate or student) undertakes under the mentorship and guidance of a *murshid* (spiritual teacher or guide). My observations of young people's online Sufi experiences raised a number of questions.

First, I wondered, was it possible to experience an *intimate* spiritual journey on *public* digital forums. And was the phenomenon I was researching more an expression of Sufi *identity* than of Sufi *belief*? Second, there exists a great diversity within contemporary Sufi practice. Specific faith practices of individuals are determined by the *tariqa* (or Sufi order: plural *tariqat*) that they belong to and into which they are initiated by their teacher. The *tariqa* also gives identity both to the collective and to the individual. Although all Sufis root their beliefs in the foundational Islamic texts – the Quran and the Sunnah – different Sufi *tariqat* have their own specific traditions, within which are embedded further diversities in practical Islamic theology, transformative ritual and spiritual self-reflection. On the internet it becomes possible for these diversities, which were traditionally quite separate, to converge creating spaces for agreements and disagreements. For the academic observer this becomes an opportunity for exploration – what was the outcome of such convergences where none hitherto existed? Finally, within Muslim practice, it is argued that Sufism has always been more inclusive towards women – was this true online as well? And were such digital religious spaces more egalitarian towards the young?

Methodology: A first look

To answer these questions and others, I undertook a 'netnographic' exercise where I embedded myself as a researcher and a forum user on a social networking website, the stated aim of which was to preserve traditional Islam including the teachings of a range of Islamic historical personalities such as the *sahaba* (companions of Prophet Muhammad), *ahle bayt* (family of Prophet Muhammad), *tabiun* (second generation of Muslims who came after the *sahabah*) and the *awliyah* (friends; usually referred to Sufi sheikhs and leaders of *tariqat*). My methodology (which I will discuss in detail later in this chapter) involved observing discussions over different periods of time; initiating new discussions; and qualitatively analysing what was said. In order to facilitate more in-depth narrative analysis, I explored three case studies in which users discussed specific areas of their Sufi practice and understanding.

The first case study involved a discussion in which participants debated the relationship between logical thinking and faith. The participant who initiated the discussion wondered whether this was the difference between Sufi practice and Wahabi practice, which took a more literary approach to interpreting Islamic foundational texts and also in its rejection of the more esoteric practices of Islam. This conversation was perhaps initially aimed at critiquing Wahabi practice; however, it quite quickly moved into a more philosophical discussion about the possibility to rationally and logically arrive at a religious standpoint of deep belief in God. Was such a belief (that was logically arrived at) easier to sustain? The second case study was a discussion thread, initiated by a female user, which referred to Friedrich Nietzsche's idea of a 'dead' God. The user wondered whether it was perhaps formal and structured religion that was dying rather than God, and that God was perhaps becoming more personalized and internalized to individuals. The third case study looked at mechanisms on the website to include participation of female users, specifically the private 'sisters' area' and is based on a number of discussions that took place in this private area (as opposed to the previous two case studies, which were based on single discussion threads). Women and girls spoke about faith and its relevance to everyday life. Discussions ranged from recipes for dishes to cook in Ramadan (month of the Islamic calendar in which Muslims fast from dawn to dusk) to poetry and general chit-chat. I spoke to women about my research interests both on Sufism and also on Muslim women and their feminisms (Cheruvallil-Contractor 2012). I also initiated a discussion about women and knowledge – asking forum users their opinions regarding French feminist philosopher Michèle Le Doeuff's assertion that women have been sidelined from the processes of knowledge (1998, 1989). Women's responses mirrored what Muslim women in the real world say about feminism – they agreed that Muslim women are denied rights and may have limited social roles due to patriarchal cultural norms that are prevalent in many Muslim communities. They also felt an urgent need for Muslim women's voices and role models to be made more visible. However, they did not think that feminism was an appropriate label for their struggle; indeed a few stated that feminism was often 'angry' and that 'it lacked in *adab* [or respect]' and therefore did not fit in with their Sufi worldviews. Instead they described their struggle as a reclamation of their faith by returning to women's rights as stated in the foundational Islamic texts.

My observations of online discussions and my participation required me to position myself both as an insider – a Sufi who was using online forums and who could therefore be a part of these discussions, and as an outsider – an academic who was observing. Methodologically, I was building relationships of trust, thus I also had to be conscientious about not breaching this trust. As the research progressed, my straddling of two positions required methodological manoeuvring that I shall reflect on later in this chapter in some detail. However, before I progress to a detailed methodological discussion, I present a summary of my research findings aimed at contextualizing this research for readers.

Summary findings: Who are these online Sufis?

Sufism was a key aspect of these young people's identities but this was constructed and experienced in many different ways. Below I suggest a range of positions that young people took, or had, in relation to their Sufi practice and their purpose for articulating this online. As with most sociological categorizations, this 'range' comes with the caveat that each category is fluid rather than rigid – the online Sufis I observed could fit into more than one category and could also change categories:

- For some young people their Sufi belief was an underpinning aspect of their life, and yet an aspect that was neither fully articulated nor formed. These young people knew they were Sufis but did not understand what it meant to be Sufi or the deep reflective practices that are characteristic of Sufism. They came online to find a safe space where they could 'learn' and 'ask questions' without the fear of being 'converted to' non-Sufi Muslim stances.

- Others characterized their Sufisms as being different from other forms of Islam, such as the Saudi-inspired Wahabi or Salafi Islam, which they criticized as too literary or dogmatic. They often came to defend, and to thus consolidate, their stance. Since the forum was open-access, users from other traditions were able to join the forum and participate in discussions. As users defended their specific belief practices from criticism, this led to debates that could often become tense.

- Some young people were more 'knowledgeable' and were able to articulate their awareness through poetry and prose, sometimes their own and on other occasions through their use of quotations and commentaries of Sufi scholars, saints and historical figures. They had reasonably mature understandings of Sufism that they often stated they had developed either through classical Islamic studies they had undertaken (in the real world) or in some cases only after joining the site.

- Others rooted their Sufism more strongly in Islamic theology. For these Sufis, their faith practice was a natural extension of divine doctrine as clarified in the Quran and as practised by Prophet Muhammad and recorded in the Hadith. Fiqh (Islamic Jurisprudence), Shariah (Islamic Law) and Sunnah (Prophetic example) were consolidated into their Sufi epistemologies. Sufism became an inner struggle, or *jihad*, to purify oneself and one's Islamic practice.

My exploration of young people's online Sufism enabled an understanding of how the transmission of Sufi practice from offline to online contexts was changing the ways in which young people were experiencing Sufism. In some cases the discussions simply mirrored offline communities. This was evident, for example, when online users made requests for prayers around exam time or when someone in their family was ill – which was similar to prayer requests being sent to extended family or being announced in mosques after prayer congregations (Cheruvallil-Contractor 2013).

In other cases, as exemplified in the case study discussions, these online Sufi discussions could be transformational. There were undertaken with great openness by young people who were knowledgeable and had the ability to reflect and be self-critical. Furthermore these discussions were open-access allowing others who were less aware to also participate and to acquire new knowledge. The democratization of knowledge and the egalitarian processes of knowledge-sharing are characteristic of the internet. In my research this is evident, for example, in user narratives of having known and learnt Sufism only after visiting the website. With regard to discussions such as those about the nature and existence of God, these forums gave users an opportunity to engage in self-critical philosophical debates that they may not have had the space to discuss elsewhere.

As these young people carry their virtual reality discussions into their real lives, they may be able to engender transformational social change in practice and perceptions of Sufism and Islam. It seems these young people have indeed initiated a new journey – reclaiming and revitalizing Sufism. While retaining the mysticism, philosophical roots and theological underpinnings of Sufism, they are also bringing it up to date with technology, thereby facilitating its continued relevance to their changed social contexts. Although online relationships and communities may never fully replace real world ones, using the tools of the internet and their own wisdom, common sense and, indeed, their naivety and curiosity, these online Sufis have reclaimed for themselves Sufi practice, wisdoms and community, rooting these firmly in the Islamic faith and in (this case) their Western social contexts (Cheruvallil-Contractor 2013).

This research indicates the increasing role of the internet in creating 'safe' social spaces for young Muslims to discuss and debate their faith to an extent that would not be possible offline. The internet brings an element of populism in the process of *ijtihad*. Young people can use the internet to access diverse scholarly opinion and thus inform their own understandings of religious doctrine. This is not without concern, for example El-Nawawy and Khamis (2009: 3) report that the internet 'can also lead to further confusion'. However, it is perhaps more significant that ultimately these young people are able to present narratives about their beliefs, in this case Sufism, that are both coherent and enlightening and which, significantly, *are their own*. According to Bunt (2009: 119), online Muslims: 'have applied technical innovation to galvanise an audience unsatisfied with convention, for which the Net is a natural place to acquire knowledge and converse with peers.'

Methodology: A detailed exploration

So now for a more detailed discussion of the methodology I used!

This research involved observation and participation within discussions on an online Sufi discussion forum. Before diving deep into the methods it is important to note that not everyone in the Umma (global Muslim community) has access to the internet (Bunt 2009) and even where access to the internet is available this may not be reliable and constant. Thus, a limitation of the 'virtual Umma' is that the views captured on it are representative of those who have access to the internet – probably young, technologically savvy Muslims and within this group more so those living in the West or in urban contexts in the Middle-East, South Asia or South East Asia. This was generally ratified by the limited statistics around user demographics that I was able to access about this website. These statistics indicated that a large number of *registered users* were based in India and Pakistan. However, qualitative examinations of forum discussions clearly indicated that the most *frequent users* were from Britain and Europe, with significantly more men than women participating In discussions.

As an ethnographer, I have always worked within what I call a Feminist-Pragmatist epistemological stance. I discuss this stance in some detail in my work on Muslim women (Cheruvallil-Contractor 2012). This stance combines the egalitarian and non-hierarchical feminist research methodologies that were developed out of a need to give voice to the marginalized, whomever they may be. The feminists recognized that top-down research stances were not always equipped to challenge marginalization and asserted that what was required was collaborative research that worked *with* and *for* the research participants (Ramazanoğlu and Holland 2002; Webb 2000). I combined this with the practical approach of the American pragmatists who sought to embed research in everyday practical life and social experience (Dewey 1958; James 1916; Geyer 1914). My research thus takes a collaborative approach that works well in the Sociology of Religion, wherein sociologists explore deeply held religious and spiritual values that are experienced and felt by believers but which outside of religious/spiritual contexts are difficult, if not impossible, to measure or weigh. This is where my Feminist-Pragmatist epistemological stance becomes relevant. It situates knowledge in the experiences of individuals, and in the consequences of their actions, thereby giving weight to those who *feel, experience, say* and *do*. Such an epistemological stance is immediately relevant to the conceptualization of digital methodologies that are emerging because everyday people are taking their lives, opinions, social networks and, indeed, their religious practices online. As researchers we are simply following *their* lead – the lead of the people. That the digital has become a normative aspect of everyday life necessitates digital methodologies.

This research process was driven and informed by those Sufis who participated in this research and my experiences of discussing their faith with them. Thus 'experience' rather than 'observation' becomes the thrust of this research – individuals are 'meaning makers' and in my research stance, the researcher and the researched work together to clarify people's interpretations of their shared world. There are problems with a research stance, such as this one, in which the boundaries between researcher and researched are blurred and criticality, perhaps, becomes less possible, but then as a feminist researcher I question whether criticality is ever possible. There are also strengths to such collaborative research approaches including better engagement with research participants, greater control for them and more democracy in the research process.

From a practical point of view, the research involved the identification of an online discussion forum that was used by Sufi Muslims. This was the first hurdle – how does one identify, and then choose a website to work on, out of the plethora that are available? In the case of this research on Sufism, there were a number of different types of websites that I could have worked on. These included websites that were dedicated to the teaching and learning of Sufism; online libraries; websites for specific *tariqat*; forums (some that were dedicated to specific socio-religious groups and others that were more general); and discussion groups on larger networking sites such as Facebook. I finally chose the website that I worked on for the following reasons:

1 I felt that a forum would be better suited to a sociological exploration as it would give access to the opinions and discussions of everyday people. A teaching and learning website or an online library, by giving access to religious texts and resources, would perhaps have been more suited to a theological exploration.

2 Although the forum I chose subscribed to a particular form of Sufi thought, it was open-access and also had an environment that allowed engagement from different Sufi and, indeed, non-Sufi groups. Its members came from a diversity of Muslim denominations, Sufi *tariqat* and different countries.

3 This was an 'active' and busy forum that included a wide variety of discussions on Sufism and also other more general subjects. The forum discussions would generate sufficient data for analysis.

4 This forum was open-access and discussions (unless they were private) were publicly accessible, even to non-members.

5 There was a private space for women. This was important as I was keen to access women's voices and opinions in my research.

TIP 1

Give careful thought to choosing the online/digital site for your research. In doing so, take into consideration your research objectives, intended outcomes and possible ethical implications.

I observed and then analysed discussions on this forum – what were online Sufis saying and how did this impact on their Sufi practice? I sometimes participated in discussions and occasionally initiated discussion threads. This was a qualitative research project and as in offline research it was vital to capture coherent, but also multiple, narratives. Yet, it was simultaneously also important to ensure that the research was feasible and doable within the resources and timeframe available. I therefore undertook two staggered sets of observations over two three-month phases. During these two phases, I often visited the website two or four times a day spending between thirty minutes and an hour reading and, where required, recording the discussions. I kept a journal of the discussions noting emerging patterns. Particularly interesting discussions, or those which stretched over a few days, were bookmarked for easy access. Accessing the website in two separate phases allowed me to see how the discussions were reflecting current affairs. So, for example, when my research coincided with exam periods there were more prayer requests from students who wanted to do well in their exams, and when one period of time coincided with the football World Cup, there were dedicated threads discussing this. Furthermore, the length of each phase (three months) allowed me to follow, observe and analyse longer discussions.

Gradually patterns began to emerge across the discussions, and I realized it was possible to begin categorizing these discussions: general chit-chat; current affairs; inter-denominational debates; philosophical explorations; etc. Identifying these patterns facilitated a sieving process that allowed me, as the researcher, to start structuring what was a very large and continuously growing qualitative dataset. These patterns also set the foundations for the qualitative analysis that I later undertook. I have previously mentioned three specific discussions that I used as case studies. The narrations of these online Sufis are important because according to El-Nawawy and Khamis (2009), current research about online Muslim communities is sometimes limited in scope because it rarely analyses content. The case studies allowed me to 'follow' these selected discussion threads and to subsequently highlight this in my analysis of online Sufism.

Although this research was situated in digital contexts, it mostly followed a classical ethnography framework, the difference being that for this virtual ethnography or 'netnography' project, the methods had to be altered to suit the online world. So 'participant observation' and 'discussion groups' (both traditional methods) were combined into a mutated form of online content analysis of discussion threads. It was still possible to observe what people were doing and discussing, but this was typed text rather than the spoken word or actions. The signifiers I looked for and the observations I made were now digitized – 'forum posts', 'emoticons', 'font size' and 'font colour' were the signs I looked for rather than the spoken word, emotions and body language. Was a participant 'SHOUTING' because s/he was using capital letters or was s/he simply emphasizing a point? What did a different font size or different font colour mean?

Over the research period as I became more familiar with the website, I also learned that it had its own social, linguistic and cultural milieus, and indeed social systems and hierarchies. For example, all users had online profiles that included their profile picture, signature statements, etc. However, I soon discovered that users had online personalities that extended beyond their 'online profiles'; these online personalities were more nuanced and were developed over months of using the forum. So users were identifiable as having specific roles – the scholar, the kind consoler, the congenial younger sister, the good-natured problem solver, the humorous joker, the leader – within what was essentially a community in its truest sense.

TIP 2

It is well worth spending time to embed yourself (in an anthropological sense) in the online/digital site of the research as this will enable you to know and understand the 'culture' of the online site.

As in traditional anthropology, I embedded myself within the community I was researching, and during this time I had to constantly reflect on my positionality as a researcher. As mentioned previously I was an insider as an online Sufi myself; I was also an academic researching this group – an outsider. Throughout the research, I needed to consider what impact my participation or lack of it was having on the discussion I was observing. In the end, I took different approaches to dealing with this. In some discussions, as in case studies 1 and 2, I did not participate and simply remained a silent observer. In others, as in case study 3 where I worked with women, I was active – I initiated and even encouraged discussions on specific subjects.

Ethics: Blurry boundaries and new definitions

There are significant ethical considerations that a researcher must be aware of in online research about religion and religious experience. Religion is an emotive and sensitive subject. With regard to Muslims and Islam, this is further complicated by sociopolitical tensions around Islamophobia, radicalization and extremism. The communities being researched are 'research weary' (Sangera and Thapar-Bjökert 2008: 544) or 'exhausted by so much research that is about them rather than for them' (Alvi et al. 2003: xv) and are suspicious of the intentions of the researcher. As a researcher who works within a feminist-pragmatist epistemological stance, I am conscious of the need to establish relationships of trust and mutual acceptance with research participants. This is much more difficult to do in online contexts where face-to-face interactions are not possible. Once this trust is established, it must be protected. This too is difficult to do in the online world where the blurring between the public and the private requires new conceptualizations of accepted ethical norms around confidentiality, anonymity and protecting the interests of the research participants. The public–private blurring can mean that although comments are posted in 'public' forums, the intentionality behind posts may not always be for them to be public. Intentionality, however, is difficult to measure, and in some cases participants may not be fully aware that they are posting their opinions publicly. Furthermore, as reported by Allen (in Chapter 4), people often say things online that they would not say offline.

Researchers must also be aware of anonymity – which is something that many online forum users may take for granted. Users may perceive their comments as not being traceable back to them and that they are using online profiles that are abstract and not linked to their real names, for example a user may call herself theonlinesufi or greenrevolution (these are just examples for illustration purposes and are not real profile names). However, technology can be used to trace the real people behind the online profiles and netnographers must constantly remain aware of possible inconsistencies within understandings and expectations of anonymity that exist in the online world.

I was able to gain access to the women-only private space and analyse discussions taking place there. Access to this space was vetted by the forum moderators who had various checks and balances to try and determine whether a user was female. As a woman, I was privileged to be given this access. To reflect briefly about positionality, it is interesting to note that had I not been a woman, I would not have been able to undertake this research, unless I had pretended to be one which would have been unethical practice. The discussions held here were not in the public domain. Hence it was important to be clear about the purpose of the discussions so that users were fully aware that the discussions were part of academic research. With regard to my own ethical practice, the website and its users will remain anonymous in all publications linked to this research project. Where quotes are used, these are all paraphrased to limit the possibility that an individual participant is identified.

TIP 3

As part of ethical considerations for a research project, it is important to include checks and balances to ensure the safety and security of the researcher.

Finally, I consider my position as a researcher working in this space where public and private spheres are blurred. When in the past I have gone out on extended research fieldwork, I have had to prepare and then abide by a 'safety framework', which states for example that colleagues must at all times know where I am, that I must not venture in private places where my personal safety may be at risk. In one sense such concerns are not relevant to online research at all – it can be undertaken from the safety of one's desk. Yet there is a different kind of visibility and exposure that the researcher must deal with. Although he or she is researching people who are only known by their online profiles, the researcher must make his or her real-world identity known – people knew who I was, although I did not know who they were! Most academics have visible staff profile pages that are easily accessible and that often publish professional contact details – emails, phone numbers, social networking IDs such as Twitter handles or Facebook accounts. Although this has not been an issue in my work, with increased occurrences of online bullying and trolling, researcher visibility and possible vulnerability need to be given appropriate consideration when planning the research, especially on sensitive subject matter such as religion.

Secondly, unlike Facebook where people use their own names as profiles, on forums such as the one I was researching, people's profile names could be virtually anything. So it is possible that forum users may not be who they say they are (this may also happen on Facebook despite the safeguards it has). For example, what if not everybody in the sisters' privacy corner was female – what impact could this have on discussions that were being held?

Concluding thoughts and reflections

As more religion 'goes' digital, we will see the establishment of academic communities-of-practice. One area that we will constantly and collectively need to reflect upon will be our research methodologies and strategies. In my work on online Sufism, I discovered a community that had social systems, hierarchies and what may best be described as a culture of its own. To research this community, I first had to become part of it, I had to understand its language and know its people. I then used traditional research methods that I tweaked and adjusted to suit the needs of my digital research site. In doing so I had to constantly reflect on their appropriateness and fitness-of-purpose. More significantly I had to reflect on the dynamics and particularly the ethics of doing research online. I developed and successfully implemented my research strategies in my project, and I hope that these will prove insightful to other researchers undertaking similar work. Yet I am also convinced that this is an evolving field that will continue to develop as more and more of our everyday lives are transferred online. A final thought: in writing this chapter I have become intensely aware of the crossovers between the online and the offline. In undertaking digital, sociological research it is no longer sufficient to delineate between the real and the virtual – indeed for participants in my work the virtual is also the real.

7 Studying Digital Hinduism

HEINZ SCHEIFINGER

Introduction

The multifaceted Hindu tradition has a strong online presence that allows for a range of activities from accessing information to actually engaging in worship (see Scheifinger 2012). In tandem with this development, digital media is now becoming integrated into the lives of many to the extent that in modern societies it often makes little sense to talk of the online and the offline as being separate (Campbell 2011; Consalvo and Ess 2011; Lundby 2011). Because of this, sociological investigations into the convergence of Hinduism and digital media – 'digital Hinduism' – are of prime importance. Studies can provide us with insights into how aspects of Hinduism are being transformed, how the religious lives of some Hindus are being altered, and how the wider Hindu tradition is being affected. Furthermore, because of the inextricable relationship between religion and new media – a development that is related to the embeddedness of new media in some modern societies – effective digital Hinduism studies can accomplish a number of further objectives. They have the potential to contribute to the sociology of contemporary Hinduism, to the field of religion and new technology, and to the sociology of religion. Moreover, a productive study of digital religion will also provide us with broader insights regarding the nature of, and changes within, modern societies in general (see Campbell and Lövheim 2011).

It is characteristic of my research into digital Hinduism that I do not adopt an all-encompassing sociological theory and then attempt to explain findings in the light of this theory. This is because I believe that if researchers fully align themselves with a specific theoretical standpoint and proceed to interpret their findings in the light of this alone, then there is the danger that the interpretation of the data can be extremely limited. Instead, I adopt an approach that Bryant (1990) would refer to as 'new pragmatism' (cited in Craib 1992: 248), which I believe can contribute more to the understanding of social phenomena. I agree fully with Ian Craib that 'the social world is made of different types of phenomena, and each type needs a different theoretical understanding and explanation' (Craib 1992: 251) – and this is also the case regarding different aspects of digital religion. Therefore, I use different theories as tools by working with those theories that are especially relevant to the area that I am investigating and which can help me to understand the data from my empirical research. In turn, when relevant theories are selected, the data from my research also has the potential to contribute to the theories that I am using (see Craib 1992;

Beckford 2003). I will demonstrate this approach by providing examples of the consideration of aspects of digital Hinduism through the lens of a key feature of a prominent theory of globalization, and in the light of a central assumption associated with rational choice theory.

Globalization

In one area of my work, I have considered the implications of being able to conduct a *puja* (a Hindu rite of worship) online. Although performing the ritual online is very different to doing so in the traditional setting, there are still similarities. In both cases the *pujas* have a symbolic aspect and they both allow for the experience of darshan (the act of obtaining grace from a deity through gazing into their eyes and at the same time being seen by them), which is the most important part of the rite and also a religious practice in its own right. However, my research also revealed that there is a common view that online darshan is not as beneficial as darshan at a physical site. The philosophical reason that explains why, for some authorities, there is a difference between receiving darshan from the original image of the deity in the traditional physical setting and from an image of the deity online, is the belief that the original image has some intrinsic power and that an online image of the deity cannot have this.

My research also indicated that issues of purity and pollution that are central in most forms of Hinduism are less pronounced when conducting online worship, although they are still important. The deity itself cannot be polluted whether it appears online or at a traditional temple (see Scheifinger 2010: esp. 336). However, the offline environment can be polluted by those who visit in an impure state and this consequently affects all worshippers who visit there. In contrast, online worship by those in an impure state does not affect the physical site and its visitors – but there is the further belief that those who worship online in an impure state will find it more difficult to gain benefit, and, according to some authorities, worshipping online in an impure state could even result in harm to a devotee. Because deities cannot be polluted through their images appearing online, the immediate main implication of an online image of a deity being accessible to everyone is that those who would previously have been prevented from receiving darshan of a specific god or goddess (because of their ethnicity or position outside of the Hindu caste system) are now able to receive darshan (see Scheifinger 2009). In the future this could increase the perception held by some that Hinduism is a universal religion as opposed to an ethnic one (see Scheifinger 2010).

Due to space constraints, I will only comment upon these findings in light of a key feature of one influential theory of globalization – that offered by Anthony Giddens. Time and space play a key part in Giddens' important work on globalization. He emphasizes that in modernity, 'place' and locale no longer simply coincide (Giddens 1990: 19) and that time and space have become separated. He refers to this as 'time-space distanciation' (Giddens 1990: 20) and its key feature is that of 'disembedding' – 'the "lifting out" of social relations from local contexts of interaction and their restructuring across indefinite spans of time-space' (Giddens 1990: 21). Online phenomena might initially appear to have undergone such a process – indeed more so than when transmitted via new technologies that existed prior to the development of the internet. However, although I have indicated above that online *pujas* are certainly a noteworthy development, the fact that it is still preferable for worshippers to attend the physical site suggests that online Hindu images have not become 'disembedded' from the local site (see Scheifinger 2009). Thus, a central feature of Giddens' theory is challenged by online Hinduism.

Rational choice theory

An entirely different facet of digital Hinduism can be investigated by drawing upon another theoretical approach, that of Rational Choice Theory (RCT). RCT is a term that can be applied to a family of theories related to the economic approach to understanding society formulated by Gary Becker (see e.g. 1986). Regarding religion (a field of study in which RCT has been especially influential), one of RCT's central assumptions is that religious organizations compete with each other in order to gain members in a religious market that functions in rational economic ways just as other markets do (see Iannaccone 1995: 77; Finke 1997). The extent of market regulation is crucial in this regard. De-regulation allows all religious organizations (not just established ones) to be a part of the religious market, and crucially, it reduces start-up costs for these organizations or 'producers of religion' (Finke 1997: 48). Efficient new religious groups are thus afforded the opportunity to become successful (see Finke 1997: 51). Overall, de-regulation is said to result in a vibrant and healthy religious market and a corresponding high degree of religiosity; and this conclusion is held to be universal (Finke 1997: 48).

Although there have been a number of criticisms of RCT, I see no reason to believe that religious producers do not act rationally and compete with each other in the marketplace in order to attain, for example, prestige and influence. If this is accepted, then it is worthwhile to use RCT as a tool in order to investigate online Hinduism because the internet – through its emergent feature of cyberspace – has brought about a site in the religious marketplace that did not exist when Finke and Iannaccone made their assertions. Such an investigation thus enables us to achieve two things: to uncover details regarding the online Hindu marketplace and to determine if the aforementioned RCT principles apply in the new venue of cyberspace.

My research in this area has revealed that if a Hindu organization or individual decides to have an internet presence then it is highly unlikely that they will be able to compete easily with groups that have expertise and resources in abundance, and who have already cemented their place online. The latter part of this conclusion is key: even if a group enters the online marketplace with expertise and hefty resources, the prominent presence of some organizations on the internet is entrenched to such an extent that the current situation cannot be easily defrayed by this. In fact, the situation of a newcomer entering the online religious market is entirely different from that of a newcomer entering the offline market. In this latter scenario, there will still be large established groups that would appear to make it difficult for newcomers to achieve their goals. But, the RCT assumptions state that in this situation there is at least a free-market where new groups can and do become successful. However, although the online market is relatively unregulated, it is still subject to major constraints.

I was thus able to draw the conclusion that the RCT assumption that de-regulation automatically brings about a free-market is problematic. In addition, religious vitality was discerned online despite the absence of a free-market and this suggests that a free-market is not necessarily required for this vitality to occur. Therefore, when the online situation is considered, a distinction needs to be made between de-regulation and a free-market. The two should not be seen to be inextricably related as RCT normally posits. In short, online, de-regulation appears to result in religious vitality but does not give rise to a free-market, and thus the proposed universality of RCT is challenged.

Methodology

Although my investigation of issues surrounding online *pujas* begins with research carried out in the online environment, the conclusions drawn are also dependent upon traditional fieldwork. Full analysis of the online *pujas* which, at the outset, requires that a researcher actually performs them, can only be achieved when they are compared to traditional *pujas*. This necessitates secondary research regarding the features of *pujas*, observing *pujas* inside temples and in other contexts, and obtaining the views of individuals. Such an approach allows both similarities and differences between the two forms of worship to be ascertained, and this can indicate how an important aspect of most forms of Hinduism is changing. It is essential to get the views of individuals regarding the validity of online worship, but it is also crucial to be aware that reasons behind views as to the efficacy of, say, online darshan, are related to the particular viewpoint within Hinduism that a respondent aligns themselves with. Therefore, it is essential that instead of just asking for individuals' views, we also learn of their wider religious and philosophical beliefs and gain further details of these through further discussion with them and by undertaking supplementary literature research.

The importance of this is shown when we consider the aforementioned belief (that a physical form or *murti* of a deity contains intrinsic power and that online darshan is, therefore, not as beneficial as darshan of a physical image of a deity) and then compare this with a contrasting belief. A contrasting belief was articulated in an interview with a religious personality of the monist Advaita Vedanta tradition in which *murtipuja* is seen as unnecessary – though usually not condemned as it can provide a religious focus for those who need it. The view was given – fully compatible with the tradition's philosophy of pure monism – that there is no difference at all between conducting a *puja* online or at a physical setting ('Anonymous', interview conducted at Annapurna temple, Varanasi, India, 11 August 2005). This demonstrates that not only is it unsatisfactory merely to conduct online research when investigating digital religion, but that it is also essential to delve deeply into the reasons behind respondents' answers – something which necessitates detailed knowledge of the religious tradition under consideration. In the case given here, it allows us to avoid sweeping generalizations and can suggest the extent to which different traditions within Hinduism will be impacted upon and evolve through digital Hinduism.

When investigating online *pujas*, then, it is conventional research methods that are of prime importance and that form the bulk of the research process. However, in the investigation of some areas of digital Hinduism, extensive online research needs to be undertaken. This is the case regarding the consideration of RCT and online Hinduism that I have referred to. Secondary research is insufficient when attempting to ascertain the characteristics of the online marketplace and can give rise to contradictory conclusions. For example, the fact that some governments have attempted to restrict access to certain information on the WWW and been largely unsuccessful in this respect, implies that the online marketplace is a free-market – as does the initial observation that there is an extremely large number of websites created by Hindu religious producers. In contrast, recourse to the notion of the 'digital divide' (unequal access to the internet) challenges this idea of a free-market online. The digital divide within India alone where many Hindu websites originate and are accessed by Hindus is striking (for example, in 2009 there were less than 62 million internet users in India despite the fact that the population was well over 1 billion (Central Intelligence Agency 2014)). The observation that there are large numbers of people who simply do not have access to the internet is usually made concerning consumers, but it is just as valid when applied to producers. This alerts us to the fact that the online marketplace is not free because there are groups or individuals who are simply unable to enter the online marketplace. Even if issues regarding access to the market are set aside, when the online marketplace itself is subjected to a detailed investigation, the conclusion that is able to be drawn is that contrary to the initial indications mentioned above, it does not constitute a free-market.

Access to consumers is of prime importance in any market. Because of this, the employment of search engines by a researcher is an important first step in researching the online marketplace as this starts the process that ultimately allows a researcher to discover which websites are likely to be encountered by those going online seeking Hindu resources. This is partly because search engines are used by millions of individuals daily in order to find content online (Hargittai 2007: 769); Google claims that there are billions of searches made every day using its search engine alone [see Google author n.d.: online]). In my research, I have conducted searches using the term 'Hinduism' under different conditions using a number of search engines at various intervals during the last nine years. In addition to the use of this term being a common-sense choice, in their analysis of US religious searching on the WWW, Jansen et al. (2010: 47) demonstrate that it is common for seekers to use simple terms such as 'Islam' and 'Buddhism'. It is therefore highly likely that many people who go online seeking information about Hinduism in general would start by entering the term 'Hinduism' into a search engine.

My data shows that the change in those websites that make up the top ten of the search engine rankings has been minimal. This is an important finding because 'approximately 80% of Web users never view more than the top ten or so [search engine rankings]' (Jansen et al. 2010: 45). In fact, there are only a handful of websites that consistently appear in the top ten despite the fact that there is a vast number of websites that offer content related to Hinduism. This finding is all the more extraordinary seeing as how the Google search engine, for example, is 'continuously updating its search algorithms, which means that one specific query will not produce the same exact results on two separate occasions' (Pan et al. 2007: 807). This alone suggests that the online market is not a free-market, and further online research confirms this and reveals why it is the case. In addition to conducting the searches using different search engines over a period of time, we can look in more detail at the online marketplace using three further indicators that then allow us to engage in further analysis. These are: 'search engine saturation', which refers to the number of times that a website address appears in a search engine's index; 'link popularity', which tells us the number of links from other websites that a website has; and the actual links between websites (see Scheifinger 2008a for a detailed discussion of the three indicators).

Further research and analysis associated with the search engine data and the additional indicators reveals significant start-up costs for newcomers that aspire to compete in the online market. In order to achieve a strong presence on the WWW, it is essential to appear high in search engine rankings, but achieving this involves huge costs. A strong presence cannot be obtained in a short period through strategies such as having a large number of keywords that get picked up by search engines. Instead, in order to appear high in the rankings, links must be established with other websites. Aside from the number of links that can affect a website's search engine ranking, it is also important to note that the actual links between websites are highly significant. This is because manually following links and subsequently analysing the content of the linked websites, reveals that the external links from websites that consistently appear high in search engine rankings are often to other websites that are also highly ranked. Therefore, because linkages are related to search engine rankings, this gives rise to a situation in which those websites that are highly ranked further reinforce their position. This discussion shows, then, how the employment of a combination of online research methods is able to provide us with insights regarding the Hindu online marketplace which I have further shown have wider theoretical implications.

Ethics

One of the points that I have made in this chapter is that of the interpenetration of the 'online' and the 'offline', which is part and parcel of the increasing embeddedness of new media in modern societies. Because of this, in addition to investigating the online environment, carrying out conventional (offline) fieldwork is essential when studying digital religion – something that I have demonstrated above and which is also suggested in the final section of this chapter where I discuss an interesting area for future digital Hinduism research. As a result of this, much of my research into digital Hinduism brings up no more ethical considerations than in standard fieldwork. For example, when researching online *pujas*, interviews were conducted with informants in physical settings who were aware of the nature of my research, and observation was carried out in public areas of temples. While it was not possible to inform all of the participants in rituals that I was a researcher, as I was not a participant and was solely interested in observing and reflecting upon natural events on which I had no influence,[1] this was not ethically problematic. In addition, the example that I have given above regarding the analysis of the online marketplace also does not give rise to ethical concerns. This is because the use of search engines and the identification and analysis of websites that are publicly available is unproblematic in this regard, as is the investigation of the links between websites.

In contrast, because it involves – on one level at least – entering an environment that is different to that where traditional fieldwork is carried out, it is in the area of my work where I look at the actual practising of religion online (see Scheifinger 2008b) that new ethical issues are encountered. As intimated above, it is a commonly held belief by Hindus that images of deities online are able to provide darshan (Scheifinger 2009; 2010). Because of this it is clear that, for some individuals, there is a degree of sacredness attached to the online environment created by a website which provides the facility to undertake an online *puja*. Therefore, although unlike in some other online environments there are no other participants in a ritual carried out via a conventional *puja* website, there are still ethical issues involved when conducting research in such an environment. These issues concern the attitude, comportment and presentation of the researcher who accesses an online *puja* website and who, it is believed by some Hindus, subsequently undergoes some form of interaction with a deity.

Although I have asserted that a deity cannot be polluted via the screen by a person in a state considered to be impure, this belief can be held concurrently with the view that deities can still be subject to disrespect in the online environment by those who are considered to be in an unfit state (Mishra, interview conducted at New Vishwanath temple [Mir Ghat], Varanasi, India, 17 August 2005). Such a state could include, for example, engaging in multi-tasking, wearing attire that would be considered improper when approaching a deity in a physical Hindu temple, and perhaps enjoying a glass of wine while conducting online research. I therefore make the assertion that there are ethical issues involved when a researcher accesses an online environment in which a deity can be worshipped even when no other participants are involved. This is because I hope that I am correct in saying that no researcher would enter a physical Hindu temple in an unsuitable state even if they were sure that there was no one else present to witness this.

TIP 1

When conducting research within online religious environments, be aware that there are ethical issues concerning respecting the religious tradition and its practices regardless of whether or not others are present.

Against the possible argument that my claim is irrelevant because the environment provided by a website cannot accrue sacredness, as Helland (2000: 216) points out, it is 'distinctly questionable' to tell those that are involved in our research that their subjective views are wrong (see also Grieve 2010: 46). Instead, we need to recognize that even if we as researchers start off with the belief that there are certain criteria which must be fulfilled in order for an online manifestation of something to be considered valid, the very fact that there may be people who accept the validity of the online phenomenon despite these criteria not being met, means that we need to take the new development seriously. In actual fact, it is the acceptance of such subjective views of research participants, along with the academic recognition that religious practices are undergoing alteration, which can demonstrate that religion is changing in modern societies (see Helland 2013). In the case mentioned here, there is the suggestion that the notion of sacredness that may, for example, have previously necessitated a certain mythological history attached to the environment, is changing. The case also provides one example which shows that online research gives rise to new ethical issues that need to be addressed (see e.g. Johns 2013: 238, 248; Markham and Buchanan 2012: 3).

Reflections

In this chapter, through offering a brief discussion of online *pujas*, I have shown that it is not only valuable to investigate aspects of digital Hinduism because they can indicate how a religious tradition and its practices are evolving as a result of an online presence. Instead, as in the case of the example of my investigation of Hinduism and a new religious marketplace, by looking at digital Hinduism through the lens of globalization I have shown how a study of digital religion can have broader theoretical implications. I have also emphasized that when researching digital religion it is essential to undertake conventional fieldwork. This is related to the fact introduced at the outset of this chapter that, because new technology is embedded in many people's lives, the terms 'online' and 'offline' are losing their utility. Thus, instead of focusing solely on online developments or even thinking in terms of conducting research in both the online and the offline context, researching digital religion requires us to speak to respondents and observe their behaviour in their normal, everyday religious lives that now incorporate new technology.

TIP 2

Avoid thinking of the 'online' and the 'offline' as being separate spheres, and tailor your methodological approach with this in mind. Utilizing conventional fieldwork methods such as interviews and observation is likely to be crucial.

In addition to applying general sociological theories to the study of digital Hinduism, it would also be profitable to consider it in the light of theories that have been influential in the specific field of the sociology of Hinduism. Such a theory – that of Sanskritization – informs an interesting area for possible further research, a discussion of which will conclude this chapter. Broadly, such research would aim to discover if there is any evidence that the presence of Hinduism on the WWW is facilitating Sanskritization, and, if this were the case, to look at this in greater depth.

'Sanskritization' is a process first identified by Mysore N. Srinivas in 1952 (Srinivas 1962: 42). In short, according to Srinivas, Sanskritization is the process (not always successful [see Srinivas 1962: 57]) whereby groups low in the social system in India adopt the habits and lifestyles of Hindu castes higher up in the hierarchy in order to attempt to bring about a rise in their status (see Srinivas 1962: esp. 44). Even groups (such as tribals) who are outside of the Hindu caste system can attempt this and, if they are successful, can enter the system and thus become Hindus (Doniger 2009). In connection with this, Sanskritization also refers to a lower-caste group's 'exposure to new ideas and values which have found frequent expression in . . . Sanskrit literature . . . [such as] . . . karma, dharma and moksha' (Srinivas 1962: 48).[2]

In addition to making it clear that my discussion that follows regarding Sanskritization, online Hinduism, and the potential for further research is speculative, it is also important to mention a number of further points. Firstly, Srinivas' concept has been criticized. For example, Christopher Fuller (1992) argues that those Sanskritic ideas and values identified by Srinivas 'are only tenuously Sanskritic' and therefore there is no dividing line between Sanskritic and non-Sanskritic concepts. According to Fuller, this means that 'in the end, we seem to be left with a concept of Sanskritic Hinduism that has no definable empirical content at all' (Fuller 1992: 26). However, despite this, there are still certain values that lower castes adopt, although rather than these values being 'Sanskritic', Fuller argues that they are merely those practices that the high-caste Brahmins have been able to claim to be superior as a result of their dominant position in the hierarchy (see Fuller 1992). Nevertheless, if this is accepted, through research it would still be possible to ascertain instances of the adoption of such practices by those low down in the hierarchy.

Secondly, it is clear that many outcaste or low-caste groups would not have access to the internet or have relevant internet skills. However, this observation certainly does not apply to all low-caste groups as in some cases they may be wealthy (see e.g. Shattuck 2003) and thus have attendant opportunities to access new technology and, in the case of a certain type of presence online (see below), even one example would suffice to show that the internet can help to facilitate Sanskritization. Finally, it goes without saying that Indian society has undergone vast changes since Srinivas introduced his idea of Sanskritization. However, as contemporary research has made clear, a caste system remains in India and is still of immense significance (see e.g. Sooryamoorthy 2008, esp. 283–4; Rao 2009). Just one example to demonstrate this is that entry to some Hindu temples is still made difficult for those outside of the caste system – one of the reasons why online darshan is a noteworthy development within Hinduism (see Scheifinger 2010). Furthermore, in the Hindu diaspora there is some perpetuation of the caste system (Sutherland 2003; Jacobs 2010). Overall, it is clear that there are important considerations regarding the concept of Sanskritization, which although are unlikely to be insurmountable when devising a credible research project, would still be a serious concern for any future research. While appreciating this, as my following discussion is hypothetical, I am able to skip over these considerations.

A future investigation of Sanskritization and online Hinduism could focus upon a number of different areas. The first of these concerns the presentation of groups online. Low-caste groups could use the internet to present themselves in a way of their choosing. For example, a website could have an attractive and professional appearance, and, as Charles Brooks points out, according to Srinivas, 'evaluations of purity and pollution are as much a result of appearances as they are of birth-status' (Brooks 1989: 21). A website could also, for example, demonstrate an awareness of those 'Sanskrit ideas' referred to above, and claims identifying a group's particular local deity with a universal deity could be made. Such a claim is a key Sanskritization technique (see Marriott 1955). A presence in cyberspace could also result in the shortening of the length of time necessary for Sanskritization to occur. For example, Srinivas asserts that it is common only for later generations of groups that attempt to Sanskritize to be able to pass themselves off as a higher status because 'the people who first hear the claim know that the caste in question is trying to pass for something other than what it really is' (Srinivas 1962: 57). Furthermore, Srinivas claimed that for those castes at the bottom of the hierarchy, 'their only chance of moving up is to go so far away from their natal village that nothing is known about them in the new area' (Srinivas 1962: 59). Online, the audience is far less likely to know the true origin of a group. Therefore, Srinivas's argument that 'the group must be content to wait an indefinite period' (Srinivas 1962: 57) may no longer apply in the future.

A second area of possible investigation involves the potential increase in the dissemination of 'Sanskrit ideas and values'. According to Srinivas, under British rule, 'the development of communications carried Sanskritization to areas previously inaccessible' (Srinivas 1962: 48). Therefore, it would certainly be interesting to investigate whether, in this respect, the internet could contribute to further Sanskritization. Another reason to suggest that Sanskritization could be facilitated by the internet also invites future investigation. One aspect of Sanskritization is the replacing of blood-sacrifices with alternative offerings (see Srinivas 1962: 49). The online *pujas* referred to in this chapter are purely symbolic and therefore there is the suggestion that if online *pujas* became widespread and started to replace those blood-sacrifices that still exist then this would be evidence of the internet contributing to Sanskritization.

The possible relationship between Sanskritization and the internet is also worth investigating because of the rise of Hindu fundamentalism, which has become an important development within Hinduism (see e.g. Bhatt 1997; Kurien 2007). Steven Vertovec points out that whereas Srinivas proposed that Sanskritization could eventually lead to a group improving their place in the status hierarchy, now the process is also adopted by Hindu fundamentalist groups so as to enable Hindus to 'rally around mutually accepted or commonly venerated religious or cultural institutions and tenets' (Vertovec 1997: 267). Therefore, Sanskritization has taken on a contemporary significance beyond that envisaged by Srinivas. And because Hindu fundamentalists embrace the internet (see esp. Kurien 2007), the possible role of the internet in the facilitation of Sanskritization could be especially significant.

TIP 3

It is fruitful to consider aspects of digital religion in the light of existing theories and debates regarding the religious tradition that you are interested in. This has the clear potential to highlight the transformative features of digital religion.

While details regarding the relationship between digital Hinduism and the process of Sanskritization are, as yet, unclear, one thing is certain: as in the case of the concrete examples presented in this chapter, a discussion of possible future research regarding Sanskritization demonstrates that studies of digital Hinduism have the clear potential to reveal important insights regarding changes in aspects of Hinduism which, in turn, can contribute to our understanding of the evolution of the wider Hindu tradition.

8 Young Sikhs' Religious Engagement Online

JASJIT SINGH

Introduction

To date, few scholars have examined the religious lives of young Sikh adults even though the British Sikh population is currently skewed towards youth. Indeed, according to the 2011 census, of the 423,158 Sikhs currently living in England and Wales, 105,985 (25 per cent) are between the ages of fifteen and twenty-nine, further highlighting the necessity to understand the lives of young British Sikh adults. Although there have been many studies of the relationship between religion and the internet (Campbell 2011: 232), to date few of these have examined the online presence of Sikhism. Those that have, have focused on the impact of internet forums on traditional authority structures (Jakobsh 2006), the response of Sikh discussion groups to the events of partition and 1984 (Barrier 2006), the impact of Sikh dating websites (Maclaran et al. 2008), the representation of Khalistan and of Sikh martyrs on the internet (Axel 2005; Sokol 2007), a comparison of discussion forums used by European Sikhs (Singh 2012), and the role of the internet in contemporary identity construction within global Sikhism (Jakobsh 2012). In this chapter I firstly outline the evolution of Sikhism online before describing how I examined the role of the internet in the religious lives of young British Sikhs (based on Singh 2014a). I then present some findings followed by a discussion of ethical issues when researching online.

The beginnings of the public online presence of Sikhism are to be found among the Usenet newsgroups that developed in the early 1990s (e.g. Sandhu 1990). As an undergraduate studying computer science at the University of Manchester from 1990 to 1993 I remember being so amazed at being able to access articles about Sikh history and Sikh issues on the 'soc.culture.indian' newsgroup (Sandhu 1990) that I would print these out and take them home to show my parents. At the time there were no publicly accessible Sikhism newsgroups, forums or websites with international computer-based communication being a novel and somewhat exciting experience. Although a relatively 'late entry' into the world of online religion given that Jewish and Christian discussion groups have existed since the mid-1980s (Campbell 2010: 22), the online presence of Sikhism has developed exponentially since the 1990s with a Google search of 'Sikhism' on 6 October 2011 producing 4,520,000 hits. As I will demonstrate in this chapter, much has happened in the interim with Sikhism firmly establishing itself online in a number of different forms.

The world's first website on Sikhism, Sikhs.org, appeared online in December 1994.[1] Sikhs.org appears to have quickly become a point of reference for information about Sikhism for Sikhs and non-Sikhs, with Microsoft including it as an 'Editor's choice' in their 1997 Encarta encyclopaedia (Sikhs.org n.d.). As well as a few websites, the mid-1990s also saw the formation of a growing number of specifically Sikhism focused discussion forums, many of which broke away from the earlier culture-based forums such as the 'soc.culture.indian' newsgroup. The first of these Sikhism focused discussion groups was the 'soc.religion.sikhism' bulletin board, which had arrived online on 4 July 1995 and was moderated by a group of young educated American Sikhs (soc.religion.sikhism 1995), including Sandeep Singh Brar, the founder of Sikhs.org, and Rajwinder Singh from Boston University (Bonine 1995).

Although a historical mapping of the emergence of every Sikh website is beyond the scope of this chapter, it is important to understand that a wide variety of Sikh/Sikhism-related websites have appeared online since the early 2000s including websites for Sikh organizations, Sikh camps, gurdwaras, Sikh history, *kirtan* portals and merchandise. As well as providing information about Sikhism, many of the early websites also hosted discussion forums. These were usually hosted either on Sikh 'portals' such as the Waheguroo network (kirtan.net), which offered visitors a variety of services including *kirtan* downloads, Sikh-related screensavers and articles about Sikhism, or on organization-specific websites such as the website run by the Tapoban gurdwara in Toronto (tapoban.org).

The website-based discussion groups such as Sikhsangat.com and Sikhawareness.com (Singh 2012) preceded the appearance of website free discussion groups following the launch of Yahoo groups and Google groups. As Hock explains, the distinction between these new discussion groups and previous discussion groups was that for the former 'you *went to* a Web site or a newsgroup reader to read and send messages. For the latter, messages *came to* you via email' (Hock 2005: 88). A number of discussion groups were created at this time although many are no longer active. The emergence of blogging in the late 1990s (Campbell 2010: 24) added a further type of online religious presence with individuals being able to write web logs, or 'blogs' about their own personal religious journeys.

To fully appreciate how young British Sikhs currently engage with Sikhism online it is necessary to examine some of the important and relevant developments that have occurred online since 2000, beginning with the launch of Wikipedia in 2001 (Jeffery et al. 2009). The format of Wikipedia, as an online encyclopaedia on which articles are written by anyone with access to the site, has subsequently been used to generate a number of specialized 'wikis' dedicated to specific subjects[2] including Sikhiwiki (www.sikhiwiki.org), a Sikhism-focused wiki that arrived online in 2005, and that currently boasts 5,821 articles on Sikhism (Sikhiwiki.org n.d.). Although Facebook only opened itself up to the public in 2006, in January 2011 it passed Google to become the most popular website in the world (Kiss 2011). As well as wikis and social networking sites, the emergence of video hosting websites such as YouTube, which arrived online in 2005 (Jeffery et al. 2009), have been an important development in the online presence of religion. The fact that videos of events held all over the world are now easily available and accessible has increased the amount of material available to young Sikhs allowing for lectures and talks that might previously have been missed, to be readily available online.

Methodology

Having understood how Sikhism has manifested itself online, I will now focus on the research methods used to understand the role of the internet as a means of religious transmission using a mixed methods approach in order to gather the views of a number of young British Sikhs and in order to be able to note patterns among a large cohort of respondents. As I wished to understand how young Sikhs learned about Sikhism from the point of view of young British Sikhs themselves, a largely qualitative methodological approach was chosen within a mixed methods approach. Although qualitative research is sometimes criticized for being anecdotal and for being presented casually and unsystematically, one of its main advantages is the contextual detail that it provides (Mason 2002: 1). As researchers can 'improve their confidence in the accuracy of findings through the use of different methods to investigate the same subject' (Denscombe 2007: 109) data was gathered using a number of different methods. This mixed methods approach can check against bias, allow for the development of research instruments, and also allow the researcher to 'exploit the strengths of a particular method without leaving him/herself vulnerable to criticism in connection with that method's weakness' (Denscombe 2007: 111) as well as increasing the accuracy of findings and validating the findings of one method against another.

For instance, although using semi-structured interviews allows a researcher to gain an in-depth understanding of the motivations of a particular group of people, the small numbers of interviews that can usually be conducted during a research project leave the researcher open to criticism that the data are not representative. Using a mixed methods approach and combining interviews with a survey allows data to be gathered from a larger number of individuals across a wider geographical area. As this research focuses on the transmission of Sikhism among young British Sikhs, I decided to carry out semi-structured interviews with this group using a 'multiple exploratory' case study approach that allows the researcher to study relationships and processes as they naturally occur (Denscombe 2007: 37). The case study approach also encourages the use of multiple methods, allowing the researcher to validate the data gathered through triangulation. As explained, I decided to use a number of methods in conjunction with the interviews in order to gather different perspectives on the research questions. Of the various methods used, in this chapter I will focus on semi-structured interviews to understand religious transmission from the actor's point of view and the online survey to gather a large amount of responses in order to be able to identify patterns and trends.

Semi-structured interviews

As qualitative research seeks to understand behaviour from the actor's point of view, interviews were used as one of the main methods of research. Choosing interviewees depends on a 'conscious and deliberate choice about which case to select from among a large number of possibilities' (Denscombe 2007: 37–9). As cases are selected on the basis of known attributes it is important that the criteria used for the selection of these cases are justified as part of the methodology (Denscombe 2007: 39). Given the constraints of time and researcher resources, it was decided to interview those young British Sikhs who:

a Deliver/have delivered lectures and talks at events held for young British Sikhs; and/or

b Organize/have organized events held for young British Sikhs; and/or

c Attend/have attended events held for young British Sikhs.

Although this categorization is open to critique as it limits potential interviewees to those young Sikhs who are already engaging with their tradition, I am arguing that this selection is justified as these individuals would be able to offer experiences and insights relating to the role of the 'new arenas' of religious transmission in particular. The problem with this approach, however, is that it assumes the usefulness of these 'new arenas'. As one of the main aims was to understand how young Sikhs learn about religion, it was also necessary to gather data from young Sikhs who may not attend or engage with any of the events described above, an issue addressed by the use of the online survey.

Online survey

As trust in the sponsor of an internet survey has a positive impact on response rates (Fang et al. 2009) I decided to design and build a project website (www.leeds.ac.uk/ sikhs) that would allow interested respondents to find out more about the research project while highlighting that the research was legitimate and being carried out under the banner of the AHRC/ESRC 'Religion and Society programme'.[3] Once built the website was used to host the online survey to facilitate the gathering of data from young Sikhs across the UK who do and do not attend events organized for young Sikhs.

Using an online survey to collect data had a number of advantages, especially in a research project of this size. First it facilitated the collection of data from a large variety of respondents in a short time without having to negotiate gatekeepers. Second, the online survey was relatively cheap to implement, certainly compared to paper surveys as there was no cost to distribute the survey (Couper 2000) and the survey software was freely available. Third, it was felt that the online survey would reduce or substantially eliminate any interviewer bias as there would be no need for any physical interaction between the researcher and the respondent.

As online surveys are best used in situations where a particular group of individuals is targeted, especially those that share a common interest (O'Lear 1996: 210), designing and building an online survey for this group made sense, particularly as young British Sikhs would be technologically very comfortable with the online environment. In order to gain some experience of carrying out online surveys I undertook a small pilot survey using Bristol Online Survey software in October 2008 to ensure that the survey performed correctly (Pearrow 2000) and that respondents were clear as to the meaning of the questions asked. This small pilot test was useful in ensuring that questions worked as required, providing confidence in the success of the survey once it had been implemented on a larger scale.[4]

Following the pilot, the full online survey was implemented on 20 November 2009. Having been advised that responses would be more likely if respondents were presented with a clickable hyperlink as opposed to having to type in a survey hyperlink, I initially sent out emails to every young Sikh I knew and asked them to pass this on to other qualifying individuals.[5] Following this, I contacted the administrators of British-based Facebook groups belonging to Sikh youth groups, university Sikh societies, Sikh camps and/or gurdwaras and other Sikh groups including hockey, *bhangra* and *gatka*-related groups. These emails were personalized according to the group in question, which led many of the administrators to forward these emails on to the members of their groups.

TIP 1

If possible, try to engage with individuals/groups offline before engaging with them online. If they have met you in person or have seen you speak they may be more likely to respond to your research.

As well as targeting relevant Facebook groups, I sent emails to relevant Sikh Yahoo groups and Google groups, posted messages to Sikh-related forums and also wrote about my research on Sikhism-related websites.[6] These advertising methods produced excellent results, with the survey gathering 645 responses in total having run from November 2009 up until July 2011. To try and minimize false responses I followed Nosek et al.'s (2002) advice to have a couple of questions with definite answers repeated in the survey, and to provide questions specifically designed to catch malicious participants. In addition, of the 645 respondents, 407 stated that they would be willing to be contacted regarding future research, and supplied contact details. It is argued that the fact that so many respondents were willing to supply their personal details goes some way to addressing Couper's (2000) concern that it is not always possible to know for certain who is participating in an online survey and Nosek et al.'s (2002) concern that participants may answer questions falsely or submit their responses multiple times. Given the fact that the survey was relatively long and required a reasonable amount of effort to complete it is argued that the risk of false or multiple submissions is somewhat diminished.

TIP 2

Build a web presence that highlights your role as a professional researcher who is linked to an established research institution. This creates a level of trust for respondents and can also provide further information about the research to potential participants.

The survey asked both quantitative and qualitative questions. Following Warren (2007) who notes that there is increasing potential to use internet surveys for qualitative research, and Williams (2003: 50) who argues that as surveys usually only present a limited range of responses, standardized questions may miss important aspects of the research, many questions allowed respondents the space to respond beyond the quantitative questions asked. This strategy worked well, with respondents appearing to be very comfortable in writing at length online (Warren 2007) providing long textual responses to a variety of questions that were rich in qualitative content. Warren (2007) concludes that although textual survey data cannot fill the place of conventional ethnographic techniques it should be taken seriously, particularly when using internet surveys as one source of qualitative data. In summary, the online survey presented both quantitative and qualitative data from a wide variety of respondents (Figures 8.1 and 8.2).

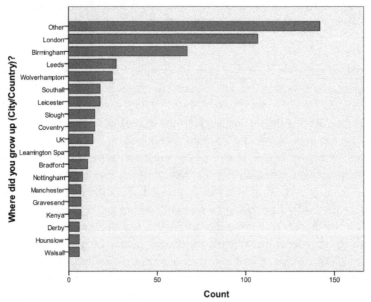

Fig. 8.1 Locality of Online Survey Respondents

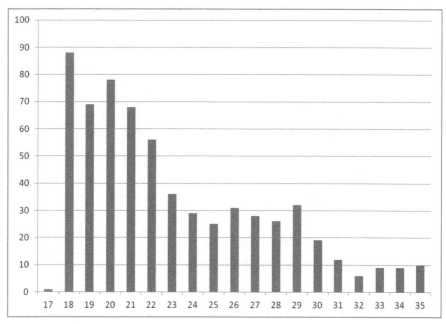

Fig. 8.2 Age Profile of Online Survey Respondents

As a method of gathering data to ensure the accuracy of themes and trends therefore, the online survey was a success. The quantitative data was analysed using SPSS, with the qualitative answers being analysed and coded using NVivo, along with the interview transcriptions and focus group data.

Summary findings

Having understood how data was gathered through the online survey I will now briefly outline how the findings highlight how young Sikhs engage with their tradition online.[7] Campbell (2010: 26) identifies five different ways in which users employ the internet to 'fulfil certain spiritually motivated goals'. First is the 'spiritual network', where the internet facilitates the formation of social networks that support spiritual activities (Campbell 2005: 54). Second, the internet can be used as a 'worship space', set aside for religious ritual where online activities become part of a person's spiritual life. Third, users might view the internet as a 'missionary tool', used to promote a specific religion or set of beliefs. Fourth, the internet can be used as an 'affirmation tool', where users can cement their religious identity and practice by connecting into a global, networked community of believers and finally, the internet is used as a 'functional technology' to support the social practices of a particular religious community.

All of these narratives can be found in the online encounters that young British Sikhs described in the online survey data. A high percentage of those who 'strongly disagreed' that they learnt most about Sikhism from the internet were *amritdhari* (43.5 per cent), came from 'religious' or 'very religious' families (82.6 per cent) and prayed more than once per day (41.3 per cent) as compared to the other categories, possibly indicating that those who responded in this way had other sources from where they could learn about the Sikh tradition. An analysis of the survey responses to questions about Sikhism-related internet usage reveals that young Sikhs go online in order to:

1 Discuss taboo subjects.
2 Obtain answers to questions about the Sikh tradition.
3 Explore differing practices within the Sikh tradition.
4 Access repositories of *kirtan* and *katha.*
5 Examine English translations of Sikh scriptures.
6 Obtain *hukamnamas.*
7 Find out about Sikh events.
8 Access event archives, recordings and instructional videos.
9 Purchase Sikh resources including books, photographs and clothing.
10 Understand the legal position of Sikh articles of faith.

Discuss taboo subjects

Many of the survey respondents stated that the internet allowed them to discuss issues which they felt that they would not be able to discuss with their parents and peers, or which they did not feel their immediate contacts would be knowledgeable about, with an 18-year-old male from Leeds stating that the internet had 'helped me learn about things that I would have found difficult to ask say a person at the gurdwara or my parents'.

Obtain answers to questions about the Sikh tradition

Young Sikhs are also able to find answers to questions that are not satisfactorily answered by parents or traditional authority figures. For a 30-year-old male from Manchester, the internet 'helped very much in asking the simplest questions. I.e. Why do we tie up our hair?, why do we shower every morning?, what effect does the daily bani's have on our psyche?'. Female respondents also stated that the internet had allowed them to find out historical information about Sikh women, with a 26-year-old female from Southall explaining that the internet had 'offered stories about strong Sikh women that I don't hear from other Sikh men who "preach" or tell stories'.

Explore differing practices within the Sikh tradition

One of the most striking ways in which the internet has impacted young Sikhs is the way in which young Sikhs are now able to research aspects of Sikhism that they might not have previously been aware of. Whereas young Sikhs might not have encountered much diversity growing up, they can now easily access a host of diverse views. A 26-year-old female from London explained that she had not realized 'how many American white people have come into sikhi which is inspirational. If they can make the effort to learn about sikhi why can't we (the ones that are born in sikh families) . . . we need to learn by their examples.' It can be concluded that, thanks to the internet, young Sikhs are much more aware of the diversity within Sikhism than previous generations may have been and are, according to a 31-year-old female from Birmingham, able to 'explore religion relatively "safely" in a non commital way'. However, the survey responses also highlighted that this accessibility to a number of viewpoints can also become confusing. A 28-year-old female from Kent explained that 'if I have a specific question its hard to find coherent answers too many sects with different maryadas and random ideas to get the true meaning of sikhi'.

Access repositories of *kirtan* and *katha*

The Internet also allows young Sikhs to easily download *kirtan* (music) and *katha* (discourse) from a variety of sources. As has been discussed, *kirtan* is an important aspect of Sikh worship with particular groups having their own particular styles of *kirtan* (Khabra 2010). Through MP3 downloads and YouTube it is now possible to listen to *kirtan* recordings in any style of choosing. Indeed, as of October 2011 the Sikhnet 'Gurbani Media Center', one of the largest repositories of *kirtan* online lists, had over 14,000 tracks sung by 544 different artists.[8] Although, the internet may not be acting as a 'worship space' in this context, the fact that *kirtan* can be downloaded means that the choice of listening to a wide choice of *kirtan* at any time is now available to young Sikhs. As with *kirtan*, a variety of types of *katha* are available, primarily by professional *kathakaars* usually trained in Damdami Taksal, or in the various Sikh Missionary colleges. The increasing availability of *kirtan* and *katha* indicates the functional usage of the internet as a distribution mechanism of religious music and discourse.

Examine English translations of Sikh scriptures

Given that the Sikhitothemax translation software first found a home online, it is not surprising that many young Sikhs mentioned the ability to examine English translations of the Guru Granth Sahib and other Sikh scriptures as being an important use of the internet. As a 25-year-old female from Slough explained, 'direct English translations from the Guru Granth Sahib have enabled me to interpret the Guru's teachings for myself' with a 28-year-old female from High Wycombe explaining that 'before the websites, I would sing without fully knowing the meaning of the shabads I was singing'.

Obtain *hukamnamas*

The increased access to translations has allowed Sikhs all over the world to receive a *hukamnama* or 'order' from the Guru Granth Sahib as and when required. Indeed, it could be argued that the taking of an online *hukamnama* is one of the few examples of Sikhs undertaking *online religion*. Whereas Sikhs would previously have had to visit their local gurdwara to hear the daily *hukamnama* or to obtain a personal *hukamnama*, it is the *hukamnama* from the Golden Temple, Amritsar which is usually presented on websites and emailed and texted all over the world. Sikhnet not only offers a daily English translation but also offers daily audio explanations in English of the *hukamnama*. Sikhs are also now encouraged to take a 'Cyber Hukamnama' for on the spot guidance from the Guru Granth Sahib. Many respondents stated that they read a *hukamnama* daily and noted the importance of the *hukamnama* in providing 'an idea of how to face the day' and to 'help stay connected'. I am arguing that the increased accessibility of *hukamnamas* has allowed many Sikhs to experience a more personal relationship with the Guru Granth Sahib as those Sikhs who might not visit the gurdwara on a daily basis can still consult their Guru as an easily accessible provider of immediate advice.

Find out about Sikh events

An important offline impact of the internet is that it allows the advertising of events to interested people. Whereas previously events might have been advertised through telephone calls and/or advertisements in the Punjabi press, the evolution of discussion groups and, in recent years, Facebook have made it much easier for young Sikhs to find out what is going on where. Anyone with membership of the right Facebook groups, or in contact with the right friends will now be automatically notified about a whole host of Sikhism-related events happening in the next day, week or month. Given that many young Sikhs have spoken about the importance of *sangat*, the fact that they are now made aware of events such as *rainsbhais*, lectures and *kirtans* taking place all over the country means that they are now regularly able to meet other like-minded Sikhs at these events through these online 'spiritual networks'.

Access event archives, recordings and instructional videos

As well as current events, the evolution of video hosting websites has meant that recordings of talks given at camps and Sikh societies are now available, meaning that even if a particular event is missed, it is still possible to listen to the lecture given. Videos of important events from the late twentieth century onwards are also now available online including the speeches of Sant Jarnail Singh Bhindranwale (YouTube

2010), and news footage of the events of 1984. In addition, the advent of these sites has allowed for instructional information, such as turban tying videos to be viewed on YouTube (YouTube 2011) by young Sikhs who have no easily accessible family members to teach them.

Purchase Sikh resources including books, photographs and clothing

The internet has made it much easier to find and purchase previously difficult to locate items. A 28-year-old male from Birmingham noted that 'Amazon – got me the books I need, emails got me the photos I needed of old granths' whereas another stated that the internet had 'greatly eased access to rare recordings by great Sikhs, access to old granths, made it possible to read *gurbani* anywhere'. Many websites now offer Sikh music and clothes for sale, including Sikhism-related hoodies, T-shirts, posters, books and DVDs (see G5 Sikh Media n.d.).

Understand the legal position of Sikh articles of faith

The internet has also allowed young Sikhs easy access to information about the legal position of Sikh articles of faith, especially the kirpan. Saldef, the Sikh coalition and United Sikhs have all published legal guidance relating to the wearing of turbans and the 5Ks and have provided legal assistance to those experiencing difficulties with wearing these articles of faith.

Reflexivity and researcher standpoint

According to Denscombe, 'one of the characteristic features of ethnography is the significance it attaches to the role of the researcher's "self" in the process of research' (2007: 69). As any account of a particular lifestyle or set of beliefs is a construction based on the researcher's interpretation of events, it is necessary to consider the background of the researcher (Bryman 2004: 500) during any research project. Denscombe (2007: 67) offers a useful list of factors that could be included in an outline of the researcher's self:

- Personal beliefs relating to the topic (politics, values, standpoint).
- Personal interests in the area of investigation (vested interest, history of events).
- Personal experience linked to the research topic (incidents affecting self or others close to researchers).
- Personal expertise in relation to the topic (qualification, experience).

The wish to undertake this research is clearly informed by the fact that I am a British-born Sikh, albeit one who has now passed beyond the phase of emerging adulthood, who has engaged with the Sikh community in West Yorkshire throughout my life. Having grown up with religiously active parents, with my father regularly being involved in the local gurdwara committee, I have been involved with events held in gurdwaras from a young age although neither myself nor my family ally with any Sikh groups or individuals.

Ethics

This research followed the guidelines outlined by Diener and Crandall (1978), which state that when gathering data for any research, it must be ensured that participants will not be harmed in any way, that participants have consented to take part in the research, that the privacy of participants will not be invaded and finally that participants will not be deceived in any way (Bryman 2004: 509). The welfare and privacy of the participants was of paramount importance throughout the data-gathering process with participants being as informed about the research project as possible before taking part. The online survey respondents had to agree to a series of ethical statements in order to be able to complete the survey as follows:

1. Please select 'Yes' to indicate that you agree with the following statements:

1.a. I am over 18 and I voluntarily agree to take part in this survey.

1.b. I give the researcher (Jasjit Singh) permission to use the results of my participation in this survey once any data which may identify me has been removed.

1.c. I understand that any information about me recorded during this survey will be stored in a secure database. No data which may identify me will be transferred outside this survey. Data will be kept for seven years after the results of this survey have been published.

1.d. I understand that I can ask for further instructions or information at any time by contacting the researcher (Jasjit Singh).

1.e. I understand that I am free to withdraw from this study at any time, without having to give a reason for withdrawal.

1.f. I understand that I do not have to answer every question.

TIP 3

When designing online surveys, ensure that you provide enough space for respondents to answer to questions. Do not miss out on useful data due to survey design.

As those taking part were generally highly technologically literate, they were welcome to contact me in case of any further questions, which they could easily do through the project website: arts.leeds.ac.uk/jasjitsingh. All participants were advised that any information given was to be treated in strict confidence and that the raw data including transcripts would not be made available to any other persons or for any other purpose. In terms of consenting to take part, survey respondents were informed that by completing the survey, they were consenting. Again, no personal details were used in the thesis itself with age and location being used as an identifying characteristic. Given that many respondents provided full, long answers to some of the survey questions (which were often up to 1,000 words long) some of which contained personal information, I had to ensure that any quotations did not identify the respondent.

Reflections

The above discussion demonstrates how I ensured that this research is both reliable and valid (Mason 2002: 188). Reliability is concerned with demonstrating that the data generation and analysis has been appropriate to the research question, and carried out in a 'thorough, careful, honest and accurate' (ibid.: 188) manner. Validity asks if the project measures or explains what it claims to (ibid.: 188). In terms of reliability, the data generation methods used all provided relevant data to examine the main research question(s). In terms of validity, the interviews and online survey generated the most detailed data. Allowing survey respondents to express themselves also worked very well, again leading to less likelihood of bias. Coding the interviews and survey responses also made it simpler to identify where common responses were being given, and proved that the results were drawn from actual responses. On the whole, I feel that the conclusions drawn will do justice to the study, and can be seen as being valid, having been derived from a number of research methods.

The biggest challenge was to ensure that users would be engaged with the research and that the online survey would gather responses. Given the huge number of choices that are available to users when they go online, the survey had to be structured and presented in a way that would appeal to users. As explained, the building of the project website certainly worked to reassure respondents that the research was being undertaken as part of a respectable research programme. Physically visiting young Sikh activists to inform them about the survey also proved useful as they informed their friends and peers about the survey through word of mouth. This also ensured that I was relatively up to date with the latest online innovations that young Sikhs would tell me about through these visits. In researching religion online it is imperative that scholars researching religion keep up to date with technological innovations online in order to understand the new ways in which religion may be manifesting itself in the online environment and to also understand how the usage of previously popular types of online interactions may be changing. On 28 March 2012, Jagraj Singh posted a series of videos on his YouTube channel.[9] Since then Jagraj Singh has released over 14,000 videos, and has appeared on Sikh television stations and on the BBC. The religious environment online is extremely fluid with social media including Facebook and Twitter being a key tool in allowing researchers to keep up to date with the latest developments.

Regarding their online interactions, it has been shown that young Sikhs go online for a number of reasons, with a useful distinction being made between whether or not the user is looking for *religious knowledge* (e.g. about taboo subjects or about the diversity of Sikh ideologies) vs. looking for *religious engagement* (e.g. with the Guru Granth Sahib) or with an event being broadcast online. This distinction between seeking *knowledge* vs. *engagement* puts the onus about the type of online interaction on the individual user. In terms of community, I found that the discussion forums and social media do not constitute communities in the offline sense, as these online communities play much less of a 'regulatory' role. Unlike offline communities, which it is usually only possible to leave following a physical re-location, online communities can be joined and left at any time. In this regard online communities only appear to be relevant if they relate to an offline equivalent, echoing Dawson and Cowan's view that 'the Internet is not a reality separate from "the real world," but an electronic extension of it' (2004: 12).

In conclusion, this chapter has outlined the methodology and research methods used to examine how young British Sikhs learn about Sikhism, why they organize events to teach Sikhism, and the impact of new technologies including translation software and the internet impacting on their religious learning. The rationale for using a mixed method approach has been explained, as has the practical implementation of each of the research methods used. The development of the online survey in particular has been shown to be the method through which most of the data was gathered, with the online presence being an important way in which many young Sikhs learned about and became engaged with the research. The online survey worked in the case of my research primarily because my target age group was internet savvy and comfortable with online engagement, emphasizing that a research strategy and methods must be tailored towards the particular group being researched.

Part 3 Digital Communication

9 Studying Apps: Research Approaches to the Digital Bible

TIM HUTCHINGS

Introduction

This chapter introduces you to some of the methods that can be used to study a mobile app using examples drawn from my own multi-method research on digital Bibles and their users. I will pay particular attention to one case study, YouVersion's 'Bible App', now installed 180 million times worldwide.

I will start by introducing the research context for my case study, explaining the history of digital Bible publishing and describing how the Bible App works. I will then outline three methodologies that could be used to study religious software, using the Bible App to show how these approaches can be applied in practice. Many different methods could be useful for this kind of project, but in this chapter I will focus on interviews, surveys and ethnography.

We must always consider research ethics when designing strategies for research projects. The study of a mobile app raises some interesting ethical problems, and I will discuss the implications of these suggested methods for the privacy and vulnerability of research subjects. Careful attention to research ethics helps maintain the safety of everyone involved in a project, but can often also lead to useful new insights about the people and contexts we are studying.

I will conclude this chapter with some reflections on what we have learned so far about digital Bibles, and where further research will be needed.

The research context

Digital Bibles for study and engagement

YouVersion's Bible App builds on a much longer history of Christian digital publishing, which can be categorized into two main traditions: 'study' (focused on textual analysis) and 'engagement' (focused on sharing the Bible with new audiences). Computers were first used to study the Bible in the 1950s, when Reverend John Ellison, an Episcopalian, worked with a UNIVAC 1 machine to create a concordance of the Revised Standard Version on magnetic tape (Computer History Museum n.d.). The first Bible study software began to appear in the 1980s, including the first electronic libraries of Bibles and references texts. As late as 2004, however, sociologist Charles Ess could still argue that the Bible software market was limited, unambitious and unhelpful. Computers could 'take on the tedium of word counts and comparisons' in textual analysis, and 'accomplish in minutes an inquiry that would otherwise take weeks or months', but this kind of work still exploited 'only the most basic potentials of the computer' – offering the appearance of scholarship, without imparting genuine wisdom or new insight (Ess 2004).

Today, commercial desktop software packages such as Logos and BibleWorks offer thousands of texts and much more sophisticated linguistic analysis tools, inviting users to purchase vast libraries of digitized commentaries and reference works. This chapter will not attempt to evaluate the extent to which these more recent products have answered Ess' critiques, but we shall return briefly in the final 'Reflections' section to the connection between textual accessibility and wise interpretation.

The 'study' tradition of Bible publishing aims to help users to analyse the text. The second tradition, 'engagement', seeks instead to use new media to attract new audiences to the Bible, or to encourage already-committed Christians to read the Bible more frequently. In some cases, digital innovations try to make the Bible more accessible. For example, the first handheld electronic Bible reader was created by Franklin Computers in 1989 (Yianlios n.d.), and transformed the cumbersome paper Bible into a lightweight, easy-to-use palmtop device. Products in the 'engagement' tradition may also be designed as tools for proselytism, like the devices created by MegaVoice, an Australian company founded in 1986, which sells solar-powered MP3 players to help missionaries share the Bible with audiences unable to read. Other initiatives teach audiences to interpret the Bible in accordance with a particular religious tradition. GloBible (released 2010) offers maps, timelines, videos and virtual-reality reconstructions of biblical sites, while BibleMesh (released 2010) focuses on video lectures from well-known pastors.

Publishers working in this 'engagement' tradition have made extensive use of social media, adopting Facebook, Twitter and other platforms to bring Bible texts into the everyday communicative environments of Christian and non-Christian users. According to Twitter staff member Claire Diaz-Ortiz, 'Pastors tell me, Twitter is just made for the Bible' (O'Leary 2012), because Bible verses are usually short enough to post in a single 140-character tweet. A Facebook page called 'Digital Bible' ranked among the most active in the world for several years and has now gathered almost 10 million followers. This page posts Bible verses, each attracting hundreds of comments and shares and tens of thousands of likes (currently found at www. facebook.com/DigitalBible).

This chapter focuses on one sub-genre of digital Bible publishing, the mobile app. Hundreds of Bible-themed apps are now available, forming a thriving marketplace that includes projects representing both 'study' and 'engagement' traditions. A search for 'Bible' in iTunes or Google's Play Store shows the variety of options now available, including study aids, collections of inspirational verses, quiz games, apps for children and apps aimed at specific Christian denominations. Most of these products are offered free of charge, but many hope to attract subsequent in-app purchases of additional content (Hutchings 2014).

In the next section of this chapter, I will go into more detail to describe one popular example of a mobile app in the 'engagement' tradition: YouVersion, 'The Bible App'.

A case study: YouVersion, the Bible App

YouVersion was created in 2006 by Oklahoma-based LifeChurch.tv, and launched its first mobile app in 2007. LifeChurch.tv is one of the largest multisite megachurches in the United States, and YouVersion just one of LifeChurch.tv's free digital ministries and software products (www.lifechurch.tv/digital-missions/). YouVersion does not include commentaries or other explanatory resources, and does not offer tools for textual analysis. Instead, this app follows in the 'engagement' tradition identified above, encouraging users to spend time with the Bible through easy access, personalization and social interaction. According to YouVersion's blog, the Bible App has already 'helped millions grow closer to God's Word through a personal experience with Scripture', and the company's ambitions are framed in language of global revival: 'it's our passion at YouVersion to equip this generation to become the most Bible-engaged in history' (YouVersion 2014a).

On YouVersion's website, bible.com, YouVersion is introduced as 'a simple, ad-free Bible that brings God's Word into your daily life'. Download this app, and 'God's word is with you . . . you'll have your Bible with you no matter where you go'. This invitation promises a causal connection between the convenience of a mobile device, increased frequency of Bible access and a more personal relationship with God, and this association is repeated across YouVersion's public communication.

YouVersion invites users to access the full text of the Bible through their tablet or mobile device in hundreds of different versions and languages. Users can listen to audio recordings of the Bible being read aloud, add their own highlights, bookmarks and annotations to the text, and sign up to reading plans created by Christian pastors, writers or musicians. These reading plans guide the user to selected passages each day, accompanied by a brief spiritual reflection. Successfully completed reading plans can earn the user a badge to display on their YouVersion profile, while alarms and emails are automatically triggered to alert those who fall behind.

The Bible App can also be used to share verses through Facebook, Twitter, SMS, email and other media. YouVersion's own lists of most-shared verses show that users prefer to share passages with inspirational, uplifting messages. The most-shared verse of 2013, for example, was Psalm 118:24: 'This is the day that the Lord has made: let us rejoice and be glad in it' (YouVersion 2013a). In 2014, the most-shared verse was Colossians 3:23, which begins 'Whatever you do, work at it with all your heart . . .' (YouVersion 2014b).

According to YouVersion, the Bible App has been very successful in encouraging users to commit more time to Bible reading. YouVersion published results of a user survey as an infographic in July 2013, and used this data to argue that 'Proximity Brings Engagement'. Seventy-seven percent of survey respondents agreed that they 'turn to the Bible more because it's available on your mobile devices' (YouVersion 2013b).

In April 2014, YouVersion introduced a new communal dimension. Bible App 5 allows the user to 'explore the Bible with your closest friends' (YouVersion 2014a) – up to 150 of them. Each user can now see and comment on how their contacts are using the Bible App, encouraging a kind of mutual accountability. According to YouVersion, 'Bible App 5 helps [Bible] conversations become part of our daily life— commenting on the bookmark of a friend who's going through a tough season, getting new insight as you read a friend's note on a familiar passage, finding common ground with a friend who just highlighted the same verse'.

Bible software raises a range of questions for scholars of digital religion. For example, what factors guide the design and marketing of products like YouVersion? How does the business model of digital Bibles impact the established industry of Bible publishing? Does using a digital Bible really encourage more frequent reading, and what other effects might be noticeable? If digitization does affect the user's relationship to the text, what does this mean for religious authority, the process of religious formation, the communication of religious ideas or the place of religion in everyday life? Addressing these issues requires a combination of research approaches, and this chapter will now introduce some of the methodologies we could use.

Methodology

Introduction

To study a digital Bible, we could focus on the designers, seeking to analyse the motivations, negotiations and processes through which their products have been developed. We could analyse the relationships of collaboration and competition between the different publishers working in the industry of Bible production. We could focus on the products themselves, and examine the ways in which the structures of software and hardware guide the user's engagement with a digital Bible. Alternatively, we could look at the users, and seek to trace their digital reading habits, the networks of communication they build around and through their digital Bibles, and any adjustment in their relationship with the text.

Each of these areas of study requires a mix of different research methods. My own research has relied primarily on interviews, surveys and digital ethnographic methods, and I will discuss these methods in this section. An alternative approach, data analysis, will be discussed very briefly under 'Ethics' in the next part of this chapter.

TIP 1

Different research methods will provide different kinds of information, so think carefully about what each research method can and cannot tell you.

Interviews

My study of the design of digital Bibles has included attention to their official websites and blogs and analysis of the products themselves, but I have also been able to interview designers. The websites and blogs of software products may include a brief outline of their history and development, but this information is rarely complete. By talking directly to designers, researchers can seek access information about product history, goals and strategies.

I contacted different companies by email, explained the purpose of my research, and asked for a recorded interview with the project leader or a senior designer. These interviews were conducted by telephone rather than face-to-face, to minimize my own research costs and the inconvenience created for my interviewees, and each lasted around thirty minutes. My interviewees were often at work during our conversations, so it was essential to establish a time limit for the interview in advance in order to plan how long I could dedicate to each question. My interviewees were willing to talk at length about their projects, and proved invaluable as sources of product history and intentions and as demonstrations of company rhetoric and discourse.

To complement these management interviews, I decided to talk to users about their own experiences with Bible software. Users of a digital product may be located anywhere in the world, so contacting a useful sample of research participants is not straightforward. Users could be contacted offline, through local religious communities, and a snowball sample could then be generated by asking each interviewee to recommend additional people for the researcher to speak to. Alternatively, research participants could be recruited online by locating central communication venues frequented by software users, such as a product forum or Facebook page. In some cases, the managers of a software product may agree to collaborate with a researcher to distribute a survey. These options would provide useful information, but would reach only certain kinds of users, limited in the first case by geographical location and religious affiliation and in the second case by intensity of product commitment.

Surveys

For my own research project, I decided instead to design a short twelve-question online survey, intended to take no more than ten minutes to complete. This survey began with a very brief summary of my research question, including my name and my university affiliation and an assurance that the research project had been approved by my university's ethics committee. I distributed this survey as widely as possible through blogs and social network sites for a period of two months and received a total of 250 responses, primarily from Britain and North America. The majority of these responses were recorded immediately after the survey link was publicized by a widely read blog, a large church, and a well-known technology writer, and the demographics of my respondents reflected the audiences of those three supporters.

This survey was valuable in its own right, particularly through the inclusion of one open-ended question: 'In what ways, if any, have digital media changed your relationship with the Bible?' Two Hundred and Twenty respondents answered this question, and I was able to code their answers to identify themes. The primary purpose of my survey, however, was to find interviewees without relying on a convenience or snowball sample. I asked survey respondents to leave their email address if they were interested in an interview, divided those respondents according to gender, and used a random number generator to select an equal number of male and female respondents for follow-up interviews. As a result, I was able to interview a relatively diverse group of software users, including British and American respondents from different age groups, geographical regions and religious traditions.

These research methods were useful, but they provided only partial answers to my research questions. Management interviews have to be understood as acts of public communication, opportunities for companies to enthuse about their achievements. My management interviewees were unlikely to discuss their disappointments and failures, or to share information they considered sensitive. User surveys and interviews were also valuable, but again relied on what users are willing to report, which relies in turn on how those users wish a researcher to perceive them – and how they perceive themselves.

Ethnography

Ethnography offers a richer, more nuanced source of data, at the expense of narrowing the scope of the study. By taking part in group activities as a 'participant observer' over a period of months or years, the ethnographer builds rapport with members and attempts to gain a personal understanding of what it means to do the things the group does (Hammersley and Atkinson 2007). Interaction with group members is essential, to test the ethnographer's understanding of group roles, activities and dynamics. In an ideal ethnography, the participant observer learns to see the world as group members see it, while retaining enough critical distance to be able to translate that holistic perspective into a form that can be understood by outsiders.

Digital ethnography is a well-established methodology for the study of online communities (Hine 2015; Boellstorff et al. 2012). A digital ethnography preserves the key ethnographic principle of long-term participant observation, but brings digital media into the 'field site' of research. This approach can help researchers to uncover depths of meaning in practices routinely misunderstood, dismissed or romanticized by outside observers. Ethnography can also contribute to our theoretical understanding of digital culture, by challenging concepts that rely on less nuanced evidence. Daniel Miller has suggested, for example, that digital anthropology can undermine overarching sociological theories of the 'network society' and 'networked individual' by returning our attention through ethnography to the importance of smaller, more diverse cultural contexts (Miller 2012). Digital Bibles like YouVersion certainly appear to generate transnational networks of religious communication, so this could be a helpful test case for Miller's argument.

Digital ethnographies can be restricted to a single, clearly bounded online site – perhaps a corner of a virtual world, a Facebook page, a product-users forum or an email list – but they are likely to require a more flexible, multi-sited approach that combines attention to online and offline spaces. 'Multi-sited ethnography' is willing to take 'unexpected trajectories in tracing a cultural formation across and within multiple sites of activity' (Marcus 1995: 96), and this approach is particularly relevant to studies of digital media. By following the circulation of people, objects, ideas, stories, identities and conflicts, and conducting 'strategically-situated single site ethnographies' (Marcus 1995: 110), the researcher can begin to identify the different sites in which relevant activity is taking place and map out the connections between them.

Using ethnographic methods to study digital Bibles means finding ways to engage with these products as a participant observer. However, identifying spaces for participation is not straightforward. The YouVersion Bible App is used worldwide, in many different languages, and the app might be used differently within different religious traditions and cultures. A meaningful ethnography would need to identify one or more specific subgroups of users to join, or specific sites where users interact, without aspiring to understand the whole population of YouVersion users.

Bible App 5 encourages users to build small social networks with friends within the app, and ethnographic research could be ideal for studying activity within these subgroups – if the researcher can find ways to access them. The ethnographer could also seek to participate in social media conversations on Twitter, Facebook or the YouVersion blog, but we cannot assume that participants in any of these spaces understand themselves as a coherent 'community' that a researcher could 'join'. Assessing the extent to which users do perceive themselves as part of a global YouVersion community would be an intriguing issue for an ethnographer to address.

An alternative approach could focus instead on the offline contexts of app production, as a complement to the management interviews discussed above. Spending time working alongside YouVersion's staff and volunteer teams would offer valuable insights into their motivations, challenges, internal dynamics and work practices. This kind of workplace ethnography would help trace the processes of negotiation through which the strategy, software, content and public communication of YouVersion are developed, disentangling the roles played by theology, finance, partner organizations, technical limitations and more.

The potential value of a workplace ethnography is considerable, but so are the challenges. Such a research project would require a high level of support and trust from YouVersion's leadership and staff, and would be subject to restrictions regarding the kinds of information that could be published. The process of negotiating access would itself be a fascinating component of the research, revealing a great deal about the priorities and processes of the organization.

Offline ethnography could also help to learn how an app is actually used. Digital Bible users access software as a solitary practice and share messages online, but they also integrate their digital Bibles into their households, churches and home groups. Through regular participation in church events, a researcher could observe how digital devices are used during services; youth group meetings and Bible studies; build up relationships with congregation members; and engage those members in conversations about their Bible reading.

I recently contacted leaders of a large, student-oriented church in my own city and secured their permission to attend services as an observer, interview some of the leadership team and conduct a focus group with the congregation. Congregation members at this church are encouraged to bring their own Bibles in order to read texts discussed during the sermon. Many now leave their paper Bibles at home and use their smartphones and tablets to access Bible apps instead. Some tweet their own responses to the preaching. Through my conversations with congregants, I found that this integration of digital devices into the church spaces had not been straightforward. A few of the church's leaders still resented what they perceived as competition for the congregation's attention, while some church members had reservations about the effects of digital text on their own understanding of the Bible.

This section has recommended a wide range of research approaches to the digital Bible: management and user interviews, user surveys, online ethnography, workplace ethnography and congregational ethnography. Each approach promises valuable insights, but each also raises challenges, particularly around questions of access, objectivity and representativeness. Each approach offers an opportunity to study the design and use of religious software from one angle, exploring the practices and perceptions of one category of people. By combining multiple approaches, we can begin to build up a more complete understanding.

TIP 2

Try to combine multiple research methods in each project, to approach your research question from different angles.

Ethics

These approaches to the study of digital media also raise ethical questions, particularly around issues of privacy and vulnerability. The Association of Internet Researchers released a report on 'Ethical Decision-Making and Internet Research' in 2012, authored by Annette Markham and Elizabeth Buchanan, and we can use this report as a valuable starting point for discussion. Markham and Buchanan argue that ethical decision-making is an ongoing process (2012: 12), which should be conducted as a consultation between academics, university review boards and participants in the research context. Research ethics must be contextual, sensitive to the vulnerabilities and expectations of particular stakeholders and participants.

Markham and Buchanan identify privacy as one of the key tensions for internet research ethics. In general, public and private communication should be distinguished when considering the ethics of research. When researching a communication that could reasonably be understood as private, the researcher should explain their research to community gatekeepers and participants, ask their permission to continue, and protect the participants' identity. When researching public communication, none of these approaches are necessary. That sounds straightforward, but the tension between what is 'public' and what is 'private' can be difficult to untangle. Users may have different expectations about the publicness of their communication, and accessibility is not always a reliable guide – even if a message is posted to a forum that can theoretically be visited by anyone, the author might intend to communicate only with a small circle of contacts.

In my doctoral research, I studied an online community that used a publicly accessible forum as an 'online church'. When I discussed the question of privacy with participants, I discovered that some felt very strongly that their communication was not 'public'. They were writing for a particular community of people, with whom they had been communicating over a long period of time. We agreed that I would ask community members for their permission to quote anything they said, on a case-by-case basis, and in the end, no one refused when I asked.

Digital Bibles can also raise complex questions of privacy. Company blogs, I would argue, are written for a public audience – so no permission is needed to quote them, and there is no need to protect them with anonymity. A YouVersion user's community in the latest version of the Bible App is limited to 150 users, so messages posted here should be treated as if intended for a private audience. But what about Twitter? A Twitter user might be writing for an unknown audience, or with specific people in mind; the difference will depend, in part, on how many followers that user has. But tweets can be 'retweeted', so a user should in theory always be aware that their words have the potential to circulate onwards through new networks beyond their initial audience. Does this make those messages public, or private? Ethnographic research is helpful here, because long-term participant observation can help the researcher identify where the boundaries between public and private communication lie in a particular community or network.

Markham and Buchanan's report identifies six 'key guidelines', of which the first is most important: 'the greater the vulnerability of the community/author/participant, the greater the obligation of the researcher to protect the community/author/participant' (Markham and Buchanan 2012: 4). The social benefit of the research and the needs of the researcher must be balanced against the rights of the participants being studied. Applying this to the tension between public and private, we can argue that greater attention must be paid to the participant's expectations of privacy if the research could make the participant vulnerable. In the case of my online church research, participants explained that their participation in the online community would be jeopardized if they did not feel safe to communicate with each other – so thoughtless academic research could lead to a clear case of harm, both to individual participants and to the community as a whole. Indeed, offending those participants by quoting their words without permission would also have harmed my own work and future studies by other academics by deterring that community from permitting any further academic research to take place there.

Users of Bible software may in some cases be left vulnerable by academic research, so their safety must be considered carefully. Some Christian organizations, such as the Digital Bible Society, use digital software for missionary work in countries where Christian resources are scarce or where conversion to Christianity could be dangerous. These projects are developing their own software and hardware, passed on from person to person in distinctive ways. It could be fascinating to study the ways in which faith formation is taking place through these digital resources – but in this case, there could be very serious implications for any individuals identified by an academic researcher. Users in majority-Christian countries are likely to be less vulnerable, but care must still be taken. If a user holds personal opinions about the Bible not shared by their congregation, family or workplace, then exposing those opinions could cause them distress.

Companies and organizations may also be made vulnerable by research, and here ethical concerns are more complicated. If a researcher concludes that a Bible publishing project is ineffective in achieving its stated aims, publication of those findings could affect the project's public reputation or financial security. If a researcher is relying on a company's goodwill to maintain access to data, interviewees or opportunities for participant observation, then gatekeepers' perceptions of the likely conclusions and impact of the research may well be critical to the researcher's chances of completing it. On the other hand, of course, the researcher must maintain the integrity and independence of their work. In most cases, the questions academics are most interested in are unlikely to be damaging for a company – but there may be a need for scholars to consider how our choice of methods restricts our critical voice.

These questions of organizational vulnerability, researcher independence and digital ethics are particularly acute around the use of data. Evelyn Ruppert, John Law and Mike Savage (2013) have called on sociologists to attend more closely to the 'social life of methods', looking not just at what data can tell us but also critically examining how the processes of data recording and analysis contribute to the shaping of our social worlds. For example, YouVersion tracks users' activity, producing data that can be shared with content providers, fed back to users in the form of prompts, or shared by users themselves through social media. Christian ideas of accountability and witnessing are being used here to valorize technologies of organizational- and self-monitoring, suggesting a role for religious studies scholars in debates over the increasing role of surveillance in contemporary society. Discussions of digital research ethics should expand to encompass the ethics of the organizations we are studying – but organizations may well be resistant to this kind of critical analysis of their less-publicized activities.

TIP 3

Think of your research ethics as a kind of research. Designing an ethically sound project means finding out how your research subjects are vulnerable and how they think about privacy.

Reflections

Commentators have speculated that the impact of digital technology on the perception and interpretation of sacred text could be considerable. According to Rachel Wagner, for example, sacred text apps 'encourage users to see sacred texts themselves as selectable "apps" or mini-programs that users have freedom to run, "play" with and in a sense control' (Wagner 2012: 200). This argument contrasts in some interesting ways with Charles Ess' critique of the digital Bible study market (2004), quoted above. Ess argued that the tools of computer-aided study did not greatly affect traditional practices of Bible interpretation, but Wagner suggests that the digital format of Bible software could have a significant impact on how the Bible is understood.

This kind of speculative argument is intriguing, but very difficult to test through empirical research. In my own survey and user interviews, I found that many did indeed feel that digital media had affected their relationship with the Bible, but they did not express these perceptions in terms of play or control. My interviewees praised the convenience, speed and portability of a digital Bible, while often regretting the loss of the personal connection they had once felt to their Bible as a physical object. A paper Bible could carry additional meanings as a long-term possession, a gift or a personal symbol of lifelong faith. For a few of my interviewees, a paper Bible also served as a public symbol of Christian identity, and the banality of reading on a screen deprived them of an important mode of Christian witness. In keeping with the findings of research on e-reading in educational contexts, some interviewees also found it harder to memorize passages of text read on a screen or to remember where each passage is located in the library of Scripture.

These are useful initial findings, but further research will be needed to explore the impact of digital reading on the user's interpretation of the meaning of the biblical text, or to support larger theoretical arguments about changes in the structures of religious authority. The kinds of online, congregational and workplace ethnography proposed above could help here, by allowing the researcher to participate in the different contexts in which practices and discourses of interpretation are enacted.

This chapter has outlined a range of research methodologies, including management interviews, user interviews, surveys and ethnography. These are all well-established research methods, widely taught and extensively critiqued. Applying these methods to the study of digital religion requires adaptation and flexibility, attending to the sometimes subtle ways in which an email interview or participant observation in a chatroom can differ from the face-to-face contexts more commonly considered in textbooks and training courses. The difficulties faced by the researcher in applying an established research methodology to a new context can often provide valuable clues into social norms and practices: who are the gatekeepers here, how do participants feel about their roles or their privacy, and what modes of communication are favoured for what kinds of interaction?

As noted above, researchers of digital religion must also begin to consider the processes through which user data is gathered, analysed and used. As well as critical analysis of corporate data strategies, we must also find our own ways to work with the large volumes of digital data being collected. Bible software companies such as YouVersion record data on Bible reading that could not have been collected without the aid of digital technology, and that data can only be accessed through collaboration with the companies that own it. If academics can persuade Bible software companies that their research skills are useful enough to merit access to user data, then we may begin to see some truly remarkable new frontiers of research.

This quantitative and critical study of data and data processes will demand more radical innovation in research methods than the more familiar approaches I have emphasized in this chapter. In this area, digital religion researchers currently lag behind their colleagues in the digital humanities and science and technology studies. We must be attentive to the advances taking place in areas of research that parallel our own, so I will end this chapter with a call for greater commitment to interdisciplinary conversation. The study of digital religion has always been diverse, collaborative and networked in its methodologies and disciplinary contexts, and this willingness to learn from other fields must continue into the future.

10 Videoconferencing as a Tool Facilitating Feminist Interviews with Muslim Women Who Wear the Niqab

ANNA PIELA

Introduction

In recent years Muslim women wearing a niqab have been the focus of policymakers, journalists and academics' attention. The niqab has become a politically loaded symbol of Islam, denoting the otherness of women who wear it (Abu-Lughod 2002). Its place in contemporary societies has been frequently debated in the last decade, infamously during the 'Jack Straw controversy' in 2006 (Khiabany and Williamson 2008). The controversial 'burka bans', recently introduced in France and Belgium, and proposed in other European countries, have led to much academic discussion questioning the legality of such prohibitions (including Ferrari and Pastorelli 2013). Furthermore, research has been conducted with non-Muslims and Muslim non-niqab wearers to investigate their perceptions of the niqab and the women who wear it. However, to my knowledge there are no UK studies that focus on views and experiences of women who wear the niqab themselves. Given the volatile attention on the niqab, it is unclear why there is so little research with them in Europe and globally. This is certainly against the grain of the social science research tradition whereby voices of the researched are not only included, but treated as central in research investigations (Ramazanoğlu and Holland 2002). The scarcity of systematic study of niqab wearers' voices may be related to the fact that they are a minority among Muslim women who choose to wear Islamic attire (Tarlo 2007) and they are therefore a hard-to-reach and potentially vulnerable population despite the fact that their numbers have been recently growing both in Europe and South Asia (Lewis 2007). Only very recently have two substantial publications based on interviews with UK-based niqab-wearing women been published (Bouteldja 2014; Open Society Foundations 2015).

I argue that this paucity of inclusive research *with* those most immediately concerned in the niqab controversies, also noted by the Canadian Council of Muslim Women (2013) is conspicuous; while research on wider (largely non-Muslim) population's perceptions of the niqab and niqab wearers in the European and American sociopolitical context is useful in its critical capacity (as it challenges established 'truths' about supposedly liberty-based European/American Judeo-Christian values), the lack of sincere dialogue with women wearing the niqab indirectly contributes to the construction of these women as 'walking deficits' (Ghorashi 2010: 13) unable to voice their own motivations. Thus, the existing research on the niqab but without the women who wear it tells us much more about the West, its isolated cultural monologue and prejudices, than about women who wear the niqab.

It is possible `that these women's voices are not deemed important for the furthering of this pan-European and American debate, in which everybody else – politicians, media, academics, Muslim and non-Muslims – seems to claim a stake. Perhaps women who wear the niqab have never really been part of the debate; in Morey and Yaqin's words, 'the voice of the Third World woman is effectively silenced, evacuated from an argument that is about her but in which she is seldom invited to participate' (2011: 179). I argue that providing insight into niqab wearers' spoken narratives about their lives and beliefs will also inform wider debates on the place of religion in allegedly secular British society. The aims of the study were threefold:

- To acknowledge and address the ways in which women who wear the niqab understand the role of the niqab in the forming of their social identities through the use of ethnographic methods underpinned by feminist perspectives.

- To increase the understanding of niqab wearers' perceptions of their role and place in the British society.

- To respond to wider political debates in which the niqab is often (ab)used as a symbol of religious patriarchy and otherness.

Recognizing the detrimental role that some secular, white, middle-class Western feminists played by interpreting Muslim/Third world/non-white women's experiences as similar to their own, I have drawn in this research from theoretical work that emphasizes the significance of multiple subjectivities and exclusions (for example, Spivak 1993). Although a small-scale qualitative study such as this one (Piela forthcoming) is by no means a sufficient effort to bridge this gap, it begins to build up evidence on self-expressions of women whose views have not been addressed, despite their obvious central role in the matter.

Videoconferencing: An online research method on the rise

In this section I briefly introduce videoconference interviews as a relatively new type of online interview. There is a well-developed body of methodological literature on various uses of the internet in social research, as well as challenges posed by this type of research. A widely accepted differentiation in approaches to the internet as a research tool is utilitarian: whether we think of the internet as a technology facilitating data collection, or as a site of research where data collection methods may also be (although not necessarily) based on internet communication (Association of Internet Researchers, henceforth AoIR, 2012). The former focuses on various online means of communication, including asynchronous ones like email (James and Busher 2009).

The latter has an emphasis on 'online communities' fostered by participation in asynchronous discussion groups (Savicki, Lingenfelter and Kelley 1996); and synchronous 'chatrooms' (Salmon 2010). Studies on various online communities have burgeoned since the 1990s (Dawson and Cowan 2004); there is even a study of an online community of Indonesian women who wear the niqab (Nisa 2013). Asynchronous and synchronous online interactions have their particular advantages and limitations: the former entails space and time displacement, but potentially invites deeper reflection as the respondent has more time to prepare an answer; the latter only entails space displacement but does not offer extra time for reflection (Salmon 2010).

Text-based online interaction was popular long before high broadband speed necessary for videoconferencing was as widespread as nowadays. This also means that the bulk of literature on 'online research methods' is focused on text-based interactions, often in the context of ethnographies of online communities (Turkle 1997; Markham 1998) and videoconferencing, as a relative newcomer to the research scene, is a relatively under-addressed method (Deakin and Wakefield 2014). Videoconferencing is an interesting tool as it raises some methodological issues relevant to online text-based research, but due to its audio aspect, also telephone interviewing, which has a much longer history (Holt 2010) and face-to-face interviewing, due to its video facility that allows visual cues to be exchanged by the researcher and participant. It potentially overcomes criticisms aimed at asynchronous communication, including loss of spontaneity (James and Busher 2009); text-based communication charged with loss of visual cues (Hanna 2012) and traditional interviews, seen as resource-hungry: expensive, time-consuming, and difficult to organize. Criticisms of early videoconferencing applications that had no recording facilities have become obsolete with the advent of freeware that allows this, removing the need to rely on voice recorders (Hanna 2012). In this sense, it seems at least theoretically to resolve most issues that prevented other types of online interviewing from becoming as popular as the traditional face-to-face interview. However, as James and Busher suggest (2009), online research, whilst versatile, always poses specific challenges, and videoconference interviews are no exception to this observation. In particular, concerns over excluding populations who do not have access to or chose not to use new communication technologies are still valid here. This category may include those who do not own a videoconferencing-enabled device such as a PC, laptop, tablet or smartphone.[1]

Feminist interviews and videoconferencing

Qualitative research is often lauded as particularly suited for feminist research (Bryman 2008) due to its focus on partial, situated knowledges (Haraway 1988). As I aimed to identify niqab wearers' own interpretations of their identity, a qualitative approach was useful in addressing my research questions. By positioning myself at the interactionist and constructivist end of the paradigmatic continuum, away from the early 'masculine' sociology standpoint defining the researcher as a 'tool', and the subject as a 'data-producing machine' (Oakley 2003: 248), I set particular parameters for this study. In-depth interviews emphasize nuance, complexity and roundedness of data rather than surface patterns (Mason 2006), and I considered them as a useful method in the context of the project.

When I realized that in order to interview some women, I would need to utilize videoconferencing, I considered how this may impact on the feminist focus of the project. From its conception, the intention of the project was to throw light on displaced, ignored and often silenced voices of Muslim women who live in the UK and wear the niqab (Piela 2013, 2014a, 2014b and forthcoming). This aim required conducting qualitative fieldwork in order to generate in-depth, personal narratives with these women. There are many caveats inherent in these motivations which I needed to avoid: misrepresenting and essentializing women in the sample; suggesting that the sample is representative of the population of Muslim women who wear the veil in the UK; and representing the project (and myself) as neutral and value-free. My approach assumed that the interactions between the researcher and participant were always going to be shaped by power relations, and those, by our complex intersubjectivities. Nagar (2002) argued that the fear of misrepresentation caused a widespread departure from fieldwork among feminist researchers; however, this can be prevented by delivery of politically engaged, materially grounded and institutionally sensitive research, and addressing critiques regarding voice ownership and authenticity in research. Furthermore, the claim to feminist research warrants attention to politics of knowledge production and constant reflection about power, knowledge, content and context of the research (Sultana 2007). Edwards and Mauthner (2002: 19) write:

> Indeed, discussions of the research process related to ethical issues have become a feature of feminist research, especially qualitative empirical work. Ethical decisions arise throughout the entire research process, from conceptualization and design, data gathering and analysis, and report, and literature on the topic reflects this.

To make research balanced, the focus is not exclusively on the participant; not only do feminists insist on the need to scrutinize the researcher, but the audience of the research as well: ethnographic writing ought to be 'a vehicle for readers to discover moral truths about themselves' (Denzin 1997: 284).

AoIR's updated ethical guidelines about internet research (2012: 4) state that:

> the greater the vulnerability of the community / author / participant, the greater the obligation of the researcher to protect the community / author / participant. Because 'harm' is defined contextually, ethical principles are more likely to be understood inductively rather than applied universally. That is, rather than one-size-fits-all pronouncements, ethical decision-making is best approached through the application of practical judgment attentive to the specific context.

This encourages the question why might the participants be vulnerable, and whether the participation might potentially affect their lives. As stated before, Muslim women who wear the veil, whilst themselves empowered and articulate, are under attack from some media commentators and politicians who endeavour to gain political capital on fomenting resentment towards Muslims. Those women who do speak out publicly, are immediately silenced, maligned and dismissed (Piela 2014a). This potentially puts women participating in research, if identified, under the risk of being targeted. AoIR guidelines state that it is therefore of utmost importance to anonymize the interview transcripts as soon as possible, by removing characteristic information (people names, place names) and to store the voice recordings securely, encrypted and physically protected. Deakin and Wakefield (2014) suggest that in research with people that involves videoconferencing interviews, it is perfectly possible to conduct fieldwork with anonymous participants, who may wish to only supply their username to the researcher (but it is also possible, if perhaps awkward, to achieve in traditional interviews). These commitments, as well as aims and objectives of the research project, ought to be declared in the informed consent form that needs to be delivered to the participants prior to the interview (Salmon 2010). Sufficient time must be provided for them to read the information sheet about the research, ask questions and potentially withdraw from participating upon obtaining pertinent information or at a later stage, without having to provide reasons. I emailed the informed consent forms in advance to both participants to allow them ample time to read the information. As the next sections of this chapter demonstrate, some aspects of videoconference interviewing, especially the use of video transmitting and recording facilities, warrant further ethical reflection due to their potential repercussion.

A highly sensitive situation of this kind calls for a particular ethical framework, and I propose here an approach termed *feminist ethics of care* and underpinned by work of several feminist writers who focused on values such as 'reconciliation, reciprocity, diversity and responsibility, and with an awareness of power' (Edwards and Mauthner 2002: 23). One such author is Nel Noddings who emphasized the primacy of responsibility and relationships that ought to form an empathetic way of responding to others ethically (1984). Another author who elaborated on this ethical model is the ethnographer Norman Denzin; he argues that the researcher ought 'to step into the shoes of the persons being studied' (Denzin 1997: 273). In this sense, the feminist ethics of care seems to have its origins in the Kantian deontological theory that has respect of the individual as its central principle, in contrast to consequentialism, which is concerned with consequences of an action when evaluating it ethically (Lippert-Rasmussen 2005).

Practical considerations

As the presented project was a small pilot study with no attached funding, the costs of traditional interviewing were an important factor, similar to projects of Deakin and Wakefield (2014) who also used Skype to interview. Most participants lived in close proximity but I knew of two women who wore the niqab and were interested in participating but lived far away. One of the participants (who I refer to as Fatma), who I had previously met in the context of this research but had yet to interview, had gone to live overseas for a long period of time. She regularly returned to the UK to visit her family, and she preferred to be interviewed via Skype as this removed the need to meet me in person and decrease the time spent with her family. Fatma used to work with a friend of my friend who 'vouched' for me, essentially fulfilling the role of a key informant (Hammersley and Atkinson 2007). Another participant (who I refer to as Zohra, and who I had not met before; a common acquaintance put us in touch) lived in the UK so travel was more possible, but she was busy with personal and professional commitments that prevented her from being able to be interviewed during the day in a formal setting. This was similar to the research experiences of Deakin and Wakefield (2014). Skype was then an obvious option, as two potential participants constituted a large proportion of the relatively small sample of twelve. Since women who wear the niqab are a hard-to-reach population, especially for a non-Muslim researcher, I was determined to find a way to enable these interviews to take place but also to disrupt participants' lives as little as possible (Gatenby and Humphries 2000). As videoconferencing would be closer to the other interviews I had conducted in this project, and would allow for better methodological consistency, than for example, email interviews, I decided to ask Fatma and Zohra whether they would be interested in a Skype interview, and they both agreed. All pre-interview conversations about the details of the potential participation took place via email and mobile phone.

To be able to conduct a Skype call, Skype usernames have to be exchanged prior to the call. Then, once the user is signed in, they have to find their interlocutor using their username or other credentials, such as email. This is followed by adding them to the contact list. Only then is it possible to call or video-call them. Needless to say, webcams (video cameras commonly installed in laptops and smartphones) and microphones have to be tested prior to the interviews. Mindful of such technical glitches capable of jeopardizing an interview (Hanna 2012), I downloaded and installed voice-recording software called MP3 Skype Voice Recorder in advance but also recorded both interviews on a voice recorder. This was a sensible precaution as following the interview with Fatma I realized the software had not recorded the interview due to my mistake and my only recording was the one produced by the voice recorder.

Time difference is another important factor when interviewing a participant living in another time zone, like Fatma; the researcher must ensure that calculations are correct in establishing the time of the interview, especially if there is no telephone contact between the researcher and the participant.

Opening the interview

In my experience, during the opening part, Skype interviews are more awkward than traditional interviews. This is to do with the need to ensure that the communication is properly set up. As a result, the opening phrases are usually more related to the sound and video quality than an established ritual of introductions and pleasantries. Below I include the transcripts of one of these openings:

AP:	Er . . .
Z:	Hi.
AP:	[unclear 00.00.07]
Z:	Can you hear me OK?
AP:	Yeah. I can hear you very well. Erm.
Z:	You can hear me . . . yeah . . .

While this opening would be unusual in a traditional interview, or a telephone interview whereby usually the quality of the connection is quite reliable, a Skype connection is dependent on the quality of broadband at both ends, and the specification of software that both interlocutors are using. A video call slows down the data transmission, which may result in sound cutting out or becoming distorted. This means that in practical terms, a researcher has to be prepared to ask, sometimes several times, about the quality of sound at the participant's end, as well as resolve any potential issues that arise. Some solutions to these problems may be restarting both the machines, or switching the video off temporarily. If the video has to be switched off for the duration of the interview, the interview assumes the qualities of a telephone interview.

TIP 1

It may be a good idea to arrange a test call a day or two prior to the interview to ensure that the technical aspect of the videoconference call does not present difficulties on the day.

I did not experience any serious problems of this kind, and the interviews commenced easily and informally. In the case of Fatma, who I had met before, we talked about her recent move abroad and her new circumstances. Both interviews posed a challenge in that the point of division between the introductions and the interview was very fluid. Fatma had been working on a PhD in social sciences, and before we moved on to the interview we had an hour-long chat about the challenges she was facing. She asked me several questions about elements of the PhD such as the literature review and the bibliography. I answered her at length, because as a researcher committed to the feminist principle of balancing the power relations in the research process, I welcomed the co-production of the agenda of the interview with the participants (Gorelick 1991). Similar to Limerick, Burgess-Limerick and Grace (1996) I saw these interviews as gifts to me from the participants and I was happy there was a way I could reciprocate.

In the case of Zohra, it was a long pre-interview conversation. We had spoken on the phone beforehand, as she wanted to know more about the project before committing to participating. She also requested samples of my previous written work to help her make this decision. The first part of the Skype interview was the last opportunity for her to potentially change her mind and withdraw, which would have been quite easy given the circumstances (Bertrand and Bourdeau 2010). Zohra used that time to interrogate me about my motives for doing research on this topic and my interest in working with Muslim women more generally. This necessitated a reflexive and thorough account on my part about my own positionality (discussed at more length in Piela 2014b). I understand positionality as 'researcher's location within existing hierarchies of power and the ways in which the researcher's identity and affiliations are positioned among and by others' (Sehgal 2007: 331). An examination of this location is considered a part of 'good feminist research practice' (England 1994; Oakley 2003). Zohra's careful interrogation reminded me, that 'any piece of research is as much about those undertaking it as the participants in the research' (Haw 1996: 320). The research has certainly been informed by the fact that I am non-Muslim, female, Polish (and therefore with English as a second language), of no religious belief, white, married, and with an academic feminist background. I assume it was easier to recruit the participants because I was a woman, as norms related to modesty might prevent them from accepting an interview invitation from a male researcher. Furthermore, because I was not a British citizen and spoke with a foreign accent, I shared the stigma of the 'Other' with them. The fact that I had an academic affiliation was likely to provide some credentials to the project. However, these advantageous characteristics should not obscure the fact that research always remains a setting in which power relations play out and there is always a potential for exploitation (Franks 2001). The research position I found myself to be in would be difficult to define in clear-cut outsider or insider terms, partly due to my poststructuralist perspective on identities, and partly due to what Styles (in Hammersley and Atkinson 2007: 86–7) describes as 'outsider and insider myths' that rely on a 'moral rhetoric that claims exclusive research legitimacy for a particular group'. However, I was particularly aware of the enormous significance of the risk of misrepresentation of the participants in the research, which may have very real and dire consequences such as Islamophobic stereotyping and verbal and physical abuse in the streets of the UK (Chakraborti and Zempi 2013).

TIP 2

Prepare for a Skype interview being longer than a traditional, face-to-face interview, as the participants are likely to slip into informal conversation or discuss issues of interest to them.

The importance of the interview setting in videoconference interviews

These two Skype interviews demonstrated the relational character of the public/private divide and highlighted the implications of this particular method for research with Muslim women who wear the niqab. The idea of such a dichotomy, whereby public and private spheres are separate and opposing, has been critiqued by many feminist authors as contributing to exclusion of women, linked to the private sphere due to their 'biology' (Pateman 1989), from social participation outside the family, i.e. the public sphere; some contemporary feminists question whether this divide exists at all and argue it is artificially maintained in the interests of male hegemonic liberalism (Pateman 1989; Tétreault 2001). The discipline of web studies also contributed to deconstruction of this dichotomy; contemporary spatial reconfigurations of social, political, economic and cultural life blurred the boundaries of what is perceived as public and private, and computer-mediated communication has further emphasized their fluidity (Gunter 2009; West, Lewis and Currie 2009; Youngs 2009). As presented in this section of the chapter, this project has somewhat complicated and questioned the concept of 'public' as 'outside the home' and 'private' as 'inside the home'. However, it also has to be borne in mind that a similar division guides niqab-wearing Muslim women's decision on whether to put on or take off the niqab. The niqab will usually be worn in places where 'non-mahram' men may be encountered (Open Society Foundations 2011; Canadian Council of Muslim Women 2013), and this will overlap with traditional conceptualizations of the public sphere, i.e. outside the home. Female-only gatherings outside the home will often be an exception as the niqab may be taken off there.

When interviewing Fatma and Zohra, I realized that due to the video function, our individual homes, where we were physically located, were no longer separate – they became temporarily visually linked and because of that, they were no longer private. Exclusions that applied to the participants' homes (no non-mahram men present) suddenly no longer applied, as they had no authority over who was present in my house. The person in question was my husband in the adjacent room, who, according to the participants' religious belief, was not allowed to see them with uncovered faces. This potentially triggered norms associated with the public sphere and therefore raised questions for the participants whether to keep the niqab on during the interview, as illustrated by the following extract of the interview with Zohra:

Z: [So you are] doing video, are you on your own?
AP: Erm. Sorry, I'm doing video yes, er, what, what, what did you say after that?
Z: On your own, or do you, are you, have you got people there?
AP: Erm, I'm, I'm yeah, erm, I closed the door on, on everybody else, so I'm, I'm on my own. [laughs]
Z: Oh, ok, erm. You can do it on video.
AP: I don't mind, if you're, if you're not . . . comfortable with video it's fine, erm.
Z: No, no it's cool, it's cool, it's just, erm . . . I'm not usually, erm, the way that my hijab is, the way that I've covered my head, is not the usual way, but erm, so that's why I was asking if there was anyone else there, because if somebody came in then I wouldn't feel like, you know.
AP: Er, my, my husband knows not to go in, er, he understands.
Z: Oh, that's good, that's good, yeah. Erm ok we, erm, let me hang up and I'll call you on video and then we'll, we'll get on with it, yeah?
AP: Sure.

Z: OK, one minute, I don't . . . Hi!
AP: [Laughs]
Z: Ok, ok let's do this.
AP: I got you there.
Z: OK.

In this particular case, this situation was easily resolved as I was aware it was my responsibility to create an interview setting that was female-only in order to enable the participant to enact her religious belief. A failure to achieve this, for example by having a male walk into the room during the videoconference interview, would potentially cause harm to the participant as her religious norms would be compromised. This was unlikely at my home where I could exert control over the setting, and had secured cooperation and support from my husband in this undertaking. However, in an alternative scenario, for example interviewing via Skype from my work, this may have been problematic as due to the 'open door policy' a male colleague or a student could enter my office. Furthermore, when using the video facility, it is imperative to first consider whether we need the video recording of the interview for our research purposes, and if we do, consult with the participant whether they feel comfortable with this request. I never considered video recording my Skype interviews with Fatma or Zohra, for two reasons: first a video showing a woman who normally wears the niqab in places where she can be seen by non-mahram men, without her niqab on would be a very sensitive piece of data and second, I was interested in generating spoken accounts. I suspect that I would not have got the consent if I had asked, as Zohra mentioned that she would not feel comfortable being video-recorded.

On a different note, it is important to consider where in their home (or workplace) the researcher is conducting the videoconference interview. Although it is likely to be more informal than in a traditional setting, we still convey an impression (Hammersley and Atkinson 2007). Deakin and Wakefield (2014) argue that with the advent of mobile technologies, the place of the interview becomes more fluid and temporary; we can select the 'shot' we will appear in much more easily. In order to maintain a professional image, I endeavoured to position my webcam in such a way that no distracting or untidy background came into view. Instead, I chose a neutral, plain wall. (A background consisting of bookshelves full of thick tomes may convey a strong suggestion of authority on the part of the researcher. As it was my aim to build rapport, as opposed to a researcher–researched division, I chose to avoid including such elements. However, such choices ought to be made accounting for the wider context of the research). The researcher's clothing is another factor that is selected with a full understanding of implications it may have (Hey 1997; Delamont in Hammersley and Atkinson 2007). The decision what to wear was a dilemma for me – on the one hand, formal attire would look artificial in a home setting, but on the other, I wanted to mark the 'speciality' of the occasion and show respect for the participant. Eventually I settled for 'smart casual' clothing in both cases, although both interviews commenced in late evening and finished before midnight. This was different to interviews I conducted in traditional settings such as a Muslim school or a mosque, where I chose very formal, conservative clothing so as not to challenge sartorial norms adopted by many Muslim women (in particular not displaying flesh other than face and hands, and wearing loose clothing concealing the curves of the body). On a more technical note, if the interview is conducted during the day, attention should be paid to the level of lighting in the room – too much light will darken out the footage transmitted to the participant.

TIP 3

Before the interview, consider carefully how to construct a setting that will facilitate the interview, i.e. where you will be located, who else is present and likely to interrupt, and what you will wear.

Leaving the field

A final ethical consideration specific to Skype interviews I discuss in this article is the issue of the management of the researcher–participant relationship. In ethnography it is termed 'leaving the field', but it may just be the decision when to end the interview (Letherby 2003). Feminist researchers in particular have grappled with the ethical dimension of retaining the relationship, or a friendship, with women participants (for example, Hey 1997). Letherby suggests that the researcher should allow the participant to decide whether to continue or discontinue contact. In videoconference interviews, 'the field' is a much more blurred concept and so it may be difficult to pinpoint the moment when we are leaving it. After a Skype interview has been concluded, both the researcher and the participant are on each other's 'contact list'. Keeping the participant on the contact list (and remaining on theirs) may be useful in terms of future contact with them, but it may cause undesired levels of visibility, in particular if the researcher used a personal Skype account that is often updated with new statuses and avatars. I had been using my Skype account for both professional and social purposes, so it was set up in a neutral manner and I judged it appropriate to retain the participants on my contact list.

As both Fatma and Zohra expressed interest in keeping in touch (Fatma declared she might ask me for some more advice regarding her PhD, and Zohra said she would invite me to an art performance in which she played a part), I retained them on my contact list. Alas, that invitation never arrived, but interactions continued on a smaller scale. Fatma emailed me some media articles about the niqab, and we exchanged some bibliographic references. I followed Zohra on Twitter, and we exchanged some brief greetings there. As I have finished the first piece of writing in which I quote them, I will be emailing it to them soon, in order to share the analysis. Thus, as Letherby suggests (2003), the researcher–participant relationship does not end with completion of fieldwork, because the researcher still has responsibilities towards the participants. It must, however be borne in mind that these decisions about the manner of 'exiting the field' are highly relational and contextual, also in videoconferencing settings. Some criticisms of relaxed procedures and continuing interactions are levelled by feminist researchers who see them as leading to 'false intimacy', and potential feelings of betrayal if generated data is used in a manner unexpected by the participant (Stacey 1991; Harrison, MacGibbon and Morton 2001).

TIP 4

After the interview, consider whether you will leave the field as you would in traditional research, or maintain some form of contact via Skype. What are the implications of each decision?

Concluding thoughts about the use of videoconference interviews for feminist research

Skype appears to be of value for a feminist project as it facilitates engaging women who may belong to a hard-to-reach category that is highly geographically dispersed. In cases of projects with little or no funding it enables participation of those women who are interested in being interviewed but travel costs are prohibitive. Similarly, Deakin and Wakefield (2014: 608) talked about being able to engage 'otherwise inaccessible participants'. From the researcher's perspective, employing Skype may help to increase the sample where it is difficult to find sufficient numbers of participants willing to be interviewed in a traditional way. The main challenge I encountered in this project was recruitment: at first, I found it very difficult to find any women who wore the face veil at all. I utilized many methods of locating them, including giving out leaflets locally, but eventually I found that the most effective way of recruiting participants was through existing networks. Unfortunately, some of the women who were interested in the project lived quite far from my location so Skype was an option I was keen to consider. Where also face-to-face interviews are conducted, the aspect of exclusivity of videoconferencing (which depends on resources and skills) may be to some extent mitigated (Deakin and Wakefield 2014).

Furthermore, in some cases Skype may be useful for a feminist researcher who wishes to disrupt the participant's daily routine as little as possible. It may also be preferable to some participants who are more relaxed in the familiar home environment (James and Busher 2009) but at the same time does not require the researcher to intrude. By offering flexibility in respect to arranging and changing times of the interview at short notice (Hanna 2012), it enables the participant to fit it into the most convenient timeslot. Furthermore, it removes the need to take time to travel to the interview and so puts less pressure on participants with many commitments. Hanna (2012) argues that videoconference interviews allow more intimacy as they can be conducted from home (although they can be also conducted from a workplace or an internet café). This removes the need to encroach on the privacy of the interviewee's home or to find a neutral, formal location appropriate for conducting an interview and convenient to both the researcher and the participant. Potentially the informality of the home setting can contribute to diminishing inequalities in power relations. James and Busher (2009) argue that online interviewing is more egalitarian due to participants being better placed to influence the direction of the interview. Furthermore, Bertrand and Bourdeau (2010) argue that Skype equalizes power relations in an interview as it gives the participants an easy way of withdrawing from research (by exiting the videoconference) without repercussions. Overall, Skype offers an interesting option for feminist researchers, provided that ethical aspects of its use are thoroughly considered. Like Deakin and Wakefield (2014) I expect that it will become much more popular in the future.

Many issues and considerations are shared by videoconference and offline interviews, including recruitment, obtaining informed consent, preparing a setting and an interview topic guide and exiting the field. Additionally, videoconferencing may help mitigate difficulties related to access and distance (Hanna 2012). However, at another level, it seems that new technologies in research may have a transformative potential, as has been seen in the case of the blurred public/private boundary during the interview with Zohra. This potential requires careful unpicking in terms of possible implications for the researcher and the participant. In offline interviews where participants had a higher degree of control over the research setting (i.e. a Muslim girls' school or a mosque), they were able to ensure that norms regarding religiously dictated modesty remained intact. Power relations became more complicated in settings where neither participants nor the researcher had control (i.e. a conference room in a local authority building) as it was impossible to ascertain the level of potential privacy there). Videoconferencing interviews where the interviewee does not exercise any control over the setting shift the ethical duty of care on to the researcher who must ensure that privacy is maintained, in particular where vulnerable populations are involved in research (AoIR 2012).

11 Religious Organizations on the Internet: A Model to Analyse Communication Effectiveness

DANIEL ARASA AND JUAN NARBONA

The goal of Institutional Communications is to establish quality relationships between an institution and its public. It is an activity necessary for an entity to convey its identity and values, and to achieve the relevance, credibility and transparency required for public interest (La Porte 2009). Like other realities, religious institutions also need to communicate to reach their faithful and to defend their values in the pluralistic society in which they operate. Like many other civil and commercial institutions, diverse religious confessions act as agents for social change. Their goal is that the faithful and in general, public life, respect and are guided by spiritual values. The public presence of religious institutions is exercised in diverse ways: through the statements made by leaders, the actions of local communities, or through social initiatives (made by colleges, hospitals, non-profit organizations, etc.). In all of these cases, religious organizations interact with other social agents and attempt to influence the social environment and reaffirm their institutional identity through the means of communication.

The internet and religious institutions

For many years, press offices, public relations, marketing and publicity departments have been the traditional arenas from which institutional communication have been promoted. Recently, however, the field and outlet where this concentration has been developed is the internet (Duhé 2007; Hart 2005). Currently, religious institutions and leaders are using their websites to offer spiritual attention and guidance, to deal with the media, to be in contact with their public, to spread their message, and to draw the attention of new followers (Campbell 2010).

There are several examples of the religious institutional presence on the internet that reflects a progressive interest for this media. In the case of the Catholic Church, the official Vatican website was established in 1996, when the internet was in its early stages. The Church of Jesus Christ of Latter-day Saints (Mormons) also established their site in 1996. In 1998, the Unitarian Universalist Buddhist Fellowship; in 1999, the Dalai Lama; in 2002, the Russian Orthodox Patriarch and the World Jewish Congress (source: www.web.archive.org).

The internet offers a plethora of benefits to religious organizations: it allows them to transmit their values in the virtual world and has the ability to reach a global audience; it offers the opportunity to present their own beliefs among people from different social environments; has a low cost production and maintenance of content; offers the possibility of obtaining donations; allows for the collaboration of the faithful in the dissemination of materials, and so on. Therefore, this chapter discusses the institutional communications that are undertaken by religious organizations and proposes a model to analyse the effectiveness of their online communication.

The rapidly growing importance of virtual communication has increased the need to establish an analytical model that allows one to study the communication and effective transmission of online corporate messages. In 2003, Cantoni, Di Blas and Bolchini (2003: 7) proposed the Website Communication Model (WCM) as a theoretical framework to analyse websites as a tool for institutional communication. Shortly after, this theoretical model was applied to studying the activity of various dioceses (Arasa 2008) and other structures of the Catholic Church (Arasa, Cantoni and Ruiz 2010).

This study demonstrated that diocesan websites more closely resemble open intranets for Catholics than websites made for general audiences. Moreover, they concluded that, among other things, there is no contradiction or opposition between information and evangelization in official religious websites. In short, the proposed theoretical model proved to be an effective tool for studying religious communication.

Since then, however, the use of the internet has evolved. Today, due to social media, relationships on the web are open to interaction and dialogue. Official websites and social media are actually two different spaces of communication that utilize different languages, through which it is necessary to *virtually* transmit an image of the same *real* identity. In a short period of time, organizations have perceived that the communication paradigm has changed: it is not enough to simply inform; it is necessary to converse. This evolution has progressed from the 'information society' to the now so-called 'conversation society' (Bloem et al. 2009).

TIP 1

Organizations' communication has evolved from an *information society* to a *conversation society*. It is necessary to 'communicate' less and 'listen' more.

New communication platforms have developed to bring about this dialogue. Among the major and most extended platforms are blogs, micro-blogs, social networks and content communities (Cheong et al. 2012). Even though these channels are well known, we offer a brief description of the most important ones: social networks (e.g. Facebook and Google +) are sites for users to share text, video and photos through personal accounts; micro-blogs (e.g. Twitter) are personal accounts where brief messages are exchanged; online communities (e.g. YouTube, Pinterest or Instagram) are pages for public users to share videos or photos in a special way. These tools foster interactivity and the exchange of ideas and materials.

In this new context of communication, institutions offering religious values ask themselves many questions, including:

- What kind of content should be transmitted online?
- Should a religious institution have some official presence on social networks? And if so, are these effective tools for dialogue with users?
- How is an organization's religious identity reflected in a virtual world?
- What quantitative and qualitative data can be extracted from online activity to improve the communication strategy of a religious entity?

An organization's website and various digital outlets produce so much data that it becomes difficult to get an overall picture that can respond to the above questions. Furthermore, daily informative activity (such as the need to update the webpage, publish posts or respond to readers' comments on a social network, etc.) makes it difficult to track a clearly defined strategy, which is only performed if goal achievement is analysed progressively and systematically.

The Online Communication Model (OCM)

The internet offers a great arena for analysing the effect of determinate messages on a specific audience, especially the communication of religious beliefs. Among other things, the large amount of data generated from the internet allows one to draw conclusions regarding the quality of relationships between the institution and its public.

TIP 2

The statistics of websites and social media must be analysed. A periodic study of content and user feedback helps reorient and improve communication.

To draw conclusions, it is necessary to analyse the website and social media of an institution through a precise methodology that takes into account the nature of these means. We propose then the 'Online Communication Model' (OCM) as a model to analyse how an institution transmits values, persuades and interacts with a community through its official website and official social channels (Narbona 2014).

The OCM divides the analysis of an institution's virtual communication into two different settings: the corporate and the public. The first is composed of the official website(s) and the second is formed by the social media outlets. The corporate sphere is the 'official' or institutional dimension, in other words, the main sphere that is entirely controlled and managed by those responsible for communications of the entity in question. The 'public' sphere is called such because the institution shares its space with many other entities and individuals that directly participate in the communication via interaction and user-generated content.

To analyse the sphere of corporate online communication, we can compare the website to a bar (Cantoni, Di Blas and Bolchini 2003). A bar is nothing other than an ensemble of the following:

1 Drinks and food for consumption.
2 Plates, glasses, silverware, tables, etc., that facilitate the consumption of beverages and food, and activities (television, billiards, cards, etc.) that can make the experience more enjoyable.
3 Personnel who manage the business (waiters, dishwashers, cooks, etc.).
4 Customers who go there regularly.

Mirroring this image, the analysis of the corporate setting in the OCM also distinguishes four elements of a website:

1 An offer of content and services (news, contacts, materials to download, etc.).
2 Tools that allow the user to access what is offered (hardware, software, etc.).
3 A group of developers or people who launch and maintain the website (website manager, webmaster, etc.).
4 Clients or users who interact with issuers and each other.

At the foundation of the OCM is the institutional communication *project*, which holds together all online strategy and action, unifies and coordinates the website with the rest of the entity's activities. A fifth element is added to the analysis, a *setting* or *context*. This is a necessary addition since a website gains meaning not only for what it is, but also for what it is not, that is, for the elements that differentiate it from its competition, and for its context. Finally, the development of a plan demands a periodic *assessment* that evaluates how adequately the communication project corresponds to the mission of the organization, as well as the constraints that may derive from the external environment.

Content and services, tools, developers and clients form the 'pillars' of the website. Pillars I and II refer to 'things' or material objects, while pillars III and IV refer to persons. This model ensures a complete analysis of:

1 Each of the individual elements (both tools and content) and the elements that form a webpage.
2 The interplay among these components that gives meaning to the site.
3 The relationship with the external environment.

This part of the model is schematically represented in the graphic below represented in Figure 11.1.

Once the elements of the corporate sphere (institutional website) are analysed, we embark on the study of the public sphere (social media). If the first is similar to a bar, the second can be likened to a public market, where each vendor, in his own capacity,

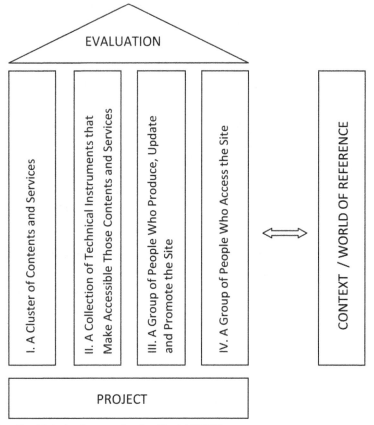

Fig. 11.1 The Website Communication Model (WCM)

offers his goods at a rented space to the passers-by, and exchange takes place. Competition occurs in the same space with other entrepreneurs and the relationships are much more fluid. In this new setting, the analysis follows the same structure of the four pillars, with a minor modification to pillars III and IV.

Contents and services (pillar I) in the public sphere are aimed to attract users by inciting dialogue, interaction and feedback. The desired relationship with users demands that the contents be persuasive. We will therefore use the nomination 'persuasion level' for the analysis of the various proposed social media elements and their reception by users. We have thus considered two dimensions for our social media study: the proposed elements [posts (pt), tweets (tw), videos (vd), photos (pht)] and the reactive elements [comments (cm), likes (lk), retweets (rtw)] upon which a relationship is formed. Currently, the main social networks offer managers detailed statistics on the user activity of their channels. These results facilitate the analysis proposed below.

The study of the *persuasion level* comprises:

1 Official identification: the entity's formal and graphic presentation of itself through its logo, URL choice, stylistic unity among the different media outlets, etc.

2 Currency: rate of content turnover (*#pt, tw, vd, pht/# days or months*).

3 Relevance: thematic classification of posts and likes, with comparisons of both percentages over the total (*pt/# pt x 100; lk/# lk X 100*).

4 Sources: origin of content (original, from official site, from other outlets, etc. in %).

5 Dissemination (*#rtw to third parties/# tw*).

A study on the *usability level*, which measures how well the tools facilitate access to contents, is proposed for pillar II. Even though tools or channels are standard, administrators can perform operations to enhance the level of *usability*. These are:

1 Search Engine Optimization.

2 Use of multimedia: the combination of images, videos, and text to form the content (*#pt or tw with vd or pht/total # pt or tw*).

3 Applications: description of services that allows you to add some of the social media.

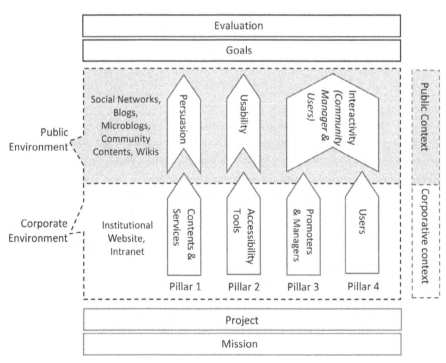

Fig. 11.2 The Online Communication Model (OCM)

Pillars III and IV are combined in the public setting since developers and users alike transmit and receive communication. The relationship established among both parties necessitates the measure of the *interactivity level* through the following analysis:

1 Supports: rate of user agreement with content (# *lk*/# *pt x 100*).

2 Comments: measure ratio of sent messages by readers (*#cm/# pt x 100*).

3 Dialogue: exchange of comments between the community manager and users (*# cm or conversational rtw/ # pt or tw x 100*).

4 Links: in micro-blogs, relationships between the number of people followed and followers (*following/followers*).

Combining both spheres, the Online Communication Model is summarized in Figure 11.2.

Application of the OCM to a religious non-profit organization

After presenting a method of analysis, let us now look at an example of a religious institution and the online activity that it may develop. *Catholic Relief Services* (CRS) is one of the most active religious humanitarian organizations on the web. This entity is sponsored by the Bishops' Conference of the United States of America (the organization that brings together leaders of the Catholic Church in that country). Inspired by the Christian message of charity, CRS drives development activities in both the US and abroad. The aforementioned institution given as an example is one of twelve non-profit institutions analysed in a study carried out by one of the authors of this chapter (Narbona 2011).

To raise awareness of its activities, CRS maintains an official website, a blog, and Facebook, YouTube, Google+, Pinterest and Twitter accounts. In every instance of online activity, this religious and humanitarian organization reflects its Christian inspiration, which distinguishes it from many other organizations in its sector. The evolution of CRS's website and social media presence gives an idea of how such an organization may make use of the internet on an institutional level.

CRS's official website began to show activity in February 1998. In its first version, the website defined the institution's identity, summarized their activity, and provided some contact information. It did not, however, include any visual elements to brand its Christian inspiration. The static nature of the online information prevented interactivity (for which users were not yet ready). In 2003, two important elements were developed: the logo, a candle, which stimulated religious values such as worship of God and light for the world; and the slogan – *giving hope to a world in need* – which encapsulated its mission.

These two elements express a defined online identity and have remained constant until today. It was not until 2006 that the directors of the website created a specific section for religious audiences, and in 2008, they added an online service to pray for a particular cause. Analysis of the website's evolution has demonstrated an increase of the spiritual aspect (religious icons, doctrinal content, etc.) in the virtual sphere.

In their social media networks, CRS has maintained a coherent image in the use of their logo and overall presentation: 'Catholic Relief Services is the official international humanitarian agency of the U.S. Catholic community.' Regarding content, the informative dimension predominates (29 per cent of all posts, tweets, videos and other content are informative). Then about 17 per cent of content is an invitation to action, while 15 per cent of all content proposes a religious reflection. Even though content strictly connected to religious messages is not the majority, they nevertheless provoke the greatest user feedback: 24 per cent of all comments, retweets or likes come from religious content, while 19 per cent come from news, and only 9 per cent come from action. It can, thus, be concluded that internet users appreciate when a religious institution offers spiritual content and are willing to interact when, for example, a verse from a sacred scripture or a quote from a religious figure is presented online.

Therefore, by studying how an institution presents itself through its official website and social networks, as well as the readers' reactions to each type of content, it is possible to reformulate the institution's communication strategy and improve its visibility. In order to do so, however, a systematic form of analysis must be performed.

In Figure 11.3 we present an example of a numerical analysis of the activity on the Catholic Relief Services' Official Facebook Page, during the months of August, September and October 2011. Similar analyses could be done for other platforms (blog, Twitter, YouTube, Google+, etc.).

Pros and Cons of the OCM

The Online Communication Model offers, as a principle advantage, a general overview of all online activities of an institution that are generally dispersed in diverse scenarios. The model also offers a cross-study of several particular aspects of communication, such as the visual presentation of the organization in diverse channels. With regard to social networking, there is no doubt of the usefulness of possessing statistical data to guide the effectiveness or ineffectiveness of a communications plan and the proposed content. Conversation, participation and collective intelligence should not only be proposed as elements of the communications strategies, but they also should be evaluated to see if the desired interaction is actually being achieved. This is particularly important for religious institutions because by their nature, they desire to positively influence users of online communication.

The proposed model is generic enough to support future forms of communication that will arise from the internet. The latest formats (i.e. WhatsApp or Snapchat) delve deeper into the intimate sphere of the individual. These new areas of communication cannot be ignored by institutions (religious or secular), keeping in mind that the dominant channels (i.e. Facebook or Twitter), can both evolve or disappear. A model based on the study of persuasion (content), usability (tools), and interactivity

SOCIAL NETWORK (FACEBOOK): https://www.facebook.com/CatholicReliefServices

	About	Persuasion level				Usability level			Interactivity level			
		Refresh	Relevance	Sources	Applications	Exclusiveness	SEO*	Multimediality	Support	Comments	Intervention	Dialogue
August	Logo: Yes Name: Catholic Relief Services URL: /catholicreliefservices About: Catholic Relief Services is the official international humanitarian agency of the U.S. Catholic community Contact: Yes	0.5 post / day (17 posts / 31 days)	a) News: 31%, 39% b) Call to action: 18%, 7% c) Services: 0 d) Testimonies: 24%, 24% e) Events: 0 f) Context: 5%, 3% g) Donations: 11%, 15% h) Values: 11%, 12%	a) Original: 11% b) Instit: 24% c) YouTube: 0 d) Twitter: 0 e) Blog: 41% f) External: 24% g) Others: 0	10 applications: 1) Friend's activities; 2) Join CRS; 3) Take action; 4) Pray with us; 5) Donate; 6) YouTube Box; 7) Photo; 8) Give; 9) Events; 10) Questions	11% exclusive contents (2 exclusive posts / 17 posts)	Catholic Relief Services (November 30, 2011) - Google: 8th position - Yahoo!: 4th position - Bing: 4th position	76% posts multimedia (13 / 17 posts)	3% fans support (954 likes / 37,612 fans = 0.03 fans / supporter)	6.2 comments / post (106 comments / 17 posts)	a) 106 comments b) 37,612 fans c) 954 active supporters d) 0.2% fans comments e) 10% active fans comments	3 interventions 0.17 intervention / post
September		0.4 post / day (12 posts / 30 days)	a) News: 17%, 5% b) Call to action: 17%, 7% c) Services: 0 d) Testimonies: 25%, 20% e) Events: 8%, 6% f) Context: 0 g) Donations: 8%, 6% h) Values: 25%, 56%	a) Original: 17% b) Instit: 41% c) YouTube: 0 d) Twitter: 0 e) Blog: 25% f) External: 1% g) Others: 8%		17% exclusive contents (2 exclusive posts / 12 posts)		58% posts multimedia (7 / 12 posts)	2% fans support (873 likes / 37,612 fans = 0.02 likes / supporter)	5.2 comments / post (63 comments / 12 posts)	a) 63 comments b) 37,612 fans c) 873 active supporters d) 0.1% fans comments e) 7% active fans comments	2 interventions 0.2 intervention / post
October		0.5 post / day (15 posts / 31 days)	a) News: 40%, 43% b) Call to action: 13%, 12% c) Services: 0 d) Testimonies: 6%, 4% e) Events: 13%, 8% f) Context: 13%, 32% g) Donations: 0 h) Values: 6%, 7%	a) Original 20% b) Instit: 53% c) YouTube: 6% d) Twitter: 0 e) Blog: 20% f) External: 0 g) Others: 0		20% exclusive contents (3 exclusive posts / 15 posts)		13% posts multimedia (2 / 15 posts)	2% fans support (811 likes / 37,612 fans = 0.02 likes / supporter)	6.9 comments / post (104 comments / 15 post)	a) 104 comments b) 38,626 fans c) 811 active supporters d) 0.2% fans comments e) 12% active fans comments	5 interventions 0.04 intervention / post
Results		0.5 post / day	a) News: 29%, 29% b) Call to action: 17%, 9% c) Services: 0 d) Testimonies: 19%, 15% e) Events: 7%, 5% f) Context: 7%, 9% g) Donations: 6%, 7% h) Values: 15%, 24%	a) Original: 16% b) Instit: 39% c) YouTube: 5% d) Twitter: 0 e) Blog: 30% f) External: 8% g) Others: 2%		16% exclusive contents		49% posts multimedia	2.3% fans support	6.1 comments / post	- 0.2% fans comments - 10% active fans comments	0.14 intervention / post

CATHOLIC RELIEF SERVICES

* The positioning results of the page in the search engines (SEO) responds to a search slightly posterior to the period of analysis.

Fig. 11.3 Analysis of CRS's Official Facebook Page Using the OCM (August/October 2011) (developers and users), can adjust to the changes that the web 3.0 and its subsequent developments contribute to online communication.

However, this model has a few limitations. For example, it is challenging to establish fixed criteria for qualitative analysis, specifically when studying an official website, where it is difficult to compare different types of institutions. This is particularly important in the communication of religious values in which, unlike for commercial institutions, numerical results do not always correspond to successful communication. The quality of the message (what is communicated), faithfulness to doctrine or a founder, opportunity, etc., is fundamental. However, it is almost impossible for the model mentioned above to take all of these factors into account (including, but not limited to, the difficulty of creating a list of 'quality standards' to serve all institutions or beliefs). Another limitation of the OCM model is its singular focus on official channels, as it is known that many discussions and debates regarding an association (including religious associations), occur outside of the managed websites (a clear example being Wikipedia). Thus, for obvious reasons, not all areas of dialogue can be studied. However, the OCM requires that this uncontrollable background noise be taken into account in the official communication. For example, a celebration on the Jewish calendar can be heavily influenced by the attention given by international news (e.g. an anniversary of Nazi persecution, a peace agreement in the Middle East, etc.), and a potential debate can jump to social channels and influence the online communication of a Jewish community.

The data required for the study is, for the most part, public. As a result, there is no problem in analysing the online communication of one or several institutions and creating a comparative study. Although helpful, doing an analysis can cause some ethical problems, specifically regarding the mission of religious organizations. The extracted data can initially suggest conclusions that are not in agreement with the principal mission of the organization (i.e. generating debates because they are well received as opposed to promoting values that pertain to a particular religious tradition; or spreading ideas that are well accepted among the faithful, regardless of whether they are unorthodox or inconsistent with the doctrine of the institution being analysed). Despite the limitations mentioned above, the Online Communication Model offers a comprehensive look at the strengths and weaknesses of the communication networks of religious institutions.

The challenges of online communication for religious organizations

Institutional communication helps translate an organization's identity into an image: an image that forms in the user's mind in various facets. For the internet, these aspects come from the virtual world, including news content, related links, quality and subject of photographs, institutional logos, language used, interactivity or lack thereof, etc. In this 'image building' process, the main ethical problem involves the temptation to not reflect reality, and rather to mask it, thereby selling smoke that obscures the representation of the institution's true nature and identity. A religious institution can end up deforming its message in order to gain more followers in the virtual world. For example, in the aforementioned case of humanitarian organizations, it would be possible to focus the online message merely on solidarity activity in order to raise funds, consequently marginalizing the religious foundation that drives the mission of that entity.

It is true that certain human and spiritual values (e.g. the defence of life before birth) may trigger public rejection, and online, this opposition can become public and generate a debate. To guarantee that the virtual world transparently reflects (without exceptions) the real institution and the values upon which it is formed is indeed an ethical issue. In our opinion, the proposed model can help to evaluate this matter. In the aforementioned study on CRS (like the other Catholic-based humanitarian entities analysed in the same report) it was found that the expressed references in the social networks to Jesus Christ or the Catholic religion were quite scarce, but nevertheless the existing ones were very well received by the public.

Interactivity poses another problem. The Web 2.0 is characterized by dialogue and participation. Religions normally propose a truth, which is proclaimed and can be rejected or accepted. Even though debate and discussion are normally permitted, doubts are raised about the web being an adequate tool for generating public opinion about religious topics. Can just any user authoritatively judge the values asserted by a religion? What may the effects be of an open discussion on religious belief for a particular faith group and its authority?

The question regarding dialogue especially affects the person responsible for the religious entity's institutional channels on the web. His/her role consists in managing the information and speaking on behalf of the institution. For organizations that concern us, does that person have adequate formation to speak on behalf of the institution? Can his/her claims be attributed to the institution for which he/she works?

Although the ethical issues raised by online institutional communications are many, we will mention one that specifically affects religious entities. Commercial institutions have found the internet to be a well suited vehicle for online sales; non-profit institutions are spreading their messages and obtaining donations online; in a similar manner, civil institutions offer services and inform the population online. For the majority of religions, institutions serve to organize a community of believers and offer them the necessary means of salvation (preaching, forgiveness of sins, access to sacred books, spiritual council, etc.). In this sense, to what extent is the internet capable of virtually containing these realities that form part of – or are the foundation of – each religion?

For example, the sacraments offered by the Catholic Church cannot be imparted online, and they are the means through which that organization intends to transmit divine grace to its followers. Similar examples can be found in other religions. If these realities cannot be offered through the internet, we must conclude that something essential is missing for a religion to show itself – in all aspects of its identity – in the online world. The 'physicality' of religious practice (i.e. the physical dimension through which communities are formed, different creeds are transmitted, and worship is carried out) implies an insurmountable barrier for the 'virtuality' of the web.

> ### TIP 3
>
> Each religious institution should know the 'virtual limits' of the services offered. Religion also has a physical dimension.

Proposing a method to analyse the online activity of a religious institution as we did, opens the door to many other future studies. The social dialogue that currently exists in social media, with hundreds of millions of conversations, makes it clear that organizations can hardly do without these tools if they want to be effective and have a social presence. The 'virtualization' of an ordinary process (buying a ticket, speaking with a friend, requesting a doctor's appointment, etc.) is already affecting religious organizations, even though the limits and challenges that come from separation from the physical world are numerous.

The process to become present online has already begun. In the coming years, the development of already existing online channels and the emergence of new outlets will offer new tools to religious organizations and communities to improve the effectiveness of their communication. How these tools are being used and what effect they are having on the faithful will need to be studied.

Glossary

Institutional Communication the organized communication of an institution or its representatives directed to individuals or groups in the social environment in which it operates. It aims to establish quality relationships among an institution and its publics and gain a social reputation and public image that corresponds to its activities and purpose.

Interactivity the ability of specific communication technology to create a mediated environment in which participants can communicate with each other (one-on-one, one with others, or many with many) whether in real-time or not, and participate in the reciprocal exchange of messages.

Online Communication Model (OCM) the WCM updated with the evolution of the internet. Along with the institutional website, the OCM also analyses the organization's official channels in social networks and other online platforms.

Online persuasion the ability for an online presence to bring a user to action, i.e. to become a subscriber, lead or client.

Usability quality indicator pointing to what extent a particular object is easy to use. It is used on the internet to evaluate how much time is necessary to learn to use a website, how effectively it is used, how much time does it take to memorize how it is used, what is the percentage of error when being used, how enjoyable is its use, etc. Some components of usability are: navigability, pertinence of content, comprehensibility of information and structure of the webpage and graphic appeal.

User-generated content content generated by internet users (video, audio, text, etc.).

Website Communication Model (WCM) website analysis model proposed in 2003. It distinguishes four components in each website: contents and services, system tools, developers and users.

12 Researching Authority in Religious Organizations from a Communicative Perspective: A Connective Online–Offline Approach

PAULINE HOPE CHEONG, BORIS H. J. M. BRUMMANS AND JENNIE M. HWANG

Religious organizations contend with the day-to-day leadership challenges of proselytization, teaching and mobilization of their members. These challenges are amplified in today's globalizing world where religious leaders must instruct and maintain relationships with their followers in geographically dispersed branches and multi-sited campuses. This chapter presents a communicative perspective that starts from the premise that religious organizations are constituted through the interactions of their members. By conceptualizing religious organizations as emerging *in* communication, we view religious authority as an order and quality of communication, which means that authority is co-constituted between leaders and followers who acknowledge the asymmetric and consequential nature of their exchanges. After we have explained our way of conceptualizing religious authority in organizations in the first part of this chapter, we will discuss and illustrate how mixed modality research methods can be used to study the connective online–offline communicative behaviours of leaders and their devotees, which are crucial to understanding how religious authority is co-constituted in contemporary mediated contexts. To conclude, we will reflect on the various challenges we have encountered in our research.

Researching religious authority in organizations from a communicative perspective

Divergent from the predictions of secularization theory, we are not so much witnessing the demise of religious enthusiasm amidst scientific developments, but the apparent persistence and rise of religious authority and social collectivities alongside technological modernization in many contemporary societies (Kluver and Cheong 2007; Norris and Inglehart 2004). To be sure, some forms of religious organizations are changing and being restructured, yet their disestablishment in a mediated world is not definite. To the contrary, some prominent religious organizations have grown exponentially in recent years and have become 'mega' churches and temples, with expansive international footprints of satellite branches, transnational affiliates and 'multi-sited' campuses (Warf and Winsberg 2010). Although much of these churches and temples' global influence is reflected in their impressive infrastructure and distinctive material presence in urban hubs and suburban neighbourhoods, the day-to-day operations of these religious organizations remain opaque. As Tracey (2012) noted in his recent review of literature on religion and organization, the 'role of agency in the creation and legitimation of new forms of organization with the capacity to exert a remarkably powerful influence over their members' and the 'deep-rooted taken-for grantedness' of large international religious organizations remains under-researched (p. 118).

To deepen our understanding of religious authority in organizations, especially in this globalizing world of transnational religious networks, our recent research looks at the communicative dynamics of religious organizing. Specifically, drawing upon prior communication research on the constitution of non-profit organizations (e.g. see Chaput, Brummans and Cooren 2011; McPhee and Iverson 2009), we contend that religious organizations are not merely abstract, objective entities with material infrastructure. Rather, they are co-'enacted' (Weick 1979) in the ongoing, and often mediated, interactions between leaders, members and non-members, which make these socio-material systems present as identifiable unities on a local and global stage. A religious organization is, in other words, dynamically brought forth in everyday communication that allows the reproduction of a collective 'self' with symbolic and material characteristics, such as a coherent discourse expounding a specific philosophy and recognizable artefacts (Cheong, Hwang and Brummans 2014). Thus, our communication-centred perspective implies that in contemporary mediated or 'media saturated' (Couldry 2012) environments, we have to pay attention to how religious organizations are discursively and materially co-enacted by various actors via their representations and performances in digital and social media interactions, grounded in their embodied realities.

Following this line of thought, we do not conceive of religious authority in traditional ways (e.g. see Weber's tripartite typology of traditional, charismatic and rational-legal authority). Instead, we view religious authority in more relational and emergent terms, as an order and quality of communication, co-constituted between leaders and followers who acknowledge the asymmetric and consequential nature of their exchanges (Brummans, Hwang and Cheong, 2013; Cheong, Huang and Poon 2011a). Accordingly, authority is accomplished through verbal and nonverbal communication that not merely describes or reports but impels and establishes precedence or hierarchy, where role and status distinctions are sustained and contested in ongoing negotiations (Taylor 2011). Our communicative perspective provides insight into the relational dynamics of authority. It helps us understand that authority is fluid, geographically distributed and multidirectional – 'initiated' by leaders at the top of the organization or generated at the 'grassroots' level.

Cultivating multilevel perspectives on religious authority

We have used the term 'strategic arbitration' to signify a more top-down approach, where religious leaders constitute their authority by expanding their social identity from commanders to arbiters of knowledge and encounters, both online and offline. Such clergy agency in connecting both online and offline encounters is observed where internet use facilitates the co-creation of information and expertise, under conditions that do not destabilize church or temple practices. This is achieved by religious leadership retaining discretionary power to help their congregation give meaning to their experiences and shape informational and interpersonal outcomes (Cheong, Huang and Poon 2011a). Examples of strategic arbitration in our research on Buddhist and Christian organizations include the reconfiguration of spiritual mentoring to include the use of online resources yet stress the necessity of personal ties; the heightened emphasis of priestly performances in mass as well as on digital sites perceived to be sacred; and the authorship of new sacred texts across digital platforms for multimedia branding to present a consistent organizational story (Cheong, Huang and Poon 2011a, 2011b).

Besides strategic arbitration, we have used our communicative perspective to study how religious authority can extend and endure across time and space in the sense that it can be co-constituted at the grassroots level by various agents who make a sacred figure present in her absence in their everyday interactions. In this case, we draw upon research that shows how authority is established by invoking figures of authority in organizational communication, as certain human and nonhuman agents can 'presentify' an organization because they have gained the legitimacy to speak and act in its name (Benoit-Barné and Cooren 2009). Authority is thus accomplished and sustained through emergent talk and actions such as dis-local directives, labels and principles. We have extended this research by investigating how traditional, digital and social media enable members and non-members of religious organizations to co-constitute their authority by invoking a spiritual figure such as a Buddhist dharma master (Cheong, Hwang and Brummans 2014).

Now that we have explicated our communicative perspective, let's see how it can help us research the communicative dynamics of religious authority in organizations by looking at an actual organization. In the next section, we will illustrate the usefulness of our perspective by using it to investigate religious authority in the Buddhist Compassion Relief Tzu Chi Foundation ('Tzu Chi'), one of the largest Chinese spiritual organizations in the world.

> **TIP 1**
>
> Recognize potential connections between online and offline data to gain insights into communicative practices that constitute religious organizations.

Using a connective online–offline approach to research religious authority: An illustrative case

Founded in 1966, the nun Cheng Yen established Tzu Chi believing that Buddhism should be used to alleviate spiritual poverty and material deprivation. The Mandarin word *cíjì* ('compassion relief') captures the organization's overall mantra: 'to cultivate sincerity, integrity, faith, and honesty within while exercising kindness, compassion, joy, and selflessness to humanity through concrete actions'; to 'promote the universal value of "Great Love" '; and to 'employ the humanitarian spirit of Chinese culture to its utmost' (Tzu Chi Foundation 2011: para. 2). The organization's four missions include charity; medical care; education; and 'humanitarianism', that is, promoting kindness and love through community voluntarism and media work (including self-produced publications, radio, television and internet programs). More recently, Tzu Chi has also started to focus on environmental protection and conservation. While its headquarters are located in Taiwan, Tzu Chi operates in many countries in the Americas, Africa, Europe and Asia, and is 'the largest non-government organization in the Chinese speaking world, with 10 million members in more than 30 countries' (O'Neill 2010: 2).

To study religious authority in Tzu Chi, we used a connective online–offline data collection approach, so that we could trace communicative processes such as strategic arbitration and invocation in transmediation – i.e. in the appropriation, reconfiguration and retransmission of messages across different media platforms. The idea of 'connectivity' has been used in connective ethnography to integrate research that is conducted across online and offline spaces (Hine 2007). It has also been used to understand work practices in corporate settings, because a focus on connectivity adds 'layers of understanding' and captures more accurately how offline practices are embedded in online practices, and vice versa (Dirksen, Huizing and Smit 2010). Our connective approach is consistent with what scholars have identified as the 'third' wave of research on online religion (Campbell and Lövheim 2011), which suggests that researchers focus on the implications of newer media technologies for religion, with an interest in understanding the potentially symbiotic relationship between online and offline practices. In this case, data collection and analyses are grounded in material and historical conditions, yet they also take into account negotiations occurring at online–offline intersections.

Our connective mixed-methods approach follows the guidelines developed for conducting naturalistic inquiry (see Lindlof and Taylor 2002; see also Lincoln and Guba 1985). Our online–offline research was preceded by extensive archival and literature research. After this, we conducted fieldwork in Taiwan over several summers, including participant and non-participant observation, as well as interviewing at the Tzu Chi headquarters in Hualien and other parts of Tzu Chi. For example, we observed important socialization rituals at an international volunteer training camp and worked with volunteers in Tzu Chi recycling centres. We also interviewed volunteers from all walks of life, besides key leaders and members of staff. In addition, we took copious field notes to keep track of our own sense-making processes. As far as our online research was concerned, we did an extensive analysis of Tzu Chi's official website, but also of its digital and social media platforms. In this case, we relied especially on thematic analysis of web features and online interactions. Combining all these methods produced a 'corroboration' of similar results (Brannen 2005), providing rich insight into how both online and offline communication enable the co-constitution of religious authority in Tzu Chi.

First, our methodological approach enabled us to explore how Master Cheng Yen's authority is constituted via face-to-face and mediated communication, in particular via a religious 'branding' process that allows her identity to be constructed, narrated and represented to build a distinctive and compelling story (Twitchell 2004). We noted, for example, how omnipresent her image is in the Tzu Chi organization, both online and offline. Our naturalistic research shows that her portraits can be seen everywhere in Tzu Chi buildings across Taiwan as well as in Tzu Chi's various media. As we wrote in one of our recent articles,

> What may strike any newcomer to Tzu Chi is how omnipresent Master Cheng Yen is, even though she mainly resides in Hualien. When entering Tzu Chi buildings, the charismatic nun can be seen on posters and photos, on book covers and pamphlets, in Da Ai television programs on TV sets overhanging hallways; and most importantly, her voice can be heard everywhere, as if it were filling the organization throughout (First author's fieldwork journal, 15 July, 2007).
>
> Brummans, Hwang and Cheong 2013: 356

In parallel, analysing Tzu Chi's main portal online revealed how the Master's image occupies a significant part of the website and on the home page, where she is portrayed as the central figure governing the universe as she is imaged as being larger than the globe.

TIP 2

Trace religious communicative practices thematically across platforms of digital media.

Moreover, the Master's brand is co-constructed via transmedia authorship – the broadcast of her speeches and subsequent reproduction of her sayings, both verbatim and in condensed form, across multiple media. Every morning, Master Cheng Yen starts the day by giving a speech from her pulpit in Hualien. This speech is then broadcast as a talk to her followers worldwide (as well as translated for subtitling by Tzu Chi's Foreign Language Department). Our research shows that members watch these speeches individually on television and on YouTube, or even in groups, because the videos and self-produced television programs are synced and accessible from various branches. This shows how carefully the Master's teachings are documented, translated and disseminated by Tzu Chi's Da Ai ('great love') Cultural and Humanitarian Centre across a variety of traditional and digital media. Tzu Chi's publications range from print to digital monthly and quarterly magazines, (e-)books, self-produced radio and television programmes for adults, audio CDs and DVDs for children, to condensations of Master Cheng Yen's teachings into Jing Si ('still thoughts') aphorisms, which have been compiled into several volumes and translated into eleven languages.

These findings highlight how the Master's omnipresence is accomplished through transmedia branding. We see how this branding requires a lot of 'work', communicatively speaking. That is, the Master's omnipresence does not appear by itself, but is co-constituted through the people and things that make Cheng Yen's authority present in discursive and material ways.

Next, to deepen our understanding of how the Master's authority is 'presentified' (Fairhurst and Cooren 2009) through the use of online and offline communication, we interviewed key members of Da Ai, including editors, media producers and web personnel. In-depth, semi-structured interviews allowed us to understand how different media are used to produce Tzu Chi's programmes (e.g. via terrestrial, cable and satellite television and newer forms of mobile applications) and to investigate how Da Ai employees perceive and appropriate various forms of media to spread the Master Cheng Yen's 'universal love'. During these interviews, we asked Da Ai members a number of questions, for instance, about (1) their everyday work activities; (2) their motivations to join the organization and the challenges they face; (3) the perceived impact and consequences of their work; (4) their collaborations with other spiritual organizations and/or commercial media; and (5) their interactions with the Master and other organizational leaders.

Discussing questions like these gave us deeper insight into how Tzu Chi members account for and appropriate media to publicize Master Cheng Yen's teachings across diverse platforms. In particular, we discovered how Tzu Chi leaders appropriate digital media to cultivate *yinyúan* ('karmic affinities') all over the world, for example by producing positive, non-sensationalistic news and using their nine satellite transponders to disseminate their messages. In brief, one way to research religious authority in organizations is therefore to examine how a religious leader's authority is discursively branded or 'authored' in and across media. In this case, it is important to analyse how different forms of media, including digital media, are appropriated to make this religious figure present.

A second way to understand the communicative constitution of religious authority is to investigate how the authority of a religious figure is reproduced because organizational leaders and employees invoke this figure in their daily interactions. For example, through our interviews, we learned that Da Ai members consider their media work to be the enactment of Master Cheng Yen's vision, meaning that they draw upon insights derived from the Master's teachings and from their personal meetings with her in their organizational interactions and constantly invoke her words to justify the redemptive purpose of their work. It is thus useful to examine members' invocational practices, because these practices play a vital role in the co-enactment of a religious organization. Invocation does not merely imply speaking and acting in a revered figure's name, but also trying to speak, quite literally, *in* this figure's voice (using his or her same discourse, intonation, rhythm, etc.), and acting in ways that are similar to his or hers, practices that are vital to the organization's communicative reproduction.

The limitation of these two ways of researching religious authority is that they do not account for the role of non-members in the establishment of this authority. For this reason, we also investigated how lay people invoke the Master in digital and social media interactions. To accomplish this part of our research, we first located and examined all the relevant social media sites in English and Chinese, including Facebook, Twitter and YouTube. However, to make our analysis more feasible, we decided to focus on the Chinese and English Facebook sites. We then archived and counted the posts, noted the frequency with which posts were updated, and compared the most 'popular' posts (i.e. posts that received more than the average number of likes or comments). Subsequently, we analysed these online data by using a constant comparative method of individually reading the online data to categorize data, returning to the data for re-examination and confirmation, and then discussing our interpretations to ensure convergence and consistency. These research team discussions enabled us to select representative excerpts to illustrate our insights (Lindlof and Taylor 2002).

These social media analyses helped us understand how Tzu Chi members and non-members used Facebook posts to publicize and celebrate Tzu Chi's activities and accomplishments, as well as to galvanize members into communal action and global prayer, which all reinforce their identification with the organization. For instance, we observed how Facebook users contribute to the co-enactment of Tzu Chi's linguistic domain by posting positive comments and prayers, responding to and liking others' comments, and expressing their support through the use of terms and symbols that are unique to Tzu Chi members (e.g. emoticons signifying hands placed together in pious prayer). Most importantly, our analysis of social media interactions indicated that Tzu Chi members and non-members frequently invoke Master Cheng Yen's teachings by posting and responding to her daily speech or citing her aphorisms and accompanying links, thus making her authority present, even in her physical absence.

This third and final way of studying religious authority illustrates how invocational practices enable laypersons to co-constitute the authority of a spiritual leader in their online interactions. Hence, contrary to popular beliefs about the capacity of social media to weaken hierarchy and authority, this kind of analysis may reveal how mediated expressions and interactions on Facebook can contribute to the co-enactment of a religious organization by co-constituting the authority of its leader. To be fair, some of our data did not support this conclusion, because we did encounter some 'negative cases' (Huberman and Miles 1994) where interactants' communicative activities diverged from the main body of evidence in our online data (e.g. they posted a message that criticized Tzu Chi). These cases were nevertheless few and far between. Although we found that social media certainly allow for some contestation and debate, we observed comparatively few critical or contentious comments within Tzu Chi's linguistic domain. The knowledge we gleaned from our offline fieldwork helped us compare these negative cases against Tzu Chi's overall culture, which is grounded in conflict avoidance and mindfulness. These comparisons showed how sporadic these instances of overt critique are in Tzu Chi's co-enactment. Hence, through our online and offline research, we learned that Tzu Chi members generally are not only focused on preserving their personal face, but also the face of their organization.

Research challenges

In this chapter, we have advocated a communicative perspective to studying authority in religious organizations, and we have illustrated how online and offline research methods can be used in tandem to examine the role of religious branding and invocation in the co-constitution of this authority. Compared to prior studies on Master Cheng Yen's authority, which have focused on the gendered nature of her charisma (see Huang 2009), we looked at how Tzu Chi members and non-members help to presentify the Master's authority in their online and offline communication. When conducting our research, we encountered several challenges that are worth discussing here, because being aware of these challenges may benefit researchers intending to conduct similar kinds of research.

First, it is important to recognize that digital research is a moving target, especially in this era of 'big data'. In our case, given the sophistication and complexity of Tzu Chi's global operations and the vast outreach of its media work across multiple channels, we were confronted with multiple pathways to collect online data. This raises the question of when and where to start collecting online data and when and where to stop. In light of resource and time limitations, we could only focus on a slice of social media data, in particular Facebook content (demarcated by a chronological period) in prior publications. We had to acknowledge that this choice has implications for our research process and findings as various other forms of social media related to Tzu Chi's operations exist, such as Twitter and Weibo micro-messaging, as well as YouTube and other video sharing sites. The daily increase and evolution of the corpus of texts authored by Master Cheng Yen and her followers shows how rapidly religious organizations are becoming mediatized and (re)presented multimodally online (Cheong and Ess 2012; Cheong et al. 2009). This mediatization creates new opportunities and challenges in terms of assembling and interpreting data. Consequently, conceptual, ethical and pragmatic considerations come to play in justifying how to assemble a reasonable and reliable sample of online data if we want to understand the communicative dynamics of these kinds of social collectivities, especially those operating widely on mediated and transnational stages.

Second, gaining access to Tzu Chi was challenging. Although many religious organizations' official discourse suggests that these social collectivities are open and inclusive, investigating the day-to-day operations of their leaders and members is often far from easy. In line with recommendations from other researchers who study religion among Chinese migrants (e.g. Guest 2003), we therefore advocate vigilance in building trust with local officials, clergy, and lay religious leaders and members over time to maintain good relationships or 'religious *guanxi*' (Cheong and Poon 2009). By participating in Tzu Chi activities and contributing to Tzu Chi in various ways (e.g. working as a member of the translation team, volunteering in recycling centres, etc.), we found that our relationships with members became less one-sided or opportunistic. In turn, access and trust became 'spontaneous' effects or consequences of mutual care, even though both the researchers and those who were being researched had different interests in the emerging relationships. It may thus be useful to see organizational members as reflexive agents, instead of as naive subjects or informants – i.e., as 'coproducers of interpretations that we elicit, cajole, contest, or share from [our] encounters [with them]' (Marcus 2001: 523; see also Marcus 1997). It is through the mutual 'complicity' (Marcus 2001) that emerges in our interactions with research participants that we gain insight into an organization's enactment, yet 'with overlapping mutual as well as differing purposes, negotiation, contestation, and uncertain outcomes' (Marcus 2001: 521). Hence, the 'time ordering' or sequencing of our connective online–offline approach is significant (Bryman 2001) – in our case, we chose to start with offline fieldwork, recognizing that this aspect of access in the research process may take time, effort and genuine interest, as 'religious *guanxi*' cannot be imposed or forced.

Third, related to the challenge of access is the extent to which one should take an emic or etic approach in connective research. In our case, we had to contend with the challenge of representing religious organizational life as members enact and relay it while reflexively recognizing forms of power (and resistance) as some organizational informants operate as gatekeepers by focusing on presenting Tzu Chi's positive face, which is not an uncommon facet of collectivistic cultures. Emic criteria have traditionally been the focus for ethnographic analysis and etic approaches have been yoked to attempts to provide neutral objective facts about a situation. However, we 'can also think about emic and etic criteria more broadly as part of the debate regarding inside and outsider perspectives. Drawing ideas of emic and etic criteria into this debate suggests that questions should not be limited to whether or not we are physically inside or outside a location or whether or not we are actually a member of an organization, but should also include consideration of the perspective utilized in accessing our engagement in an organization' (Neyland 2008: 82). Using naturalistic inquiry and a triangulation of multiple online and offline data sources, the picture that we have produced to date of religious authority and organizational activity is closer to developing an emic perspective that privileges Tzu Chi members' own sensemaking. However, we have also been watchful (and repetitively urged by reviewers of our work) to note critical points of contention, particularly those emergent in online data, to include a consideration of an etic perspective in assessing non-members, critics and our own engagement and representation of the organization. Accordingly, one ethical consideration is how to build and maintain intimate field relations while choosing to assess and present features of our research to wider publics and back to the organization we are studying.

Finally, the bulk of past research related to religion and the internet have tended to employ digital ethnography, while past research on religious organizations has rarely examined religious authority in online interactions. Recent reviews of literature on virtual communities, however, show a significant gap in our understanding of how organizations influence online interactive spaces, particularly the 'whys' and motivations for online behaviours (Hercheui 2011). In this chapter, we have proposed to study authority in the context of religious organizations by focusing on communicative processes, both embodied and mediated. This perspective inevitably leads researchers to investigate the diverse, multimodal expressions of religious authority, which requires the use of mixed online and offline methods. Thus, by refocusing the question from who has religious authority to how religious authority is co-constituted in the course of everyday communication, we are likely to encounter new methodological opportunities and challenges, as transmediation and media convergence evolves.

Part 4 Virtual Reality and Religion

13 Online Ethnographic Research: Avatars in Virtual Worlds

WILLIAM SIMS BAINBRIDGE

Introduction

Ethnography in online virtual worlds has become an exceedingly active research area (Boellstorff et al. 2012). When applied to religion, it can be conceptualized in two rather different ways. First, it can be seen as a valuable extension of traditional practices in sociology, useful both as a training laboratory for students and as a field for carrying out professional research oriented towards traditional theories. Second, it can become the means for transforming the sociology of religion, in the context of the widespread technical as well as cultural revolution that can be called *secularization*, in which religion loses its sacred quality without becoming irrelevant, being respected as a form of aesthetically stimulating fantasy fiction (Bainbridge 2007a, 2013b).

Beginning students and experienced researchers alike may find that many of the new forms of online community, including massively multi-player online (MMO) role-playing games, are ideal environments for undertaking ethnographic studies (Bainbridge 2010a, 2011). Narrowly defined, ethnography is the rigorous documentation of a living culture, while ethnology is the comparative study of cultures in the plural, and participant observation is more narrowly focused on the experiences of a field researcher who at least partly dwells within the social group under study. More broadly defined, ethnography encompasses many varieties of interview and observational field research in cultural anthropology and sociology, including some more experimental approaches such as ethnomethodology and action research. In human-centred computing, ethnography largely means close observation of users of a new information technology in order to refine its design, the better to meet those users' needs. Any of those definitions could describe high-quality research inside MMOs.

To anchor the discussion, this chapter begins with a description of the most influential MMO, *World of Warcraft* (WoW), which contains a tremendous amount of religion-related material, from cults to cathedrals, from shaman avatars to priests, from computational death to virtual resurrection (Corneliussen and Rettberg 2008). At its peak having 12,000,000 subscribers, WoW has been extensively studied, and other MMOs that have also received close examination by social scientists are similar both artistically and technically. Furthermore, given how significant WoW is on the internet, as the focus of multiple wikis, forums and more than half a million YouTube videos, it illustrates how the general methods and hypotheses discussed here may apply far beyond the boundaries of game-like virtual worlds.

Virtual cathedrals

In both cultural and economic terms, *World of Warcraft* is the most significant virtual world of the early twenty-first century, and over its first decade of existence social scientists studied it from many perspectives and using many methods. Anthropologist Bonnie Nardi (2010) did so in a book titled *My Life as a Night Elf Priest*, exploring through a character having religious significance. Ordinary players and ethnographers alike enter this virtual world by purchasing the software plus a monthly subscription, downloading gigabytes of program and data onto a desktop or laptop computer, then creating a character. MMOs tend not to use the word *avatar*, because this term borrowed from Hindu religion suggests that the virtual being is a spiritual aspect of the user, while *character* suggests that it has some degree of autonomous identity, like a character in a drama who is conceptually separate from the actor. Yet the connection between person and character may be intense, varying by personality and context (Bessiere et al. 2007; Pearce and Artemesia 2009; Blascovich and Bailenson 2011; Yee 2014). Most avid players in fact operate multiple characters, having a variety of abilities and cultural contexts. To start with, Nardi needed to select the race and class of this particular character. Night Elves are an ancient civilization worshipping the moon goddess Elune and following an environmentalist set of values seeking harmony with nature. Players who are priests in WoW and many other MMOs, are healers possessing magical powers to assist warriors and hunters in combat and lacking any ritual or theological functions, while artificial non-player characters (NPCs) that represent religions in WoW often perform educational functions and officiate over rituals.

When I set out to study religion in WoW, I naturally created priest or shaman characters in all the fictional cultures then available, and my two main characters were priests among Humans and Blood Elves (Bainbridge 2010c). According to a self-report survey carried out in mid-2010 of 6,014,846 characters, fully 872,659 or about 15 per cent of all characters were Night Elves, 1,028,766 (17 per cent) were Humans, and 1,039,815 (17 per cent) were Blood Elves, the three most populous races out of ten.[1] In the *backstory* or *lore* of WoW, Human civilization is in decline, having recently lost much of its territory to the Burning Legion, 'a vast, innumerable army of demons, infernals, and corrupted races who seek to destroy any trace of order in the universe.'[2] Its centre of power is Stormwind city, and Human characters begin their virtual lives not far away, at Northshire Abbey, just the other side of Elwynn Forest. My Human priest, named Maxrohn after my deceased uncle Max Rohn who was an Episcopal priest in real life, soon took religious training in the Cathedral of Light at Stormwind.

Maxrohn was used not only to study WoW, but to develop the early principles of an emerging quasi-religious practice, the memorialization of deceased persons through avatars of them in virtual worlds (Bainbridge 2013a, 2013c, 2014). Ancestor veneration was a standard religious practice in many traditional societies (Fortes 1961; Riley 1983; Palgi and Abramovitch 1984), but belief in a pleasant afterlife as in Christianity may have reduced survivors' sense of grief and obligation to the dearly departed. Secularization leaves people without an easy solution to the psychological problems of death, and running an avatar based on another person may have philosophical benefits as the living person tries to understand how the deceased might have felt and acted, within the new world. Players of MMOs tend to operate main characters for many hours, and I did ethnography of WoW for 802 hours through Maxrohn, a statistic that the game itself tallied and could be retrieved by typing '/played' into the chat interface used for text communications.

My main Blood Elf priest, Catullus, was also based on a deceased person, the ancient Roman poet Gaius Valerius Catullus, but he largely represented a stereotype of classic Pagan civilization, in which leaders were often highly cultivated yet dissolute. In WoW lore, Blood Elves and Night Elves were very different factions that had resulted from the disintegration of ancient High Elf civilization. While Night Elves were environmentalists, Blood Elves were technological radicals, using any magical powers they could master to help them regain power over other races. They enter WoW on Sunstrider Isle and quickly go to the half-ruined city of Silvermoon. While Human architecture appears like Medieval European architecture, and Night Elf structure blends in naturally with the sacred forest, Blood Elf buildings are bright, often golden in colour as if composed from pieces of the sun, seemingly built by Apollo. Catullus explored WoW for 784 hours, and was the chief organizer of a major scientific conference held inside *World of Warcraft* in May 2008, with over a hundred avatars of scholars and students in attendance at the three plenary sessions (Bainbridge 2010b).

My third main WoW character, a panda-bear monk named Erniekovacs, was the instrument for what Michael Burawoy (2003) has called a *revisit*, returning to an ethnographic field site after a passage of time, either with a fresh perspective, or documenting changes that occurred there, or, as in this case, both. A fresh perspective was afforded by basing a new character on the comedian from the early days of television, Ernie Kovacs, energized by watching many of his skits and characterizations on YouTube and on a set of DVDs. As Karl Marx (1913: 9) noted, history repeats itself, 'Once as tragedy, and again as farce.' Yet Kovacs was far more than a mere comic, often incorporating classical music and philosophy into his creative routines, and exploiting more than any of his contemporaries the new technical opportunities of the TV medium, even if it was, for example, to depict a beautiful woman with a hole in her head through which he could wink at the viewer. Two major expansions in WoW, Cataclysm and Mists of Pandaria, had transformed the landscape and added both a new kind of character, a Pandaran monk, and many cultural elements expressed through new missions. Another expansion, Warlords of Draenor, added a continent, allowed Erniekovacs to reach level 100 in experience and to visit a display created by WoW designers as a memorial for fellow comedian Robin Williams, a recent suicide victim.

As in many popular MMOs, a full exploration of the virtual world requires multiple characters, each exploring a different fictional culture and often distinct virtual geography. In WoW, the races are organized into two competing factions, the Alliance to which Night Elves and Humans belong, and the Horde to which Blood Elves belong. In day-to-day play, individuals often need to team up, which they often do informally but also may enter an MMO as a group of real-world friends who plan their activities to some extent ahead of time. High-quality MMOs provide tools to assist players in combining with strangers to form temporary teams capable of undertaking missions too difficult for individual players. In WoW, they typically bring together five players, but there also can be raid groups of forty. MMOs typically also facilitate formation of enduring groups, called *guilds* in WoW and many others (Williams et al. 2006; Nardi and Harris 2006; Duchenaut et al. 2007; Bardzell et al. 2008). For the 2008 conference, publicized through the journal *Science*, Catullus created a guild named Science. Despite the fact that I myself left WoW shortly afterwards, that guild was still in existence six years later when Erniekovacs ended his revisit in 2014. Thus, field research inside virtual worlds can examine very real social groups, as well as the fictional cultures created by the game designers.

TIP 1

In a secular society the same methods and theories may be used to study online fictional religions as traditionally were used to study real ones.

Data collection

Many traditional data collection methods work fine in virtual worlds. For example, one can write ethnographic notes either during the hours one operates the character, or afterwards. However, the user interfaces differ in how well they function simultaneously with other software such as a word processor. Several gameworlds provide the option to run them in a window, but others dominate the entire screen. In either case, it may be more convenient to take notes on a second computer. However, the data files for the research should be assembled in a coherent manner on one computer, and the majority of them are likely to come directly from the game itself.

Everything the user sees and hears from the virtual world, and potentially everything the user does inside it, can be captured automatically, although with varying degrees of difficulty and resulting in data files that vary in their convenience for analysis. Before we even describe the diverse data collection opportunities, we must suggest that some work will be required to prepare. For example, a primary data collection method involves taking *screenshot* photographs of what is seen on the computer's screen, and most high-quality virtual worlds have built-in systems for doing this. However some of them assume that the user does not want images overlaid with the on-screen text, such as mission instructions and words 'spoken' by other players or non-player characters, yet this text may be precisely what a researcher wants to preserve. A fair amount of information about screenshots can be found on websites describing the game, but there is no substitute for actually taking some trial pictures, learning the game's options for including data displayed by the interface, discovering which graphics formats are available, and even finding where the files are saved. Thus, depending on the research goals, it might be advisable to run a temporary character to become familiar with the screenshot capabilities and other data collection options, before beginning the research proper.

Some popular virtual worlds, and many less popular ones, do not make it immediately possible to record screenshots of everything. For example, in *Neverwinter*, one may take ordinary screenshots either with or without the interface display, but when the game goes into the *cutscenes* that represent conversations with non-player characters, the screenshot function is shut off. One response to this problem is to use a separate program, such as Fraps (www.fraps.com), which can capture videos as well as still pictures. One can set *Neverwinter* such that pressing the F10 key in Windows takes a screenshot without the interface, a short *macro* program added by the user into the game makes the F11 key take a screenshot including the interface, and F12 tells Fraps to take a screenshot of whatever is on the screen, even during cutscenes. It is important to set Fraps to use the same graphics format as *Neverwinter* does, so that when all the files from both sources are placed in the same folder, a picture display program can show them in chronological order. Those programs tend to pay attention to only one graphics format at a time.

Depending upon the nature of one's research, one may wind up with thousands of screenshots, so a system such as well-labelled file folders or even a catalogue is needed to manage them when assembling and analysing their data. It may be wise to keep one copy of all the screenshots arranged in chronological order, stored in some small number of folders, and then arrange a second set of copies into whatever order works best for analysis. For example, a number of missions over a wide span of time may take a WoW character to the Scarlet Monastery, and if the focus of the research is virtual sacred architecture, there should be a set of well-oriented screenshots documenting its physical structure, which is quite large and complex. Many of the brief books in the monastery's library can be read, so the researcher might want a folder for these books, with a subfolder for each one, given that a half dozen screenshots may be needed to document each. The social-cultural meaning of the Scarlet Monastery is best expressed through the missions, many of which can be completed only by teams of players, so a good deal of planning will be required, and a copy of the screenshots for each mission could be in a subfolder of a more general Scarlet Monastery missions folder. In my own research at this virtual sacred site, I found that careful documentation required returning to it at a much higher level of combat experience than the original missions required, so I could easily defeat the NPC enemy characters that would attack my character as I was trying to record data.

Much of the communication inside a virtual world traditionally has been through text, typically displayed in a window at lower left unless the user has moved it. This text includes data from the software, but most importantly, what people are 'saying' to each other. Often, there are many text chat channels, and the researcher will need to think carefully about which ones should be displayed, and how that valuable text should be captured. That can be done automatically in some of the highest-quality games, such as *World of Warcraft*, *Lord of the Rings Online*, and *Elder Scrolls Online*. Depending upon the game, this function can be turned on at the beginning of a data collection session, either by making a selection from a menu, or by entering '/chatlog' into the text chat. At completion of the session, the researcher should log out of the game as usual, then look for a file of all the text that was displayed, in a designated folder. The text is then ready for any kind of analysis that works with a general text file of ordinary language. In the case of the 2008 WoW scientific conference, chatlogs of the plenary sessions were edited to produce two chapters of the printed proceedings.

Some gameworlds have voice chat systems, although most serious gamers prefer to use separate voice communication software such as TeamSpeak, Ventrilo, Mumble, or Skype. These are primarily used for group activities in which a team battles enemies, and the players need their hands free to control their avatars, yet want to communicate swiftly: 'Run for your lives!' Of course, a recorder can be attached to the headphones through which the user speaks and listens, but then the result is a sound file that might need to be transcribed laboriously. Similarly, a video file may require much data extraction work before it can be analysed. Therefore, sound and video recordings should probably be avoided, unless the nature of the particular research project gives them a high priority.

High-quality games include many utilities for finding information, and in some cases *add-on* or *mod* programs have been written that facilitate downloading and analysing these data. Very common are in-game systems for searching the roster of characters to find some to invite to a PUG (pick-up-group) team, and these can be used manually to do a census of the distribution of characters across race, class, gender and experience level. A mod program for *World of Warcraft* that repeatedly activates the built-in search functions, called CensusPlus, will quickly tabulate all the online characters in one of the two factions, working through a specific one of the researcher's characters, so a complete census required doing this through both Maxrohn in the Alliance and Catullus in the Horde. This works only for the internet server the character is on, and as of 5 June 2014, WoW had a total of 512 servers in the US and Europe. Each is a separate version of the entire virtual world, capable of handling about 4,000 players simultaneously. Another mod, called Auctioneer, analyses the price trends in WoW's market system where players buy and sell virtual goods. While ethnography tends not to be quantitative, it certainly can be, and it is a cultural fact that Warriors in WoW are disproportionately male, while Priests are disproportionately female, at least in terms of their virtual gender.

Much of the information about an MMO can be found in specialized wikis, forums or other collaborative archives. Players of WoW often have a database called Wowhead open in another window, for example reading advice from other players on how to complete each of 12,377 'quest' missions. Each quest bears a distinctive name such as 'Make Haste to the Cathedral', 'The Call of the World-Shaman', or 'Harrison Jones and the Temple of Uldum', which is a parody of the *Indiana Jones* movies starring Harrison Ford. The online forums can themselves be the focus of many intensive studies, because they are vast repositories of diverse text-based discussions by well-developed online communities, but they will not make sense unless the researcher has considerable experience actually playing the game. In some cases, other background experience will be required. For example, as of 6 June 2014, the forums for *Lord of the Rings Online* had 952 threads (discussions) and 26,251 posts (messages) about J. R. R. Tolkien, all organized in one of dozens of forum categories, and one would need to have read the works of this creator of the mythos to understand them.

Another very rich source of data, little used by social science researchers at this point in time, is YouTube, where many players post videos of their exploits in virtual worlds, some of which are quite artistic, and others of which are well-designed tutorials. Especially notable for WoW is 'Serenity Now bombs a World of Warcraft funeral', which shows a sincere virtual funeral procession for a deceased player that horribly is attacked by a raiding party. While not common or nearly as popular as that example, a diversity of serious memorial services have been conducted across a wide range of gameworlds, such as 'Funeral Sail for Truuth Bringer' in *Pirates of the Burning Sea* which shows a memorial fleet of ships with black sails, or 'Battleground Europe Online Funeral – RIP AOTHELM' in *World War II Online* where dozens of soldiers show their respect for a deceased comrade at a virtual cathedral.

Social, cultural and ethical issues

Some MMOs serve North America and Europe, while others serve specific Asian nations, notably China and South Korea, and others are global in their reach. Thus they span many cultures, legal systems and even economic markets. At the end of 2011, one plausible estimate claimed that 3.2 million WoW players lived in China, and another 800,000 in South Korea, but since servers were located in those countries and required local accounts, it was difficult for researchers outside Asia to study their populations.[3] Of the more accessible 512 servers as of June 2014, 246 were located in the Western Hemisphere, 226 serving the US and Canada, 12 served Oceania (Australia, New Zealand, etc.), 5 served Brazil and 3 Spanish-speaking Latin America. The 266 European servers can be classified by language: 110 English, 87 German, 36 French, 20 Russian, 11 Spanish and 2 Italian. *Lord of the Rings Online*, not nearly so popular but still quite successful, had 15 North American Servers, and 14 serving Europe but located in the US, in June 2014. The Japanese MMO *Final Fantasy XIV* had 20 serving North America and Europe, and 15 serving Japan. Its older but still surviving sister game, *Final Fantasy XI* had 16 servers, each covering the whole world and having a built-in phrase book to facilitate cross-language communications between English, Japanese, German and French.

For WoW and some other popular MMOs that have multiple servers, a distinction is made between those in which the computer programming allows one player to attack another – what are called PvP or *player-versus-player* servers – and those where such attacks are prevented – PvE or *player-versus-environment*. Of the 512 WoW servers that could readily be tabulated, exactly half, or 256, were of each type. The experience of PvP play is very different from that of PvE, more violent but not necessarily less cooperative, because players often band together as humans have throughout history to defend against enemies, and even to raid them for economic advantage. Characters who 'die' in virtual worlds usually can resurrect easily, although at some cost. Yet PvP clearly violates the traditional commandment, 'Thou shalt not kill.' In WoW, the standard locale for resurrection is indeed the local graveyard, while given its Christian cultural roots, *Lord of the Rings Online* does not have players die and resurrect, a privilege reserved for Jesus, but lose morale and flee the conflict. Instead of PvP, this Tolkien-based MMO advocates human unification, yet has a custom called Monster Play, in which the darker side of a player's nature can be expressed through attacking others. Indeed, a very large fraction of the action in MMOs involves violent behaviour that would be criminal were it happening in the real world.

The social sciences set ethical standards for researchers, and yet appropriate standards can be difficult to define, doubly so in virtual worlds, and much more today compared with a decade or two ago. Back in the 1960s, a conflict model of social science was quite influential, including but not limited to the notion that as warriors in the class conflict social scientists were free to violate the privacy of their enemies. For example, some researchers studied cults covertly, even by joining them without mentioning their scientific goals (Bainbridge 1978). The logic was that every person in the religious movement had a personal agenda, and a covert ethnographer was no different in this respect. Indeed, the researcher was just as vulnerable as any of the other members, and the term *protagonist* was used to describe this model of participant observation research. Subsequently, universities found it politic to downplay social conflict and limit the freedom of employees to engage in *protagonist ethnography*. Yet, by the second decade of the twenty-first century, conflict models of society experienced a resurgence, and it may be time to lift the bans on covert ethnographic research.

Observational researchers studying virtual worlds tend not to worry very much about adherence to strict human subjects rules, for three reasons: (1) gameworlds are public places; (2) players tend to be anonymous, seldom revealing their true identities; and (3) the formal user agreements between the game company and the players limit the privacy rights of players. However, each of these justifications may be questioned. A fourth possible explanation deserves further study, as we come to understand better the place of MMOs in the emerging online global culture. It may be that the genre represents a hyper-secular counter culture, that on the one hand often denounces traditional cultures by depicting its adherents as fools or villains, and on the other hand overflows with deviant religious cultural elements, in the form of fictional cults, ecclesiastical architecture, and ancient superstitions brought to life. Thus, all participants are protagonists in a conflict, the researcher included, with the right to do as they personally judge best on the internet, which has become a cultural battlefield.

Greg Lastowka (2010) has considered a host of specific ethical issues in his book, *Virtual Justice: The New Laws of Online Worlds*, as they relate to players. Two examples that might possibly be analogous to problems researchers might face involve player exploits and property. When a player manipulates the software or data in unexpected ways to give the player's avatar a competitive advantage over others, implicit rules of the game are violated, yet many players consider such exploits to be entirely fair exploitation of computational possibilities, even while other players consider exploits to be unethical. Researchers may often commit exploits, without always being aware that they are, when they manipulate their avatars in usual ways to get into a position to gather data would otherwise would be difficult, most obviously by concentrating resources to advance the avatar to a high level of power within the game, but also by systematic collection of data that may be used to competitive advantage. The second example, virtual property, is considered at length by Lastowka, because players often invest great time and effort in building such properties as a private home or castle in some games, and valuable equipment in all of them, but then lose it if the game shuts down or if their own avatar is banned for some reason by the game company, or if major changes such as merger of internet servers collapses social groups or diminishes valuables. Similarly, researchers who invest heavily in well-planned research in a particular online world may feel that unexpected actions by the company that operates it interferes improperly with their research. Thus ethical questions around research concern not only just proper behaviour by researchers, but also the behaviour of other players and the game's company that may endanger the research.

Gameworlds exist in larger cultural contexts, and many research studies would logically be designed to compare alternatives. For example, both *Pirates of the Caribbean Online*, based on the Disney movie series, and *Pirates of the Burning Sea* take place in the Caribbean around the year 1700, yet the first of these was filled with supernatural horror elements, while the second is wholly secular and even offers critiques of the real religions of the period. Both *Dungeons and Dragons Online* and *Neverwinter* contain much supernatural horror, as well as critiques of conventional religion, but any researcher studying one would need to be at least aware of the other because both are direct translations of the influential table-top role-playing game, *Dungeons and Dragons*.

A few MMOs feature a particular real-world religion, for example Taoism in *Perfect World*, while others feature well-known fictional creeds, such as the Jedi Order in *Star Wars: The Old Republic*. The Tolkien ethos in *Lord of the Rings Online* is Roman Catholicism minus any Christian symbolism. Especially deep in its conceptions, the Norwegian MMO *The Secret World* begins with New England horror literature, specifically referencing Nathaniel Hawthorne, Edgar Allan Poe, H. P. Lovecraft and Stephen King. It does so in a way that doubly disparages Christianity. First, it depicts clergy as fools who lack any real understanding of the nature of human existence. Second, it offers a clear dogma about the supernatural, in which no benevolent gods really exist, but horrible demons gnaw away at human life and sanity. For many years, Evangelical websites have criticized videogames for promoting Asian religion and occultism (Bainbridge and Bainbridge 2007). Wherever one stands in these culture wars, the few partial exceptions like *Lord of the Rings Online* fail to refute this grim analysis.

TIP 2

Research of many kinds concerning online communities will raise new, difficult ethical issues, because the internet renders problematic such concepts as privacy, property and identity.

Demystification of religion

Social science research methods have always been more than techniques for gathering data with which to test theories; they have also been tools for transforming society. For more than two centuries, many intellectuals in Western civilization have been critical of religion. Sociology was originally conceived by Auguste Comte as a modern substitute for religion, and Sigmund Freud called religion an illusion while his Psychoanalysis movement was really a cult in disguise (Comte 1883; Freud 1928; Bainbridge 2012). More recently, cognitive scientists have criticized religious views of the human mind, suggesting they stand in the way of realization of the truth about human existence (Pinker 1997; Bloom 2004). A related New Atheism cultural movement has arisen, based on thinking in evolutionary biology as well as cognitive science (Dennett 1995; Dawkins 2006; Bainbridge 2009; Amarasingam 2010). While significant fractions of the populations of advanced nations remain religious, the sociology of religion should not ignore the secularists, but seek to understand their diverse orientations toward transcendence. It is difficult to predict whether the net societal effect would be to accelerate secularization, or work toward mutual respect between believers and nonbelievers.

In the 1980s, a perspective sometimes called the New Paradigm was introduced into the sociology of religion, contributing to the field but remaining somewhat peripheral to it over the succeeding decades (Warner 1993; Jelen 2002). One reason frankly may be that many of the scholars in the field really practise religious studies and have a degree of commitment to traditional religion, while critics of religion tend to move into other fields. A central concept of the New Paradigm was that religious explanations provided psychological compensation based on supernatural claims when deeply desired rewards could not be obtained in real life (Stark and Bainbridge 1987; Bainbridge 2006). Religions originated as radical groups based on the psychopathological delusions or entrepreneurial deceptions of leaders, or in the gradual accretion of supernatural ideas in transmission of rumours between many people (Bainbridge and Stark 1979). Once a religious tradition had been established, it would tend to differentiate into high-tension groups that provided the real energy, and low-tension groups that provided respectability, thereby socially insulating the powers of faith from depletion from too much contact with reality. Over time religion churned, as sects moderated into denominations from which new sects erupted, moving in place but neither advancing nor retreating (Stark and Bainbridge 1985; Bainbridge 1997).

Today, with the internet and the permeation of all aspects of modern life with science and information technology, the traditional hardware of religion may be short-circuiting, and online fantasy religions may actually represent a serious future possibility, providing emotional compensation, if perhaps not as convincingly as religion formerly did. But the fundamental problems of human life remain unsolved, including how to deal psychologically with death, and what foundation morality can have. Online virtual worlds explore such issues through human imagination, and thus may possibly be the source of fresh insights. Because ethnographic role-playing research places the scientist in the mental context of the people and the culture under study, it can redirect the professional viewpoint, in the case of the examples given here, possibly towards greater scepticism of conventional religion.

14 Researching Religion, Digital Games and Gamers: (E-)Merging Methodologies

SIMONE HEIDBRINK, TOBIAS KNOLL AND JAN WYSOCKI

Introduction

Few will seriously doubt that within the last decade digital games have become an important and influential part of contemporary popular culture. Among many other topics derived from the sociocultural environments digital games are embedded in, religion(s) and religious elements are recurrent topics that contribute to the game contents as well as the playing experiences in a multitude of ways. Even though at first glance the presence of religion in videogames might be somewhat surprising, a look at other contemporary media shows that religious topics are also frequently referred to in bestseller books, blockbuster movies, TV series, popular music and other media content. In the following chapter we will provide you with a hands-on approach on how to conduct research on religion in/and digital games. First, we will give you an overview on how and where you might encounter religion(s) in the context of videogames, together with some basic theoretical and methodological considerations. Then we will address practical procedures, including a step-by-step approach on playing as method.

Religion in digital games

There are two basic perspectives that can be taken when researching religion in/and digital games (Heidbrink, Knoll and Wysocki 2014, 2015):

- the game-immanent approach which considers all in-game content and analyses the occurrence of religion within the context of the game itself ('gamescapes');
- the player-centred approach which focuses on player-sided interactions within the game, in relation to the game as well as in reference to the game.

In the following, we will take a further look at these different prospects and uncover the possible areas where we might encounter religion(s) or religious elements.

'Gamescapes' – Game-immanent perspectives

When looking for religion(s) and religious elements in digital games, the in-game contexts (i.e. the area of the game itself), its 'storyscapes' (plot and narratives), 'landscapes' and 'soundscapes' (aesthetics) that together form the 'gamescape' (the gameworld which consists of the visual, auditory and story-based 'appearance' of the game), might be the most obvious approach.

'STORYSCAPES' – NARRATIVES
Most digital games tell stories. There is hardly any debate on this fact. Stories (ranging from an overarching narrative to microstories that might even transgress the in-game perspective) can be found in various game contexts (Ryan 2006: 201):

- main narrative script/plot;
- player-driven narratives created by player-sided actions and decision-making;
- in-game cut scenes or background information on the game (commercials, etc.);
- microstories told by nonplaying characters (e.g. quest texts);
- fan fiction, forum discussions, machinima.

For thorough research, however, digital games must not be reduced to their narrative quality, as they are not merely a new rendition of old media like books and films, but – due to the fact that players are not only recipients but indeed actors and decision-makers actively engaged in the process of the game unfolding – a new media by definition. Therefore both, the 'narrative' and the 'ludic' elements must be respected and games can be examined with focus on narrative and story as well as with focus on the notion of play and interactivity (Aarseth 2003; Jenkins 2004; Murray 2005/2013). The best way, however, is a combination of both approaches.

'Game designers don't simply tell stories; they design worlds and sculpt spaces,' as Media Scholar Henry Jenkins puts it (Jenkins 2004: 121). In the context of what he coined as 'game architecture', the networks of intertwined narratives play – together with the visual and auditory design – an important role in creating a notion of 'spaciality' and a sense of 'worldness' (Krzywinska 2006: 386) for the players, allowing for a deep 'immersion' (Murray 1997: 98) into the virtual game environment, that is, the impression of 'being somewhere else', of entering a new/different world.

'LANDSCAPES' AND 'SOUNDSCAPES' – AESTHETICS
To evoke those kind of experiences in the players, the 'landscapes' and 'soundscapes' that together constitute the aesthetical setting of the game, that is, 'the way a game looks, sounds, and presents itself to the player' (Niedenthal 2009: 2f.) are essential. It is therefore important to note that:

- Game aesthetics refers to the sensory phenomena that the player encounters in the game (visual, aural, haptic, embodied).

- Game aesthetics is an expression of the game experienced as pleasure, emotion, sociability, form giving, etc. (with reference to 'the aesthetic experience').

Additionally, aesthetic experience as 'the play of imaginative and cognitive faculties' (Niedenthal 2009: 2f.) is closely associated with the already mentioned concepts of 'immersion' or 'incorporation' (Calleja 2007).

The aesthetical dimensions of a digital game (the 'landscape' and the 'soundscape') as well as the importance of a coherent storyline heavily depend on the game genre and its underlying mechanics (think, for example, of puzzle games like *Tetris*, which go well with a minimum of aesthetical and narrative adornment) and are naturally predominant in games with an emphasis on creating certain atmospheres and evoking emotions like, for example, role-playing games. However, in many cases the world setting and the story is not 'told' in the strict sense (in a coherent storyline from beginning to end) but remains fragmentary and allusive, drawing from an (assumed) 'cultural archive' or 'collective memory' that comprises of an agglomeration/cluster of dominant discursive threads of contemporary popular culture. Therefore, it is needless to label, for example, tall and ethereal beings with pointy ears as 'elves'. This knowledge is part of those 'cultural archives' and can (even without a deeper knowledge of J.R.R. Tolkien, whose works serve as a kind of 'role-model' for the contemporary notion of elves) easily be deciphered and related. The (post)modern depiction of elves and the narratives around them can be denoted as 'thick text' (Kaveney 2005: 5; Krzywinska 2006: 383), a term that comprises and refers to the multitude of intertextual contexts, references, allusions and connotations within as well as across media genres, which add to the understanding of the term and concept.

The processes of creating, composing and disseminating 'thick text' can be described by applying the concepts of 'transmedia storytelling' (Jenkins 2004, 2006) and 'remediation' (Bolter and Grusin 2000). 'Transmedia storytelling' emphasizes narratives and storylines and explains how narratives are being transferred and transmitted across a multitude of media platforms, thereby reverting to topics from earlier media forms, for example literature or other popular or traditional strands of discourse. In contrast, 'remediation' focuses on the technical aspects of the media and mediatization, mainly the refashioning of earlier media such as visual art, film, television, literature, etc. by new digital media. It is assumed that digital means of communication do not merely substitute their predecessors, but incorporate them and only through this gain cultural significance (Bolter and Grusin 2000: 20ff).

While 'transmedia storytelling' targets the contents of the transfer/transformation processes, 'remediation' points at its technical requirements. In the area of videogame research, the remediation of textual and intertextual elements derived from a multitude of pre-existing media genres – such as orally transmitted myth, literature, fantasy tale, comic and movie – merge into the narrative, plot, setting, gameplay and/or mechanics of digital games.

RELIGION AND 'GAMESCAPES'

In many digital games, familiar elements often derived from (especially Western-Christian) historical and contemporary religious iconography, architecture and landscaping can be found. Looking, for example, at the different regions in *World of Warcraft*, the 'landscapes' and 'soundscapes' as well as the 'storyscapes' contribute heavily to the players' experience of a unique gameworld featuring different races and cultures as well as a multifaith religious topography (modelled more or less along the line of real-life religions). Here, questions concerning the selection, combination (re-) construction and (re-)contextualization of religious elements as well as the reception by the players offer interesting research scenarios (which provides, for example, insights into contemporary discourse on Christianity or Esotericism). Beside actual 'real-life religion', game developers also draw on 'fictional religion' derived from fantasy literature, movies etc. (e.g. Krzywinska 2008: 130).

Dealing with religion in/and 'gamescapes' means looking at the way religion is being constructed, (re)presented and negotiated through in-game narratives and aesthetics.

Further reading Krzywinska 2006 and 2008, O'Donnell 2015, Šisler 2014
Recommended games *Bioshock: Infinite*, *World of Warcraft*, *Ôkami*

Gameworld, gameplay and gaming culture: Player-centered perspectives

Adding the aspects of interactivity, interaction and player agency to the in-game elements of the 'gamescapes', we are reaching a higher level of complexity in analysing digital games. Now, the focus of the research is being shifted towards the individual players with regard to the game.

GAMEWORLD AND GAMEPLAY

The gameworld indicates the larger experience of the game that exceeds the in-game content. It includes the 'gamescapes', the mechanics and the entirety of the potential processes of communication and interaction between the player and the game. Within this gameworld, the gameplay takes place, pointing to the different levels of interaction by the (human) players in the course of the game, mainly with regard to choice, interactivity and agency. Both the gameworld and the gameplay shape and steer the 'ludic experience' (Rodriguez 2006).

> Doing something in a world, participating in its ruleset, to get involved in its world through exploration and/or through the repertoire of action of the player's avatar lets the player become part of the gameworld
>
> (Heidbrink, Knoll and Wysocki 2014: 31).

Players interact with the game code through peripherals like controllers, keyboards etc. and manipulate elements of the game. This form of reciprocal communication between digital game and player is a crucial point in analysing digital games. Within these interactive dynamics the scholar's interest can, for example, lie in the quality of the player's *agency* (Barker, Chr. 2005: 233ff.).

GAMING CULTURE

Taking another step away from the game itself and looking at the players' receptions, we enter the realm of 'gaming culture'. It is important to note, however, that the term 'gaming culture' is not to be mistaken as describing a detached/separated part of 'culture' in general (or even worse, a 'sub-culture' in a pejorative sense), but points to an organic part of everyday life. Therefore, while researching religion in the context of gaming culture, we need to consider (at least) two perspectives, namely 'culture in games', i.e. the way culture is being negotiated inside the game, and 'games in culture', i.e. the way games influence and interact with (popular) culture (Shaw 2010: 416).

RELIGION AND THE PLAYER

Just like 'gamescapes', the construction of gameworlds and specific elements of the gameplay (like 'moral decision-making systems', the designation of 'character classes', the rule set, etc.) can often be traced back to religious categories, symbols and narratives. These processes of reception concern both the game designers and the players. The gamers' notions of the game content and their correlating and negotiating of those religious discourses within and outside their own religious disposition (in discussion forums, at game conventions, on video sharing platforms, etc.) is another approach and can serve as a diagnostic tool that enables insights into individual religiousness.

Dealing with religion and the player means looking at interconnections and interdependencies between game, designers and players.

Further reading Irizarry and Irizarry 2014, Knoll 2015, Luft 2014
Recommended games *EVE Online*, *Dragon Age: Inquisition*, *The Graveyard*

Games analysis: Practical approaches

'Playing research'

As could be seen by looking at the in-game perspectives (the 'gamescapes') as well as the actor-centred perspectives (gameworld, gameplay and gaming culture), the complex network of intertextual references and discourses often refers to religion or religious issues in an explicit or implicit way. Depending on the research perspective, both a game-immanent analysis of the construction mechanisms and reception processes on the side of the game designers, as well as an actor-centred approach on the players' side, can provide interesting insights into the discursive localization, the construction and the mechanisms of reception, ascription and personal disposition towards religion on different levels.

Even though the two perspectives have been described separately, it is important to note that in most practical research scenarios it is necessary to respect both approaches, as they usually intersect. The mix of perspectives does not only concern the theoretical consideration, but also applies to the methodology and specific methods in researching religion in/and digital games. Thus a plurality of methods is called for.

The 'storyscapes' of digital games can be analysed by utilizing methods from Humanities and Social Sciences like text and content analysis, or discourse analysis; the 'landscapes' and 'soundscapes' can be researched by applying the methodical toolbox offered by Fine Arts, Musicology or Media Studies. In the same way, religion(s) and religious elements with regard to gameworld, gameplay and gaming culture can be tackled by falling back on existing methods and methodologies such as communication analysis, empirical social research, participant observation, etc.

There is one practical aspect, however, which none of the established methods and methodologies is able to cover (owing to the unique character of digital games as research scenario): the playing of the game. The following sections will give a detailed insight into what we call 'Playing Research' (i.e. playing as method) based on the considerations by Espen Aarseth (2003).

Why do we play? Games of emergence and games of progression

As has been shown throughout this chapter, games are tremendously heterogeneous when it comes to the transportation, negotiation and communication of religious symbolism. The same applies to their overall structure and the way they can be (and are being) played. This has to be taken into consideration when trying to come up with a methodology based on both game content, play and player reception.

Renowned game scholar Jesper Juul has developed a very useful framework for the analysis of game structure that is based on the concepts of 'games of emergence' and 'games of progression' (Juul 2002). He explains both concepts as follows:

> *Emergence* is the primordial game structure, where a game is specified as a small number of rules that combine and yield large numbers of game variations, which the players then design strategies for dealing with. This is found in card and board games and in most action and all strategy games. Emergence games tend to be replayable and tend to foster tournaments and strategy guides.
>
> *Progression* is the historically newer structure that entered the computer game through the adventure genre. In progression games, the player has to perform a predefined set of actions in order to complete the game. One feature of the progression game is that it yields strong control to the game designer: since the designer controls the sequence of events, this is also where we find the

games with cinematic or storytelling ambitions. This leads to the infamous experience of playing a game 'on a rail', i.e. where the work of the player is simply to perform the correct pre-defined moves in order to advance the game. Progression games have walkthroughs, specifying all the actions needed to complete the game.

Juul 2002: 324

While there are some games which can (mostly) be identified as pure 'games of progression' (e.g. the text adventure Zork[1]) or 'games of emergence' (e.g. the classic Pong[2]), most modern games combine elements of both and differ mostly in their individual emphasis on either emergence or progression, with 'sandbox RPGs' like The Elder Scrolls: Skyrim[3] or EVE Online[4] on the one side of the spectrum and 'rail shooters' like the Call of Duty[5] series on the other.

Some aspects of 'games of progression' can – at least to a certain degree – be described (and analysed) from a somewhat removed perspective, that is, by watching video footage, reading plot summaries or 'walkthroughs', due to their very linear and guided structure. Still this does not mean that research on these kinds of games 'should' be conducted solely this way, as some players will constantly try to find ways to deviate from predetermined paths to act out their own agency (Knoll 2015; Schut 2014). In any case, it is still the player who steers the progression through the game by his or her actions, making the act of play the most vital part of even the most 'on a rail' games out there and therefore an important focus of research.

Even more apparent is the importance of play and the role of the player in 'games of emergence' where only the basic rules and mechanics are provided by the game and the player is given the task of creating his or her own experiences, goals and strategies. 'Games of emergence' cannot be described by linear means and their structure is heavily dependent on the given rules as well as the player's means and motivations to interact with them.

So why again is this important for 'playing research'? First, the prevalence of systems of emergence in most modern games is a clear indicator for the importance of studying games on their own terms. Only by actual gameplay can we decipher the complex interactions of rules, narratives, game world, progression and player agency, which is the basis for any kind of further research. Second, realizing that there are many ways of playing a game (and that there is seldom one 'right' way to do so) may open our eyes for questions and research interests that would otherwise remain unnoticed.

How do we play? A step-by-step guide to playing research

In the following, we offer you a 'universal toolbox' that will assist you with your own playing research and provide you with the necessary approaches and perspectives for your projects and digital fieldwork. This 'toolbox' is by no means complete. Quite the contrary: it is merely intended as a starting point for any research undertaking and can (and should) be complemented based on specific research interests.

STEP 1: PREPARATION

- *The game*: While it should be your goal to learn as much about the game as possible by playing it, it cannot hurt to gather some information beforehand. This may include information about the genre the game places itself in, earlier games in a series, online reviews, popular discussions, marketing campaigns prior to release as well as some first hints toward the overall structure of the game (narrative, aesthetics, gameworld, gameplay, emphasis on 'emergent' or 'progressive' elements). This will help you in familiarizing yourself with the game you are about to play and also with the living culture surrounding it as well as contextualizing your first gameplay experience. Additionally, this may give you some ideas for phrasing a first *research question*.

- *The research question*: One of the reasons why playing research is such an important part of any research project on digital games, is that by its very 'explorative' nature questions of interests may arise, which otherwise would have gone unnoticed. Still, the phrasing of an initial *research question* can be very helpful, because it makes you reflect on your own intentions right from the beginning and focus on a general area of interest. Just keep in mind that this general research interest will (and should) later be specified based on your own findings and experiences in the game.

- *The tools*: There are some things you should always have available (i.e. installed on your computer or sitting at arm's reach on your desk) while playing. This includes some material for note-taking as well as recording software.

So now that you have properly prepared yourself and your workplace, let's start up the game and take our first steps into uncharted territory.

STEP 2: THE FIRST STEPS

This step is largely self-explanatory as most (if not all) modern games feature extensive tutorials to familiarize the player with the core concepts of the game. Additionally, guides for many games (either official or community-made) can be found online. The main goal of this step is to reach a somewhat competent level of playing experience; that is, you should at least familiarize yourself with the game mechanics and rules up to a degree where they no longer interfere with your ability to concentrate on the various other aspects of the game or – in the case of multiplayer games – prevent you from playing and/or socializing with other people. In the latter case, this phase should also be used to make yourself familiar with any kind of game-specific language, abbreviations and terms you might encounter as they might be crucial for your being accepted by other players. How long it takes to reach an acceptable level of competence is also very much dependent on the game, research scenario and prior experience with similar games. Some games may take a few minutes to learn, others can take hundreds of hours or more.

STEP 3: EXPLORATION

After you have made your first (figurative) steps into the game and have learned (if not mastered) its mechanics, rules and conventions, it is time to do some actual research within the game. This step is without a doubt the most important one, but at the same time it is most difficult to narrow down to a single modus operandi. The reason for this is the varied nature of game structures described above. Still, based on the concepts of games (or systems) of 'emergence' and 'progression', we would recommend two possible 'modes of play':

- *Progressive Play*: This means playing the game in order to (you guessed it) progress through it. This mode of play is most relevant when dealing with a very story-driven and linear game where a large part of the playing experience involves living through the game's narratives and micronarratives. You should not limit your observations to storytelling, however, but also pay attention to interactions between narratives and aesthetics, world building, mechanics and rules, especially when dealing with religious elements (which can be found in any of these elements).

- *Emergent Play*: This mode of play essentially means 'exploring' the game in every aspect possible. Of course, not every game features an actual 'explorable' world or a single avatar to explore the world with (many games can be quite abstract). So in this case 'exploring' just means trying out everything. *Literally*. This includes trying to act against the game rules, using the game mechanics in creative ways, testing alternative strategies to beat a mission/quest, trying out popular game modifications and deviating from given paths.

Again, both modes of play are 'ideal types' and in most cases you will have to take both (or a mix of both) approaches towards gaming in order to encompass the whole reach of possibilities provided by the game. Document what you find, reflect on your data, re-focus your *research question*. And now, start over.

STEP 4: STARTING OVER

Yes, you have read correctly. You have made it very far (farther than many so-called game scholars in the past). Perhaps you have finished the game or its main storyline. Perhaps you have reached a level of skill and competence with the game to rival other players and have become a part of the community. Or perhaps you have explored every inch of the gameworld, you know every cave, every city and every dungeon. Either way, it is time to try out a different perspective. You have played the good guy? Well now it is time to play the bad guy! You have played on the easy difficulty setting? Why not try out a harder one! You have mastered all the strategies for one faction? Time to learn a new one. You have chosen to let the final boss of this one game live at the end? Well, he is going to have a bad time the second time around.

Again – the degree to which you push this exercise is up to you and, of course, dependent on your specific research interests. Sometimes it is important to be skilled at a game, and sometimes it is not. Sometimes you have to turn every stone several times, and sometimes you do not. Just like in any other form of empirical research, the challenging part is to decide when exactly you have played enough, when you have completed your data collection, when your contact with other players suffice.

Addition: Proper documentation

One of the most important elements of any kind of empirical research is proper documentation. Playing research is no exception to this, although the digital nature of the subject matter offers some rather unique opportunities as well as some problems:

- *Recording Software*: There is no better way of documenting your gameplay experience than videotaping it. Luckily, there is a multitude of dedicated game recording software available online. Please note, that based on recording settings and desktop resolution, game video files can get very large, so make sure that you have enough disk space available on your system.

- *Screenshots*: Screenshots are another easy – if somewhat limited – solution for documenting your findings within a game. Screenshots can be made either by using the built-in features of your operating system (search online for specific tutorials) or third party software.

- *Note Taking*: Being able to digitally record your playing sessions is great in simplifying the collection of large amounts of data. But in most cases you only record what you see, read, hear, or do in the given situation but not your initial or further thoughts and reflections on the subject. To accomplish this, it is recommended to keep some kind of notes or even a research diary for your digital fieldwork so that you remember your thoughts and ideas at a later time and are able to contextualize them. You might even consider audio recording your own voice and commenting on your experiences.

- *Saving*: This might sound trivial but it cannot be overstated: If the game you are playing has an active 'save feature' (i.e. allowing you to actively save your game state at any time on multiple 'save slots' and reload any of them at a later time) then use it. Extensively. There are some things which simply cannot be easily recorded or reproduced by conventional recording and you might want to replay a single sequence, mission or just a dialogue with multiple outcomes. Saving often allows you to jump to any point in the game you would like to revisit without having to play the whole game once again.

Ethical considerations

Ethics in the context of digital games are still a 'hot topic' in a multitude of ways. On one hand there is the perspective of in-game ethics, that is, in-game 'morality', where reference to religion can occur (e.g. Knoll 2015). Digital games can be regarded as 'ethical systems' with rules that create gameworlds with values at play. Likewise their players (far from being passive and amoral) are 'ethical agents', intertwined in a complex network of responsibilities and moral duties (Sicart 2009). On the other hand, and in a more general perspective, ethics in digital games are subject to each research project, ranging from the research design, the actual conduct of the research to the analysis and publication of the results.

It is strongly advised to take all usual ethical considerations (e.g. from Anthropology or Social Sciences) like, for example, obtaining informed consent, maintaining strict confidentiality and making the subjects of research aware of their right to withdraw. Additionally, there are some general ethical guidelines concerning online research that help decide on and adapt the offline research ethics to the specifications of online environments (e.g. Buchanan 2011; Markham and Buchanan 2012).

For scholars who are about to conduct research in digital games, the following two main perspectives concerning research ethics might prove helpful.

ETHICAL CONSIDERATIONS WITH REGARD TO THE SUBJECTS OF RESEARCH

In the context of digital games, players create identities and engage with others by using an avatar, a (nowadays, usually) graphical representation of 'one's self'. Respecting a participant's right to privacy and anonymity is a basic ethical requirement of any study, and it is mandatory that this procedure also includes the person's nicknames or avatars (e.g. Boellstorff 2008: 79ff.).

The way identity structures are being negotiated in online spaces, (e.g. concerning gender, sexuality, race, ethnicity, embodiment, etc.) generally differ from the offline realm and identity experiments like gender swapping might occur. It is helpful to remember the potential biases between the player avatar and the actual player persona even though there might be no opportunity to resolve the conflicts that might arise from these biases. Participants might, for example, lie about their gender, their age, their location, or any number of demographic variables. There is no general solution to avoiding these problems, just as in most offline scenarios where the researcher usually also accepts information at face value without official verification (e.g. Wood et al. 2004; Whiteman 2012: 98f.).

Always remember: The player avatar might be the only contact point with a player. Identity in digital games can be multiple, and anonymity must be afforded to player's character names or avatars as well as their actual names (assuming that these are even known)!

ETHICAL CONSIDERATIONS WITH REGARD TO THE RESEARCHER

Even though in the course of a research project, the anonymity and privacy of the players is a first prerequisite, the identity of the researcher must be disclosed. While researching games as well as offline scenarios, covert 'fieldwork' is for justified reasons (e.g. the lack of informed consent by the research subjects) regarded as highly unethical. The way the researcher communicates his/her identity and research endeavour depends on the conditions of the virtual environment in question. If possible, it is, for example, advisable to use the avatar's profile for backlinking to official information on the research and the researcher (e.g. see Boellstorff 2008: 79ff. for an example for ethical considerations in the virtual 3D environment *Second Life*).

Being part of the gaming environment, participating in in-game activities and interacting with other actors naturally might cause problems, mostly due to the fact that the researcher naturally interferes with his or her research subjects and objects, thus influencing the research's outcome. These issues are basically an insoluble dilemma and well known also from offline fieldwork (e.g. Boellstorff 2006).

Summary

Congratulations. You are now a game scholar. Of course, the points mentioned above are mere guidelines that are aimed at opening up your perspective for the multitude of fields of interests the research of religion and digital games has to offer. From here on, there are still many things to do and to consider.

Possibly (and most likely) you will find aspects of 'playing research' that are not covered by our guidelines, and you will have to come up with your own ideas and solutions. You should certainly call to mind that 'playing research' is only the first step in your research endeavour. The next step might be actor-centred research inside the games, on online discussion forums and web communities, video portals like *YouTube* and *Twitch* as well as conventions, e-sport events and other gatherings of gamers. But the decision is up to you. The field is wide open, largely unclaimed and there is still much to discover!

KEY POINTS/TIPS FOR RESEARCHING RELIGION IN/AND DIGITAL GAMES

Reflect on Yourself!
Remember your own position and previous knowledge as a researcher as well as a gamer. Be mindful of your actions and decisions in-game and off-game as well as when interacting with other players.

Play!
Do not be an 'armchair scholar'. To understand games, their languages, their structures and the communities surrounding them, they have to be played, so do not rely only on third person accounts and game-external resources.

Observe!

Be mindful when playing a game. Be it single or multiplayer, games are carefully constructed environments of narratives, aesthetics, world-building, rules, mechanics and interactions, all of which can carry religious elements. So try everything, explore, do not be afraid of attempting to bend the rules of the game and don't miss anything.

Ask Questions!

The relevance of religious elements in digital games is a result of processes of reception and construction by players as well as the people involved in creating the games. So talk to players and game designers (if possible). Research game(r) communities and conduct interviews. Use the knowledge and experience acquired by playing, but do not let your own perspective on the games be the only one.

Contextualize!

No game exists in empty space. The design processes, influences and history of a game all have an effect on the way it is perceived by the players. And of course, player perspectives also depend on various factors like sociocultural influences, cultural and religious lifeworlds as well as knowledge related to videogames and other forms of (digital) media.

Document!

Use every means necessary and at your disposal to record and document your findings. Digital games are by nature subject to constant change and information might be lost throughout the various iterations they go through.

15 The G-d in the Machine: Studying the Representation and Performance of Judaism in Video Games using Multimodal Corpus-assisted Critical Discourse Analysis

ISAMAR CARRILLO MASSO

Research context

In the past decade, video games have become an overwhelming success in creative industries as well as an established cultural medium, which has been borne out by the creation of the BAFTA video games awards in 2003. The field of New Media Studies has, however, failed to produce, until now, a methodology to study the sociological, sociolinguistic and wider semiotic content of video games; one that can be adapted to different genres (e.g. adventures, strategy games, role playing games), and that produces verifiable results that can be shared across disciplines to encourage inter- and transdisciplinary studies of this new medium.

This chapter (based on my own doctoral dissertation, as well as 2009 and 2010 publications, and a case study published in 2014 with Prof. Nathan Abrams) will attempt to fill that void by producing a quantitative and qualitative methodology for studying video games as multimodal texts, combining Fairclough's (2003) and Kress and van Leeuwen's (2006) approaches to critical and multimodal discourse analysis, with Corpus linguistics (e.g. Baker's [2006] approach to Corpus-based sociolinguistic analysis), and multimodal transcription and text analysis (e.g. Baldry and Thibault 2006). The method will be based on the codifiable correlations between purely linguistic, aural and visual data, following the approach to video games image analysis in Carrillo Masso 2009, 2010, 2014).

I will illustrate the main elements of my methodology using examples from one video game in particular: *The Shivah: A Rabbinical Adventure* (Wadjet Eye Games 2006). Within this case study, I will focus on how Jewishness is portrayed in this new medium. More specifically, I will show that by using this new method, it is possible to bridge the gap across disciplines such as Sociology, Theology, Jewish Studies and Games Studies and to answer questions such as:

1 How can metaludic and metalinguistic practices in *The Shivah* inform our understanding of Judaism and Jewish identities, as portrayed in the game?

2 What discourses on religion are present in the game, and how do players enact them?

3 How does *The Shivah* portray different versions of Judaism?

It has been pointed out before that a multiple disciplinary (inter- or trans-disciplinary) approach is better equipped to answer complex questions. The nascent field of Games Studies or 'gameology'[1] is essentially 'the theoretical and critical study of video games across various platforms and genres' (Ensslin 2010: 207), with reference to elements unique to games such as interactivity and, of course, play. This poses several methodological difficulties, as play and interactivity create new challenges in the study of media. In 1958, Caillois observed that:

> [t]he study of the functioning of semicircular canals is an inadequate explanation of the vogue for swings, toboggans, skiing, and the vertigo-inducing rides at amusement parks. (. . .) the development of the calculus of probability is no substitute for a sociology of lotteries, gambling houses, or racetracks.
>
> Caillois 1958: 170

This sentiment was echoed by Aarseth (2001) who expressed that '[l]ike architecture, which contains but cannot be reduced to art history, games studies should contain media studies, aesthetics, sociology, etc., but it should exist as an independent academic structure, because it cannot be reduced to any of the above' (Aarseth 2001).

In this sense, 'reading' a game can be very much like understanding a painting: one can get a certain amount of enjoyment from interacting with the image itself, but to engage with it on a deeper level, one needs to understand the semiotic resources used by the artist, the context in which it was produced, and the reasons/advantages/ limitations of the chosen medium and technique (which in the case of games could be extrapolated as understanding, at least roughly speaking, the processes of game design, production and programming, as well as something of the hardware). Understanding games *as media* carries the advantage of grounding the researcher's analysis by providing clues as to what is a product of the nature of the medium (e.g. limits of a particular programming language or genre, or limits imposed by the project's budget) and what constitutes a more or less 'free' aesthetic choice on the part of the makers. From this perspective, attempting to analyse a full game is indeed a complex endeavour, as it requires a systematic fragmentation and reassembly of both medium and message (McLuhan 1964).[2]

Background information

The Shivah: A Rabbinical Adventure (Wadjet Eye Games 2006)

Rabbi Stone's synagogue is broke. The congregation has dwindled to single digits, the building is out of repair, and his sermons are depressing. He is disenchanted with

God. Then one day, a detective comes to ask Rabbi Stone questions about his relationship with one Jack Lauder, an old member of his congregation, who was murdered three days ago and left Rabbi Stone ten thousand dollars. Rabbi Stone realizes that he can be accused of murder because the money provides a motive, so he decides to pay a Shivah visit to Lauder's widow. The widow shows contempt for Stone's visit, and makes the player understand their history together: Rabbi Stone had refused to officiate Mr and Mrs Lauder's wedding because Mrs Lauder (nee Sharma) was not Jewish. An interesting search for clues all over Manhattan follows, in which Stone meets Joe De Marco, who is a member of the same synagogue Jack Lauder moved his membership to after breaking up with Stone's. The nagging question keeps coming up: Is Joe De Marco Jewish?

Rabbi Zelich, who oversees the congregation Jack Lauder belonged to, and who had both married the Lauders and buried Jack, seems to be thriving. An older man, he seems to have more modern views than Rabbi Stone. After paying several visits to Zelich, Rabbi Stone figures out a connection between Zelich and the murder of Jack Lauder, as well as another murdered member of the congregation: an accountant by the name of Goldman. Eventually Stone finds out that Jack had tried to contact him to ask for advice about Zelich and some shady business Joe De Marco was involved with. Stone discovers that De Marco was the murderer, under Zelich's orders. The game has three main possible endings, depending on the choices the player has made through their gameplay. In one ending, Stone is forced to jump to his death from Zelich's balcony to fake his own suicide. In another ending, Zelich kills Mrs Lauder and pins the murder on Stone, who goes to jail. In the last possible ending, Rabbi Stone kills Zelich in self-defence, and saves Mrs Lauder, who testifies in his favour. She eventually joins Stone's congregation.

The Shivah is a point-and-click adventure game. The point-and-click game format involves very simple mechanics and limited affordances for gameplay, which makes the dialogue and narrative more important to both set the theme of the game (crime/noir) and to develop the gameplay experience. The user plays a detective in the form of the character Rabbi Stone. David Gilbert, the game's creator, said in an interview that unlike other games, which rely on violence to solve problems, 'questioning is the rabbi's power'[3] (Gilbert, cited in Lando 2007).

In order to have a unified method to study video games, it is important to have a common definition of video games to be used. There are several definitions of video games that operate in the field of Games Studies. Gonzalo Frasca (2001) defines video games as:

[a]ny form of computer-based entertainment software, either textual or image-based, using any electronic platform such as personal computers or consoles and involving one or multiple players in a physical or networked environment.

Frasca 2003: 4

To Juul (2003: 43) the basic departure in video games from the classical model of games is that it is 'the computer that upholds the rules'. This means that video games as media allow for much more flexibility as they allow for more complex rules, while freeing the players from the 'responsibility' of enforcing them.

After examining the definitions above, and holding them against both classic and new generation games, I define a '**video game**', then, as the following: A video game is a mediated entertainment system composed of a software program run on specialized or non-specialized hardware that allows a player to voluntarily interface with the computer itself (and potentially with other players), within a virtual environment, through a computer–controlled set of rules, to experience play in one or more of its forms, all of them **realistic** (Atkins 2003), meaning 'internally consistent'.

Studying religion in games

Campbell and Grieve (2014) provide in their edited collection an overview of the study of the portrayal of religion and the religious experience in video games. Their work includes a wide variety of methods and approaches grounded in various fields of study, showing that there has been a recent spike in interest, of which this volume is also proof. Part of my method includes Critical Discourse Analysis. While this will be defined below (Figure 15.1), here I would like to point out examples of what types of questions dealing with religion that this can handle.

Scholarship has largely tended to focus on ethnicity (Jewishness) as the analytic category for the study of Jewish representations and industry participation in the

TENET (Fairclough and Wodak 1007: 271–280)	POSSIBLE APPLICATION/SAMPLE QUESTION
· CDA addresses social problems	Can we indentify problems with the discourses of production and consumption of videogames with religious content? What do they emphasize or obscure?
· Power relations are discursive	How are power relations between characters realized discursively in a particular game? Is the same discourse mirrored in fan-produced texts? How do these relate to the religious aspects of the game in question?
· Discourse constitutes society and culture	What is the relationship between the way a religious group is represented in the wider context of culture, and the way the same religious group is represented in-game?
· Discourse does ideological work	How is a particular religious group/object/situation discursively constructed in the game? How does this compare to the way they are portrayed in metaludic material and in real life?
· Discourse is historical	How have representations of Muslim characters changed in PC games since 11/9/2001?
· The link between text and society is mediated	How does the format of the game affect its discursive power, as procedural rhetoric, and how does religion relate to this power?
· Discourse analysis is interpretative and explanatory	How can we interpret the use of specific (American) guns as semiotic devices in a first person shooter such as Al-Intifada (2003)?
· Discourse is a form of social action	How do fans/gamers use discourse to exercise agency of to construct their own identities in their communities of practice?

Fig. 15.1 The main tenets of CDA with examples of their fields of application in games studies, based on Wodak and Fairclough (1997: 271–80)

media. Hitherto, where Judaism was represented in media, it tended to fall into one of the binary categories: *haredi*[4] or Reform. Since haredism is 'the most obviously distinctive and colorful' branch of Judaism (Elber 1997), it works as shorthand for an instantly recognizable Jewish religious status. Indeed, haredism tends to stand as a metonym for all of Orthodox Judaism. In contrast, since Reform Jews are represented as no different from the vast majority of Americans, they are rarely explicitly described or delineated as Reform.[5] Furthermore, such Jewish representations often display downright ignorance about the Judaism of Reform Jews. Rather, Reform Judaism is inferred by the lack of outward markers that identify a male haredi Jew, such as a yarmulke, *tzitzit* (Heb. fringes), *peyot* (Heb. sidecurls), and distinctive black hat and clothing. Almost without fail, whether Reform or haredi, Jews are represented as Ashkenazi (Eastern or Central European) as opposed to Sephardi (Abrams 2013).

However, as Nathan Abrams's study of Jewishness and Judaism in contemporary cinema argues (2009, 2010, 2013), some media are now depicting Jewish identity both ethnically and religiously. Abrams shows how contemporary Jewish culture's comfort with an increasing range of religious identification beyond the Reform-*haredi* binary was the product of the revitalization of Jewish religious beliefs, practices, and literature in the United States (and beyond) during the 1980s and 1990s. This change was a result of a number of factors, including greater enrolment in Jewish day schools, improvements in Jewish education at all levels, the expansion of Jewish studies at the university level, the publication of Jewish literature, an increase in the number of secular Jewish organizations observing Jewish holidays, and the Jewish programming offered in Jewish community centres (Rosenthal 2008). It was also a reflection of a growing post-denominationalism in which committed, younger Jews increasingly refused to be labelled by existing religious institutions and rejected established branches of Judaism in order to create something more fluid and qualitatively 'better' (Rosenthal 2008).

When researching this sort of topic, it is good to remember that there is a clear distinction between Jewishness as a racial, ethnic, political or cultural identity, and Judaism as a religion and set of beliefs, behaviours and values. At the present time, contemporary culture has produced a multiplicity of religiously defined Jews on screen. Not only have these representations increased, but they have also taken on different forms, marking a departure from the past towards more unselfconscious, self-critical, deeper, subtle, playful and even outrageous representations of Judaism. There is even some attempt to understand and explore religious beliefs and the ideas and philosophy behind these rituals, as well as to mock, mimic and reverse them. Film not only represents subjective Judaic experiences, but also serves an overt educational purpose. Jews are increasingly being identified through religious rather than simply ethnic markers (names, physical looks, professions, locations) (Abrams 2013). Key points in the Jewish religious calendar, other than just Chanukah and Passover, are depicted (Abrams 2013; Rosenberg 2012). In this way, contemporary popular culture has been moving towards a more sophisticated understanding of Judaism and its beliefs, rituals and practices, portraying a fuller range of Jewish denominational affiliations (rather than just secular, Reform and haredi) and intra-Jewish conflict such that contradictory and 'multiple cultures are shown to thrive within Jewish life itself' (Rosenberg 2012). This incremental effect of discourse (Baker 2006) has paved the road for a new, more nuanced exploration of Judaism qua Judaism in a new medium: games.

Jewish discourses in video games

Can video games as media be in any way analogous to Judaism? Is there a comparable procedural discourse in both? Rabbi Owen Gottlieb (maker of the alternative reality video game *Jewish Time Jump* [ConverJent 2013]) argues that:

> Rabbinic literature has a sense of playfulness and inquiry—of spiritual delving through wordplay. Rabbis will use this to look at the Bible [Tanakh] and tell stories in between the cracks [Talmud]. [. . .] It's playfulness for deeper spiritual understanding. Also, the great Jewish legal texts explore underlying rule systems to find out what are the implied and necessary ethics.
>
> Gottlieb 2013

The rule systems of games provide the scaffolding on which gameplay is built, so to speak. In a good game, the player has the illusion of an individual experience – the illusion of endless choice. Games, however, even sandbox games, present a series of constraints to players (for very practical reasons) that at best mirror the mechanics of the *Choose Your Own Adventure Series* of books, popular in the 1980s (Carrillo Masso 2009, 2010). This need not be a negative attribute of games. On the contrary, just as the format of a sonnet provides the limits of a poetic form within which many themes can be explored, the video game format's inherent constraints provide what Eric Zimmerman calls 'the space of possibility'[6] (Zimmerman 2013).

By analogy, we can look at the similarities between the Jewish Torah and video games as systems, in the sense that they can be seen as (larger than) the sum of three main parts: a material element whose mechanics and corporeality cement and provide a platform for the other two, and two elements, in which one can be seen as a text as product, and the other one, which can be seen as a text as process.

The reason this admittedly loose analogy works[7] with Judaism as a religion, and not with, say, Christianity, has to do with the lack of what in Christianity would be termed the infallibility of the Church. In Judaism, the Oral Torah, is considered a process, rather than a fixed revelation (Maccoby 1988: 18). Indeed, '[t]he chief characteristic of the Oral Torah (apart from its Sinaitic nucleus) in point of authority, in contrast to the Written Torah [the Tanakh], was thus its *fallibility*. This derived from the fallible status of its enactors and decision-makers' (1988: 20).[8]

The Torah as persuasive process and process of argument for the purpose of persuasion can be said to be then in some ways similar to a quality of video games that Ian Bogost terms 'procedural rhetoric' (Bogost 2007). Bogost defined procedural rhetoric as 'the practice of persuading through processes in general and computational processes in particular' (2007: 3). Continuing:

> Just as verbal rhetoric is useful for both the orator and the audience [. . .], so procedural rhetoric is useful for both the programmer and the user, the game designer and the player. Procedural rhetoric is a technique *for making arguments with computational systems* and for *unpacking* computational *arguments others have created*.
>
> p. 3, my emphasis

Bogost's definition seems to indicate the appropriateness of the analogy I have hitherto canvassed. Yet how common is this procedurality to Judaic practices in general and Jewish identities in particular? How is this process carried out?

The process of Talmudic exploration and intertextual conversation (responsa) is commonly termed 'pilpul'.[9] This Talmudic tradition of interrogation is certainly not exclusive to rabbis and sages. Indeed, in the Eastern European *shtetl*[10] of yore,

> [t]he attitudes and thought habits characteristic of the learning tradition are as evident in the street and market place as the yeshiva. The popular picture of the Jew in Eastern Europe, held by Jew and Gentile alike, is true to the Talmudic tradition. The picture includes the tendency to examine, analyse and re-analyse, to seek meanings behind meanings and for implications and secondary consequences. [. . .] The process that produces such a response—often with lightning speed—is a modest reproduction of the *pilpul* process.
>
> Zborowski and Herzog 1962

This 'attitude of thought' applied to video games can be further illustrated by the comments made by Warren Spector on the attitude that informs his work as a Jewish games developer:

> In my games, there are no absolutes. I try to weed them out. It's very consciously a dialogue between me and the players. That idea of dialogue and argumentation is, I guess you could say, Talmudic. Judaism is a religion and a culture based on dialogue, argumentation, and questioning. It's about pushing the limits of rules in order to define them, often in very personal terms, in terms that differ from accepted wisdom.
>
> Spector, n.d. in Johnson, 2014

These characteristics, which as I have shown, indicate a potentially useful analogy between both systems (Torah and video games), grounded the intellectually playful process of Talmudic argumentation, and are more clearly shown in the procedural rhetoric of the game that forms the basis of my case study: *The Shivah* (Wadjet Eye Games 2006).

Critical Discourse Analysis (CDA)

Critical Discourse Analysis (henceforth CDA) can be defined as:

a type of discourse analytical research that primarily studies the way social power abuse, dominance and inequality are enacted, reproduced and resisted by text and talk in the social and political context. With such dissident research, critical discourse analysts take explicit position, and thus want to understand, expose and ultimately to resist social inequality.

van Dijk 1998: 1

CDA is the social analysis of discourse through a variety of approaches and methods, each depending on the nature of the research being carried out (Hardt-Mautner 1995; Saha 1997; Fairclough and Wodak 1997; Pêcheux 1982; Wodak and Meyer 2001; Orpin 2005). CDA combines interdisciplinary, as well as **transdisciplinary** techniques to analyse texts (Fairclough 2005) and to look at the way dominant discourses not only represent the world, but also *construct* the world through texts.

Fairclough and Wodak (1997: 271–80) (c.f. Caldas-Coulthard and Coulthard 1996; Fairclough and Wodak 1997; Fowler and Kress 1979; van Dijk 1998) summarize the main tenets of CDA as in the table in Figure 15.1 (left column). I have paired each tenet with a sample question that links it with the study of religion in games in Figure 15.1 above.

CDA in itself is then not a single quantitative or qualitative research method, but rather a critical approach to research methods that seeks to eliminate inequality expressed and legitimized through language use (Wodak and Meyer 2001: 2; van Dijk 1993) by exposing it, and to make social changes through social understanding (van Dijk 1998: 252). The approaches commonly classified as part of CDA offer a way to interpret a problem, to narrow down a topic, and to see the motivations behind the discourse in and through different 'readings' of a text and looking at its context and surrounding elements (Fairclough 2003; 2004; 2005, and Chouliaraki and Fairclough 1999). An '[e]mpirically adequate critical analysis (. . .) is usually *multidisciplinary*' (van Dijk 1998). This makes its partnership with methodologies like Corpus Linguistics and Multimodality all the more natural, as well as making it well suited to the study of religion in CG, as a subject that crosses several traditional disciplinary boundaries and can be applied to different contexts. This context not only refers to a text's accompanying images, which should never be disregarded in an analysis (Kress and Van Leeuwen 1990), but to the discourses that exist around (and inside) the text and the accompanying images, and the sociocultural practices that envelope them both.

What is a Corpus?

A Corpus is a collection of texts (Thompson 2007). Well-designed Corpora are ideal tools to examine large amounts of language for critical analysis (Hunston 2002: 123). They can provide us with quantitative information and thus inform qualitative studies by providing the means to replicate and triangulate (Newby 2009: 123) the results. They also provide the opportunity to systematically examine features and patterns of regularity in them, which are too difficult or time-consuming to obtain by other means (Hunston 2002). Kenny (2001) argues that in fact the Corpus-based approach is more 'like a kaleidoscope', allowing us to see 'textual patterns come into focus and recede again as others take their place' (Baker 2006).

I have chosen to use a Corpus as my primary tool of data organization because Corpora also make vast amounts of data more manageable to be studied, and this makes them ideal to handle data for the study of computer-mediated communication in general, and video games in particular. It is precisely due to the large amounts of data available that it is important to keep the *relevance* of the data in mind and to have clear criteria before it is collected, bearing in mind the project-specific, relative difficulties of transcription and annotation, particularly in multimodal corpora. These challenges will be explored in more detail below.

How is a Multimodal Corpus compiled?

Depending on the modes to be studied, a Multimodal Corpus will follow the same basic principles described above, but extending them to images, video and music files. The software to access them follows different principles, but they will be discussed in more detail in the sample analyses below.

Crucially, one of the most important aspects of Multimodal corpora is the transcription process, which differs somewhat from the transcription into pure text, as it is a fragmentation of the communicative event into its constituent parts, and then the way they're grouped or clustered, as well as different relations between the parts.

In a multimodal Corpus, transcription and analysis are closely interrelated. To Baldry and Thibault '[a]nalysis synthesizes the results of transcription in order to ground statement about textual meaning' (2006). Essentially, they see analysis as the breaking down, deglossing of a text, and therefore transcription plays an important role in this process.

Outline of methodology

TIP 1

Keep meticulous records of all the texts you use in your Corpus and their provenance.

These steps, grounded in the epistemological traditions of Games Studies, Multimodal Discourse Analysis and Corpus Linguistics, are framed from the perspective of the researcher as player, so they would need to be slightly adapted to projects in which the player is a third person, and a different provision should then be made for added ethical considerations.

1. Selection of the game or games to be studied. This is an important step, as it is closely linked to deciding on the purpose and scope of your study, and designing the research questions. The questions could emerge also from the selected game, but a rationale for this selection should be clear from the start.

2. Obtaining the game. This involves making sure the game to be studied can be played on a computer you have access to, by checking the system specifications. Also making sure you can obtain legal access to playing the game in your country of residence,[11] and become aware of any other versions of the game that might be available, making a record of the one you download/purchase for your research, to avoid confusion in your data.

3. Pre-play preparation. Having selected the game you want to study, I very strongly suggest that, whether you are an expert player/gamer, or this is your first experience with CG, that you refrain from playing the game at this stage. Rather, I suggest you play at least one, but possibly up to three games of the same genre in preparation for your project. The reason is twofold: you will gain confidence in using the game interface (which is especially important if you are unfamiliar with this kind of game or games in general), and you will then see the commonalities in the genre that will have provided a sort of template for the target game design, meaning you will quickly gain an insight as to what is part of a genre, and what is unique about your chosen game when you do play it. Both will provide a degree of transparency for the medium, which should aid your immersion in the game by removing some potential initial obstacles, and also inform your analysis by giving you at least some context on games in general and this genre in particular.

4. Selection and installation of your computer-assisted software for analysis. These should include: 1) a program for recording gameplay, such as FRAPS, or Camtasia Studio 7; 2) a piece of software[12] that will let you analyse video and audio data, with a time stamping function for ease of transcription; and, potentially, 3) a program(s) such as Sketch Engine that will allow you to look at the language used in the game in some detail. Your selection of the software will of course be determined by both the game you have chosen to analyse and your research questions.

5. Play (and record gameplay). Play the game. This step is crucial, even if the main subject playing the game in your project is not you. Play the game to completion (if it is a close-ended game), and if it has multiple pre-encoded endings, I suggest you play them all. If your chosen game is open-ended, such as a MMORPG, I suggest you play for at least a pre-determined number of hours.[13] If your project is heavily focused on looking at your reactions to the game, I strongly recommend the use of a video camera to record yourself (your facial expressions or posture) as part of your Corpus.

6. Preparing video data. You may need to convert your video files in preparation for the software you will use. There are many free online converters that can be used for this purpose. You will also need to name your files carefully and keep a record of the metadata in an organized manner.

7. Transcription. You will need to budget your time, as this step can be very time-consuming, depending on the granularity you will use in your project. You may also decide on multiple transcripts to run simultaneously; one, for example, recording all verbal aspects of the game (such as dialogue or narration), while other transcripts add layers of complexity by describing important visual elements, or elements of gameplay, such as rules and interactions with the interface. Alternatively, a single transcript can be edited iteratively to add all these elements in what could be termed *layering*. Ultimately, what you choose to transcribe and how you choose to transcribe it will be inextricably linked to your analysis.

TIP 2

Remember to back up your Corpus regularly as you compile it.

As an example, we can ask a question as to how the Start screen of *The Shivah: A Rabbinical Adventure* (Wadjet Eye Games 2006) organizes potential meanings and their relations for their target users. Because of the affordabilities offered by the game's playpath they show their potential for particular kinds of interaction between player and game.

Upon reaching this screen, three elements seem to jump out of the screen: its monochromatic nature, the image on the right, and the name of the game in bold, followed by the other components of the screen. Interestingly, saliency here does not equal interactivity. The figure on the right is of a mature man with a beard and wearing a kippah, both of which elements code him as Jewish. His maturity, and the point of view of the image (slightly above the viewer's right, and looking left and up) potentially code him as a rabbi: as a mediator between the viewer and God. The monochromatic nature of the image code it as the start page of a serious game, and the font, as well as the nature of the options, code it as an old-school style game. The options offer (limited) different starting points to the potential playpath.

Our previous experience and knowledge of these objects is, above all, an intertextual one. These are all texts, verbal, visual, etc., which we encountered in other contexts, and will thus inform our interpretation of the image. By recording the gameplay experience using FRAPS and then examining this record in Transana, we can then systematize the way in which we relate to and read these images within, and beyond, the gameplay experience.

Transcribing Playpaths I will use the term 'playpath' to describe the meaning-making pathways that are created when players move through a game including the movement within one screen/level, from one level to another as they make their way through a video game. A playpath, in this sense, will refer to the progressive integration over time of the semiotic resources that are encountered as the player progresses from one linked object, space or level to another. A playpath may occur over minutes or hours, depending on the length of a play session and the skill and playing style of the player; it may occur over much longer periods of time, as well as being picked up and continued across separate occasions. 'Space is time-based' and constructed around and conditioned by a sequence of events which involves the constant reorganization of the participants' occupancy of space in relation to each other (Baldry and Thibault 2006). Thus, in a communicative event the perception of space is time-based, based on what happens along a timeline. In a video game the perception of virtual space will have to do with both the actions and movement that take place in that space. Transcription of playpaths can take the form of flowcharts of different types. For a simple playpath of the first three minutes of *The Shivah*, see Figure 15.2.

The multimodal transcription and analysis of playpaths can reveal the ways in which they integrate diverse semiotic resources to themselves as they develop and unfold. In time, possible playpaths are afforded by both technological resources (game code, programming language, interface) and semiotic resources of video games. By the same token, the recording and analysis of playpaths will provide insights into the way in which players experience games and their possible meanings through actual instances of navigating and negotiating their way through game spaces, and on how these potentials are encoded and function within the original game design. It would also be able to show the extent to which playpaths as trajectories have generic and individual characteristics in their semiotic makeup, as the preferred playing that designers envisioned can be compared to both the potential pathway and the actual one.

We need to take into account the nature of the different semiotic resources that are used and the way they are used to create a particular video game, both as individual **text** and as part of a genre. This includes a player's potential playpath, as encoded in the game design – including what I term the *preferred playing* (based on

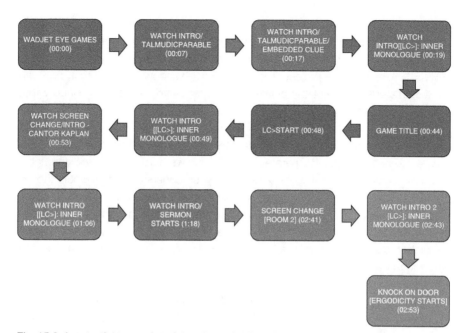

Fig. 15.2 A potential transcript of the playpath of the first three minutes of *The Shivah*. This low-granularity transcription only shows basic actions taken by a player with a time stamp for each. The various intros to the game serve as an introduction to the main character (Rabbi Stone) and the Film Noir-like setting, as well as to show the game options and to provide a clue to the preferred playing of the game. This is achieved by the designer in under three minutes.

the idea of the preferred reading of a text) as well as a *dispreferred playpath* (including cheating or play that goes against the rules). What I call the *potential playpath*, which can be taken through a particular game, as opposed to the *actual playpath*, taken by a particular player, in a particular instance of gameplay. The actual playpath is created by the player while negotiating the meanings afforded by that particular game along with particular meaning-making elements within a fixed trajectory out of a more-or-less fluid set of potentials, depending on the game's genre. This distinction is necessary because the experience of play itself does not really exist in isolation of the medium.

The above example (Figure 15.2) illustrates the relevance of the role of transcription in multimodal game analysis and hints at the usefulness of having a consistent notation system to use in your project.

A word on Transana 2.53 Transana is an open-source software package used to analyse and manage audio and video data (Transana.org). This program, which runs on Windows and Apple OS X, allows you to organize a large number of clips so that you can transcribe them, look for relationships between them and share your results with fellow researchers. Transana's screen is divided up into five parts. The top menu bar controls the program as a whole. The video window on the right displays the video and can display two synchronized videos as well. Under the main menu is the visualization window that displays the audio information in a visual form or a graph of keywords related to the project. The transcription window is below that, and can show numerous transcriptions at the same time. Lastly, is the data window that displays a data tree and allows you to navigate your data.

8. Parallel Corpus: compilation of paratexts. I suggest the optional creation of a parallel Corpus of metaludic paratexts (game reviews, forum posts, walkthroughs, manuals, backstory, fan fiction) to expand your understanding of your chosen game – all depending on your research question. This can be easily accomplished by collecting the texts chosen in the right format (.txt), and keeping a detailed record of their provenance. As the verbal amount of text contained in a short game might be insufficient to answer certain questions, a parallel Corpus would bridge that gap and help inform your analysis.

9. Treating Raw Data (Annotation and its Discontents). One of the most important contributions of Corpora to the field of CDA is that it allows researchers to study the 'incremental effect of discourse' (Baker 2006: 13). The single word used to be considered the smallest unit for analysis, but now the smallest unit for analysis in Corpus Linguistics is the 'chunk'. A chunk is the smallest meaningful unit: a cluster of words that seem to be 'strongly attracted to each other'. This allows, particularly, for explorations on collocation. In Transana, the smallest unit of analysis is the Clip – effectively, a video chunk.

In Transana 2.53 you can create **Keywords** tied to a particular Series (I suggest a series is used to speak of the whole game, and an episode, under a Series, to speak of individual video captures of said game, particularly **playthroughs**). The process of adding keywords is iterative, so you can add more keywords than originally planned if the analysis seems to demand it. Once you have created your keywords (which can also be grouped for convenience), you can start creating Clips. By highlighting the part of the transcript you wish to include in an individual clip, and then applying the pertinent keywords to this portion of video, Transana will then automatically create a small clip already tagged with the keywords you applied. I strongly suggest you keep an unannotated version of your main transcript to use with a concordancer and/or an automated tagger. This would be most useful to projects where the linguistic aspects of a game play a role in the research questions, but I think this step has the potential to inform any piece of research. It is particularly useful when used with metaludic data as a point of comparison, or to enrich the Corpus. I propose a full tagset for the annotation of multimodal corpora for the analysis of Jewish representations elsewhere (2014b), but a sample, contracted version appears at the end of this chapter.

After Machin (2007) and Lemke (2001, 2002), I propose that the following visual aspects of video games are contemplated in their analysis via the grid:

- Iconography
- Modality (Articulation of Detail, Light, Depth, Abstraction, Sensory Modality)
- Colour
- Typography
- Proxemics (Gaze, Distance and Angle of Interaction)
- Chronemics
- Function
- Kinetics
- Trajectory
- Composition
- Visual Representation of Social Actors

I also believe that it would be possible to compile a Corpus of movement, transcribing movement into a kinetographic score, a transcription based on Laban's (1975) dance and movement notation, which is in turn based on Beauchamp's and Feuillet's 300-year-old choreography notation system. This system has been used not only to notate performance movements, but also to optimize industrial processes. It could be applied to both the movement of characters on-screen, and to the movement of players, especially of console and arcade games. This would open a new avenue of enquiry for game analysis that is well worth exploring.

Multimodal Game Analysis. Once the data has been taken apart, so to speak, by means of transcription, annotation and tagging, it is time to put it back together to perform your analysis. I believe that video game analysis is hermeneutic in nature, that is, one needs to understand the parts in order to understand the whole and vice-versa. What you transcribe, what you tag and what you annotate will largely depend on your research questions and goals, but the essential aspects of Corpus-assisted analysis will remain the same: with the help of the computer, you will find patterns. These patterns, whether linguistic, visual or thematic, tend to remain largely hidden to the naked eye, because of the vast amount of multimodal information to be processed. For the reasons outlined above, I suggest here the use of CDA[14] as an approach to the analysis of games, but I do not wish to imply that it is the only one to be followed. Rather, I believe every researcher should exercise discretion in choosing what is necessary for their individual project, but for the purpose of this chapter, where I focus on the study of Jewish representations in games, I believe CDA works very well.

This method does require a lot of steps to be followed and requires then the examination of practically everything related to the game. At a first glance, this might seem to include needless work, but this is not so. One could relate the pressing need to devise a fit-for-purpose method for game analysis (Aarseth 1997, 2001), to the concept of Ashby's requisite variety (c.f. Ashby 1957 in Muse 2014). Beer (1979) applied Ashby's theory of requisite variety to management systems. In Muse's words, Beer sustains that 'regulation [of a system] could only occur through either attenuating (reducing) the variety in the system or amplifying the variety of the regulator.' I believe this methodology blends both approaches to fulfil requisite variety: First, it 'destroys' variety by capturing the system in video, effectively crystallizing the playpath as a single instance to which nothing further can be added – a video recording of a game to be studied, and no longer the whole game system. Second, it amplifies the variety that the regulator (researcher) can handle by means of a software package that can hold myriad details in 'mind', well beyond human capacity. It is for these reasons I advocate the usefulness and timeliness of applying this methodology.

Ethical considerations within this research

Both here and elsewhere my research has primarily involved using the researcher as subject. Thus, I will not discuss here the well-known implications of using subjects for your research, but three ethical considerations have emerged from this chapter, and these I will now address below.

1 **Availability and Legality:** Due to concerns extraneous to academia, certain games are banned in certain regions. Any game that has any connection with Israel, for example, be that in the design or production process, or in terms of content, is legally banned in the Arab world. Studying such games would then incur additional hurdles of a very material nature, and caution and discretion should be exercised when choosing this line of research to ensure access to the games can be safely granted.

2 **Academic rigour:** I believe that my proposed methodology certainly aids in the replicability and falsifiability elements of research, thus adding rigour to any claims of analysis (and their implications) within the context of such a sensitive topic as religion.

3 **Impact:** In a recent article,[15] Aaron Hughes claimed that Jewish studies had perhaps become 'too Jewish', meaning there was a sense of self-imposed isolation in the field, as well as a problematic lack of accountability in some of the research produced. Applying a more systematic methodology to the study of Judaism and Jewish representations in video games could be a step in the right direction to foster inter- and transdisciplinary collaboration, opening the field of Jewish studies to researchers outside the field, and inviting more transparency and accountability from within, which would provide a positive new direction.

Reflections

In video games as media, because of their affordances, variability, fluidity, and context-specificity are emphasized over global order and stability of meaning. What is absent in most discussions, however, is any detailed account of the meaning-making process that accounts for the appointment of semiotic and material resources that takes place during this process. The process is simply taken for granted and celebrated as such. Due to the complex nature of games, the need for a flexible approach that can encompass the requisite variety of the aspects outlined above is paramount. I have outlined in this chapter a series of steps to follow to analyse PC games in a systematic fashion, and suggested examples of how this method can be applied to study the representation of Judaism and Jewish characters in games.

I hope that a method that uses a systematic approach to study religion in video games can shed new light on epistemological questions on the nature of play, on human–machine interaction, and on the impact of technology on emotion and cognition, and, by extension, on our humanity as we play with religion.

Note: A Sample from a Tagset for the Study of Judaism in video game using Multimodal Corpora

Group: Ludic

LC	Left Click
RC	Right Click
>	On
[SI:]	Speaker Initials
FPP	First person-perspective
3PP	Third-person perspective
H>	Hover cursor over [object]

Group: Theological/Religious

JqJ	Jew qua Jew
CrJ	Crypto-Jew
R-S	Representation of Self
R-O	Representation of Other
JSbth	Jewish Shibboleth
NJSbth	Non-Jewish Shibboleth
JW	Jewish faith/Judaism as Faith
SoB	Sense of Belonging
RA	Rabbinical Approach
TA	Talmudic Allusion

Glossary

Crypto-Jew In the context of research on the representation of Judaism and Jewish people, I define this as a character that is not specifically stated to be Jewish, but can be tacitly read to be so, or one whose Jewishness in contested in the game. This is in contrast to the common meaning of the term, which is a person who outwardly maintains another faith (usually Catholicism or Islam) but secretly practices Judaism. **Examples:** The characters of Joe De Marco and Mrs Lauder in *The Shivah*, the Goblins in *World of Warcraft* (Blizzard Entertainment 2004–2014).

Jew-qua-Jew A Jewish character who is stated as Jewish from the start. **Examples:** The character of Rabbi Stone and Rabbi Zelig in *The Shivah*, Hyman Roth/Johnny Lips in *The Godfather* (Electronic Arts 2006–2007).

Keyword In Transana this is a searchable tag that the user creates in order to annotate their Corpus.

Metaludic 'Metaludic' information, lit. 'beyond the game', refers to game-related material (from the blurb and pictures on the box, to advertising campaigns, to fan art, blogs, etc.). It contrasts with diegetic, i.e. pertaining to the storyline or inner world of the game, and non-diegetic information, i.e. information inside the game that does not relate to the game as a story, such as commands to save the game, tutorial information and tips on game mechanics, etc.

Realistic In the context of a video game, realism refers to 'internal consistency' as opposed to life-like features.

Text 'language that is functional. By functional we simply mean language that is doing some job in some context, as opposed to isolated words or sentences [. . .]. So any instance of living language that is playing some part in a context of situation, we shall call a text. It may be spoken or written, or indeed in *any other medium of expression that we like to think of*.' (Halliday 1989: 10; my emphasis).

Walkthrough A walkthrough, as the term is used online in gaming communities, is a tutorial for a specific game, usually in written form, but often offered as a video clip. Walkthroughs are often consulted to obtain answers to difficult puzzles/missions in a game, and their use is controversial, as many class their use as a form of cheating. A **playthrough**, by contrast, tends to be produced for its entertainment value rather than for didactic purposes, or, simply put, as a record of completion. In my research I use 'playthrough' in the latter sense.

Afterword: Digital Methodologies in the Sociology of Religion – What next?

Sariya Cheruvallil-Contractor and Suha Shakkour

In Chapter 1 of this book, Campbell and Altenhofen assert the urgent and important need for a continued effort towards interdisciplinary cohesion as a way of developing common ground for conversations among scholars seeking to study digital religion. The research project that led to this volume, and this volume itself, emerged from our recognition of this. Before writing this book, we saw the need to discuss digital methodology and to leave a trail based on our research experiences, which future researchers could follow. At the very least, we hoped to save future researchers the same trials and errors faced by current researchers in this field.

This book, therefore, is intended to be wide-reaching, and so provides researchers pursuing a variety of topics within the sociology of digital religion, some context in which they can situate their respective projects. Thus, from complex discussions about positionality, to simpler tips about checking for copyright issues, this volume includes a range of practical guidelines and tips. More importantly, however, it begins the process of deconstructing current understandings around ethical issues in research to facilitate their realignment with the complexities of digital religion. So, in a way, after completing this book there is a sense of victory. Yet we also realize that while we may have advanced the study of digital religion, there remains much to do.

First, technology is constantly changing and advancing, and often the most researchers can do is to try to keep up with it. As sociologists we are being led and, in some ways, we are guided by the individuals we research to venture deeper and deeper into the internet. Second, although the internet is not universally accessible, today more people than ever before have access to it, and the skills of each new generation of users surpasses the last. Although this is great advancement, for researchers, it also means that the complex world of digital religion or belief will only become more crowded and more difficult to study. This, of course, presents us with both ample opportunity for further research, but also, perhaps an opportunity to humbly acknowledge that our work is a mere foundation upon which, we hope, other researchers will continue to build.

Notes

Chapter 2

1. The original site (www.multifaithnet.org) is no longer functioning, with the domain name having been taken over in 2007. A snapshot of *MultiFaithNet* captured by the Internet Archive at http://web.archive.org/ on 5 December 1998, can be accessed via the Archive's Way Back Machine search engine. The earliest fully functioning version is captured in the Archive's snapshot of it on 27 April 1999. In a later format, developed in association with the Multi-Faith Centre at the University of Derby, Archive snapshots can be found from 27 May 2004.
2. See www.derby.ac.uk/religion-and-society
3. Project Number AH/H016074/1/.
4. See www.limesurvey.org/en/
5. See www-01.ibm.com/software/analytics/spss/
6. See www.derby.ac.uk/religion-and-belief-in-HE
7. See www.snapsurveys.com/
8. See www.belieforama.eu
9. See www.skype.com/en/
10. www.derby.ac.uk/media/derbyacuk/contentassets/documents/research/ethic sandgovernance/University-of-Derby-Research-Ethics-Policy-and-Code-of-Practice-June-2011.doc
11. See www.surveymonkey.com/
12. See www.google.co.uk/forms/about/
13. See www.sikhsonline.co.uk/
14. See www.gosikh.com/
15. For example, through the decennial Census and the British Social Attitudes survey.
16. However, the results of the research informed development of the ECU's policy, practice and work with other stakeholders, including the Higher Education Statistical Agency's data collection on student and staff religion or belief. HESA has now adopted the ECU's recommendation, based on the practice of the project's online survey, to include the respondent category option of 'spiritual', which is not used in the decennial Census. For HESA's staff survey, see www.hesa.ac.uk/index.php/component/option,com_studrec/ task,show_file/Itemid,233/mnl,12025/href,a%5E_%5ERELBLF.html and for its student survey, see www.hesa.ac.uk/component/option,com_studrec/task,show_file/Itemid,233/ mnl,12051/href,a%5E_%5ERELBLF.html/
17. See, for example, Sheffield's Skeptics in the Pub http://sheffield.skepticsinthepub.org/

Chapter 3

1. This rate of completion for the primary survey has been replicated with a diverse group of target populations including religious minorities, LGBT minorities and hard-to-reach market segments.
2. Similar denominationally diverse samples were also obtained for Americans of Jewish and Buddhist faith.

Chapter 7

1. It is conceivable though that the rare presence of a Westerner at a sacred site could indirectly affect ritual performance. For example, participants may act more conscientiously.
2. The theory of *karma* postulates that every action has its inevitable consequence, which means that everyone's condition is determined by good or bad deeds in this life and in previous ones, while *dharma* refers to religious duty, law and custom (see Fuller 1992: 245, 268). *Moksha* is liberation from the cycle of birth and death (Klostermaier 1998: 104).

Chapter 8

1. Sikhs.org claims to be the world's first website on Sikhism (Sikhs.org n.d.). From its registration date and from the fact that Sundeep Singh Brar was involved in other online Sikh interactions at this time, this claim is most likely true.
2. As of July 2012, religion and spirituality focused wikis include Theopedia – an encyclopaedia of Christianity (www.theopedia.com/Main_Page), IslamWiki – a pro-Islamic wiki (http://islam.wikia.com/wiki/Islam_Wikia), WikiIslam – a wiki critical of Islam (www.wikiislam.net/wiki/Main_Page).
3. For further details about the Religion and Society programme, see www.religionandsociety.org.uk/
4. According to Nielsen and Landauer (1993) having five users test a website will reveal 85 per cent of its usability problems.
5. Advice on how to advertise the survey was obtained from the members of the 'Religion, Sexuality and Youth' project who had also implemented an online survey. I was a member of the Advisory Board for this project. For further details, see www.nottingham.ac.uk/sociology/rys/index.aspx [accessed 9 December 2009].
6. Facebook groups included those belonging to university Sikh societies, Sikh camps, gurdwaras and local Sikh youth groups. Yahoo/google groups included the 'learning-zone' and 'leeds-bradfordsikhs'. I also posted details about my research on a number of websites, for example Sikhnet: www.sikhnet.com/news/phd-research-british-sikhs-18-30-currently-underway [accessed 24 November 2009] and Sikh discussion forums including Sikhsangat: www.sikhsangat.com/index.php?/topic/48145-phd-research-into-british-sikhs-18-30/page__hl__%2Bphd+%2Bresearch+%2Byoung+%2

Bbritish+%2Bsikhs__fromsearch__1 [accessed 1 December 2009] as well as posting on Bhangra forums: http://simplybhangra.com/forum/5-general-chat/271-phd-research-into-british-sikhs-18-30/ [accessed 1 December 2009] and Punjabi discussion forums including: http://punjab2000.proboards.com/index.cgi?board—ixedForum&action=display&thread=15001 [accessed 1 December 2009].

7. More detailed findings are available in my recent article (Singh 2014).

8. This has been derived from the fact that there are 25 tracks per page and 572 pages of *kirtan* listings at www.sikhnet.com/songs?page=571

9. The 'Basics of Sikhi' YouTube channel is available at: www.youtube.com/user/basicsofsikhi/

Chapter 10

1. The number of people.

Chapter 13

1. www.wowwiki.com/WoW_Census [accessed 23 April 2014].
2. www.wowwiki.com/Burning_Legion [accessed 23 April 2014].
3. www.wowwiki.com/WoW_population_by_country [accessed 5 June 2014].

Chapter 14

1. http://en.wikipedia.org/wiki/Zork [accessed 17 February 2015].
2. http://en.wikipedia.org/wiki/Pong [accessed 17 February 2015].
3. http://en.wikipedia.org/wiki/The_Elder_Scrolls_V:Skyrim [accessed 17 February 2015].
4. http://en.wikipedia.org/wiki/Eve_Online [accessed 17 February 2015].
5. http://en.wikipedia.org/wiki/Call_of_Duty [accessed 17 February 2015].

Chapter 15

1. The reason I here favour using Ensslin's 'gameology' over the more strictly correct 'ludology' is that in Games Studies, 'ludology' has taken to mean a particular slant of the field that views the analysis of representation or semiotics as both superfluous and ultimately alien to the medium, and is set in opposition to what is usually termed the 'narratological approach', which tends to disregard purely ludic aspects, such as interactivity.

2. C.f. Benveniste in Cobley and Jansz (1997) and Lacan's interpretation of Saussure's work on mediation.

3. The questioning approach could be read as a Socratic approach to analysis and it was used in the very earliest AI engines, e.g. Weizenbaum's Eliza (1964–1966), etc. Although there are similarities between the two, the main difference between the Socratic method and the Talmudic approach is that rabbis formalized their inferential techniques, but did

not create an abstract system of reasoning of general application, as this logic was the design for the sacred activity of Torah study, and was not seen as an end in itself.

4. Haredi (pl. *haredim*)is translated as 'ultra-Orthodox,' a definition that does not do justice to this extensive and nuanced term, which covers a range of Jews, not all of whom are 'Orthodox' in the strictest definition of that term. See Abrams 2012: 215.

5. Some examples of this from American television would be some of the characters in the long-running television series *Friends* (1994–2004) *Will and Grace* (1998–2005), and *Numb3rs* (2006–2008).

6. Although, of course, technological constraints need to be added when talking about video games. A sonnet is mostly verbally/formally constrained, and the conventions have probably been broken as often if not more often than they have been adhered to.

7. This is, of course, a strong simplification of two very complex phenomena.

8. I deliberately ignore here the finer subdivisions of halacha (general legal ruling by rabbinical consensus) and miswah (commandment from the Tanakh) for reasons of space as these distinctions do not add to the present discussion.

9. Lit. 'sharp analysis'. It can also be translated as 'hair-splitting'.

10. Small villages with a majority of Jewish populations. They disappeared after WWII and the Jewish persecution in Soviet Russia (Rothenberg 1981).

11. Some games are banned or heavily edited for distribution in different regions, which can make it difficult, or even dangerous to use them as the object of your research if you cannot obtain legal permission to import or download them. For example, the games I use as an example in this chapter have different legal access requirements and restrictions in the UK from, say, in the Kingdom of Saudi Arabia.

12. For an overview of software packages for qualitative video analysis, look at the CAQDAS project, from the Department of Sociology at the University of Surrey. www.surrey.ac.uk/sociology/research/researchcentres/caqdas/index.htm

13. In previous work (Carrillo Masso 2009, 2010) I used fifty hours as a benchmark for the study of MMORPGs, but a different one could be making sure you reach a particular level. It is worth consulting players in a forum before deciding what this level should be, if you are unsure.

14. If you wish to explore the use of CDA to analyse Jewish representations, I suggest you turn to the work of Ruth Wodak, which provides an excellent example of this type of analysis applied to other media.

15. *Chronicle of Higher Education*, 24 March 2014.

Bibliography

Aarseth, E. (1997), *Cybertext: Perspectives on Ergodic Literature*, Baltimore: John Hopkins University Press.

Aarseth, E. (2001), *Playing Research: Methodological Approaches to Game Analysis*, Melbourne: DAC.

Aarseth, E. (2003), *Playing Research: Methodological Approaches to Game Analysis*. Available online: http://www.cs.uu.nl/docs/vakken/vw/literature/02.GameApproaches2.pdf [accessed 10 June 2014].

Abrams, N. (2009), *Caledonian Jews: A Study of Seven Small Communities in Scotland*, Jefferson, NC: MacFarland.

Abrams, N. (2010), *Norman Podhoretz and Commentary Magazine: The Rise and Fall of the Neo-Cons*, New York: Continuum.

Abrams, N. (2012), *The New Jew in Film: Exploring Jewishness and Judaism in Contemporary Cinema*, London: I.B.Tauris,

Abrams, N. (2013), 'The "sub-epidermic" Shoah: Barton Fink, the Migration of the Holocaust, and Contemporary Cinema', POST SCRIPT: Essays in Film and the Humanities 32:2 (Winter/Spring 2013): 6–19.

Abu-Lughod, L. (2002), 'Do Muslim Women Really Need Saving? Anthropological Reflections on Cultural Relativism and its Others', *American Anthropologist*, 104(3): 783–90.

Akou, H. M. (2010), Interpreting Islam Through the Internet: Making Sense of Hijab', *Contemporary islam*, 4, 331–46.

Allen, C. (2010a), 'West Midlands Case Study', in J. Githens-Mazer and R. Lambert (eds), *Islamophobia and Anti-Muslim Hate Crime: UK Case Studies 2010*, Exeter, UK: University of Exeter, pp. 147–81.

Allen, C. (2010b), *Islamophobia*, Farnham, UK: Ashgate Publishing.

Allen, C. (2011), 'Opposing Islamification or Promoting Islamophobia? Understanding the English Defence League', *Patterns of Prejudice*, 45(4): 279–94.

Allen, C. (2013a), 'Between Critical and Uncritical Understandings: A Case Study Analyzing the Claims of Islamophobia Made in the Context of the Proposed "Super-Mosque" in Dudley, England', *Societies*, 3(2): 186–203.

Allen, C. (2013b), 'Passing the Dinner Table Test: Retrospective and Prospective Approaches to Tackling Islamophobia in Britain', *SAGE Open*, 3(2).

Allen, C. (2014), 'Anti-Social Networking Findings From a Pilot Study on Opposing Dudley Mosque Using Facebook Groups as Both Site and Method for Research', *SAGE Open*, 4(1).

Alvi, S., Hoodfar, H. and McDonough, S. (2003), 'Introduction', in S. Alvi, H. Hoodfar and S. McDonough (eds), *The Muslim Veil in North America – Issues and Debates*, Toronto: Women's Press, pp. xi–xxiv.

Amarasingam, A. (ed.) (2010), *Religion and the New Atheism*, Leiden: Brill.

Androutsopoulos, J. (2008), 'Potentials and Limitations of Discourse-Centred Online Ethnography', *Language@Internet* [Online], 5. Available: http://www.languageatinternet.org/articles/2008/1610 [accessed 6 June 2014].

Androutsopoulos, J. (2010), 'Localising the Global on the Participatory Web', in N. Coupland (ed.), *Handbook of Language and Globalization*, Oxford: Wiley-Blackwell, pp. 203–31.

'Anonymous' (11 August 2005), interview conducted at Annapurna temple, Varanasi, India.

Arasa, D. (2008), *Church Communications through Diocesan Websites. A Model of Analysis*, Rome: EDUSC.

Arasa, D., Cantoni, L. and Ruiz, L. (eds) (2010), *Religious Internet Communication. Facts, Trends and Experiences in the Catholic Church*, Rome: EDUSC.

Armfield, G. G. and Holbert, R. L. (2003), 'The Relationship Between Religiosity and Internet Use', *Journal of Media and Religion*, 2(3): 129–44.

Arnau, R. C., Thompson, R. L. and Cook, C. (2001), 'Do Different Response Formats Change the Latent Structure of Responses? An Empirical Investigation Using Taxometric Analysis', *Educational and Psychological Measurement*, 61(1): 23–44.

Ashby, W. R. (1957), *An Introduction to Cybernetics*, London: Chapman & Hall.

Association of Internet Researchers (2012), 'Ethical Decision-Making and Internet Research: Recommendations from the AoIR Ethics Working Committee (Version 2.0)'. Available online: http://about.brighton.ac.uk/hss/fregc/Ethical-internet.pdf [accessed 10 February 2015].

Association of Internet Researchers Ethics Working Committee (2012), 'Ethical Decision-Making and Internet Research'. Available online: http://www.aoir.org/reports/ethics2.pdf [accessed 25 February 2015].

Atkins, B. (2003), *More than a Game: The Computer Game as a Fictional Form*, Manchester: Manchester University Press.

Atkinson, R. and Flint, J. (2001), 'Accessing Hidden and Hard-to-reach Populations: Snowball Research Strategies', *Social Research Update*, 33.

Axel, B. K. (2005), 'Diaspovic Sublime: Sikh Martyrs, Internet Mediations, and the Question of the Unimaginable', *Sikh Formations*, 1(1): 127–54.

Back, M. D., Stopfer, J. M., Vazire, S., Gaddis S., Schmukle S. C., Egloff, B. and Gosling, S. D. (2010), 'Facebook Profiles Reflect Actual Personality, Not Self-idealization', *Psychological Science*, 21(3): 372–4.

Bader, C. D., Mencken, F. C. and Froese, P. (2007), 'American Piety 2005: Content and Methods of the Baylor Religion Survey', *Journal for the Scientific Study of Religion*, 46(4): 447–63.

Bainbridge, W. S. (1978), *Satan's Power: A Deviant Psychotherapy Cult*, Berkeley: University of California Press.

Bainbridge, W. S. (1997), *The Sociology of Religious Movements*, New York: Routledge.

Bainbridge, W. S. (2006), *God from the Machine: Artificial Intelligence Models of Religious Cognition*, Walnut Grove, CA: AltaMira.

Bainbridge, W. S. (2007a), *Across the Secular Abyss*, Lanham, MD: Lexington.

Bainbridge, W. S. (2007b), 'The Scientific Research Potential of Virtual Worlds', *Science*, 317 (27 July): 472–6.

Bainbridge, W. S. (2009), 'Atheism', in P. B. Clarke (ed.), *The Oxford Handbook of the Sociology of Religion*, Oxford, UK: Oxford University Press, pp. 319–35.

Bainbridge, W. S. (2010a), *Online Multiplayer Games*, San Rafael, CA: Morgan and Claypool.

Bainbridge, W. S. (ed.) (2010b), *Online Worlds: Convergence of the Real and the Virtual*, London: Springer.

Bainbridge, W. S. (2010c), *The Warcraft Civilization*, Cambridge, MA: MIT Press.

Bainbridge, W. S. (2011), *The Virtual Future: Science-Fiction Gameworlds*, London: Springer.

Bainbridge, W. S. (2012), 'The Psychoanalytic Movement', in W. S. Bainbridge (ed.), *Leadership in Science and Technology*, Thousand Oaks, CA: Sage, pp. 520–28.

Bainbridge, W. S. (2013a), 'Ancestor Veneration Avatars', in R. Luppicini (ed.), *Handbook of Research on Technoself: Identity in a Technological Society*, Hershey, PA: Information Science Reference, pp. 308–21.

Bainbridge, W. S. (2013b), *eGods: Faith Versus Fantasy in Computer Gaming*, New York: Oxford University Press.

Bainbridge, W. S. (2013c), 'Perspectives on Virtual Veneration', *The Information Society*, 29: 196–202.

Bainbridge, W. S. (2014), *An Information Technology Surrogate for Religion*, New York: Palgrave Macmillan.

Bainbridge, W. S. and Bainbridge, W. A (2007), 'Electronic Game Research Methodologies: Studying Religious Implications', *Review of Religious Research*, 49(1): 35–53.

Bainbridge, W. S. and Stark, R. (1979), 'Cult Formation: Three Compatible Models', *Sociological Analysis*, 40: 285–95.

Baker, P. (2006), *Using Corpora in Discourse Analysis*, London: Continuum.

Baker, P. (2010), *Sociolinguistics and Corpus Linguistics*, London: Continuum.

Baldry, A. and Thibault, P. J. (2006), *Multimodal Transcription and Text Analysis: A Multimedia Toolkit and Coursebook*, London: Equinox.

Bardzell, S., Bardzell, J., Pace, T. and Reed, K. (2008), 'Blissfully Productive: Grouping and Cooperation in *World of Warcraft* Instance Runs', in *Proceedings of the ACM 2008 Conference on Computer Supported Cooperative Work*, New York: ACM, pp. 357–60.

Barker, Chr. (2005), *Cultural Studies: Theory and Practice*, London: Sage.

Barker, E. (2005), 'Crossing the Boundary: New Challenges to Religious Authority and Control as a Consequence of Access to the Internet', in M. Hojsgaard and M. Warburg (eds), *Religion and Cyberspace*, London: Routledge, pp. 67–85.

Barrier, N. G. (2006), 'Trauma and Memory Within the Sikh Diaspora: Internet Dialogue', *Sikh Formations*, 2(1): 33–56.

Barzilai-Nahon, K. and Barzilai, G. (2005), 'Cultured Technology: The Internet and Religious Fundamentalism', *The Information Society*, 21(1): 25–40.

Baym, N. (2005), 'Special Issue: ICT Research and Disciplinary Boundaries: Is "Internet Research" a Virtual Field, a Proto-Discipline, or Something Else?', *The Information Society*, 21(4).

Becker, G. (1986), 'The Economic Approach to Human Behaviour', in J. Elster (ed.), *Rational Choice*, Oxford: Basil Blackwell, pp. 108–22.

Beckford, J. A. (2003), *Social Theory and Religion*, Cambridge: Cambridge University Press.

Beer, S. (1979), *The Heart of Enterprise*, Chichester: Wiley.

Bell, G. (2006), 'No More SMS from Jesus: Ubicomp, Religion and Techno-Spiritual Practices', in P. Dourish and A. Friday (eds), *UbiComp 2006: Ubiquitous Computing*, Vol. 4206 of *Lecture Notes in Computer Science*, Berlin/Heidelberg: Springer, pp. 141–58.

Benedikt, M. (ed.) (1992), *Cyberspace: First Steps*, Cambridge, MA: MIT Press.

Benoit-Barné, C. and Cooren, F. (2009), 'The Accomplishment of Authority Through Presentification: How Authority is Distributed Among and Negotiated by Organizational Members', *Management Communication Quarterly*, 23: 5–31.

Berinsky, A. J., Huber, G. and Lenz, G. (2012), 'Evaluating Online Labor Markets for Experimental Research: Amazon.com's Mechanical Turk', *Political Analysis*, 20: 351–68.

Bertrand, C. and Bourdeau, L. (2010), 'Research Interviews by Skype: A New Data Collection Method', *Proceedings of the 9th European Conference on Research Methods in Business and Management*, Academic Conferences Limited.

Bessiere, K., Seay, F. and Kiesler, S. (2007), 'The Ideal Elf: Identity Exploration in *World of Warcraft*', *CyberPsychology and Behavior*, 10: 530–5.

Bhatt, C. (1997), *Liberation and Purity: Race, New Religious Movements and the Ethics of Postmodernity*, London: UCL Press.

Blascovich, J. and Bailenson, J. (2011), *Infinite Reality: The Hidden Blueprint of our Virtual Lives*, New York: William Morrow.

Blizzard Entertainment (2004–2014), *World of Warcraft*, Irvine, CA: Blizzard Entertainment.

Bloem, J., van Doorn, M., Duivestein, S. and Leyden, P. (2009), *Me the Media. Rise of the Conversation Society*, Amsterdam: UitgeverijkleineUil.

Bloom, P. (2004), *Descartes' Baby: How the Science of Child Development Explains what Makes Us Human*, New York: Basic Books.

Bobkowski, P. (2008), 'An Analysis of Religious Identity Presentation on Facebook', *Conference Papers – International Communication Association*, 1–24, Montreal: International Communication Association.

Boellstorff, T. (2006), 'A Ludicrous Discipline? Ethnography and Game Studies', *Games & Culture*, 1(1): 29–35.

Boellstorff, T. (2008), *Coming of Age in Second Life*, Princeton: Princeton University Press.

Boellstorff, T., Nardi, B., Pearce, C. and Taylor, T. L. (eds) (2012), *Ethnography and Virtual Worlds: A Handbook of Method*, Princeton: Princeton University Press.

Bogost, I. (2007), *Persuasive Games: The Expressive Power of Video Games*, London: MIT.

Bolter, J. D. and Grusin, R. (2000), *Remediation. Understanding New Media*, Cambridge, MA: The MIT Press.

Bonine, S. (1995), 'First call for votes (of 2) moderated group soc.religion.sikhism' [Google groups]. Available online: https://groups.google.com/group/soc.culture.punjab/msg/a937a21846729531?hl=am [accessed 12 November 2011].

Bouteldja, N. (2014), 'France vs England', in E. Brems, (ed.) *The Experiences of Face Veil Wearers in Europe and the Law*, 115–60, Cambridge: Cambridge University Press.

Brabham, D. C. (2008), 'Crowdsourcing as a Model for Problem Solving: An Introduction and Cases', *Convergence*, 14(1): 75–90.

Bradburn, N., Sudman, S. and Wansink, B. (2004), *Asking Questions: The Definitive Guide to Questionaire Design – For Market Research, Political Polls and Social and Health Questionaire*, San Francisco: Jossey-Bass.

Brannen, J. (2005), 'Mixing Methods: The Entry of Qualitative and Quantitative Approaches into the Research Process', *International Journal of Social Research Methodology*, 8(3): 173–84.

Brasher, B. (2001), *Give Me That Online Religion*, San Francisco: Jossey-Bass.

Brooks, C. R. (1989), *The Hare Krishnas in India*, Princeton: Princeton University Press.

Brummans, B. H. J. M., Hwang, J. M. and Cheong, P. H. (2013), 'Mindful Authoring through Invocation: Leaders' Constitution of a Spiritual Organization', *Management Communication Quarterly*, 27(3): 346–72.

Bryant, Christopher G. A. (1990), ' "Tales of Innocence and Experience": Developments in Sociological Theory Since 1950', in H. A. Becker and C. G. A. Bryant (eds), *What has Sociology Achieved?*, London: Sage, pp. 69–93.

Bryman, A. (2001), *Social Research Methods*, Oxford, UK: Oxford University Press.

Bryman, A. (2004), *Social Research Methods*, 2nd edn, Oxford: Oxford University Press.

Bryman, A. (2008), *Social Research Methods*, 3rd edn, Oxford: Oxford University Press.

Buchanan, E. A. (2011), 'Internet Research Ethics: Past, Present, and Future', in M. Consalvo and Ch. Ess (eds), *The Handbook of Internet Studies*, Oxford: Wiley-Blackwell, pp. 83–108.

Buhrmest, M., Kwang, T. and Gosling, S. D. (2011), 'Amazon's Mechanical Turk: A New Source of Cheap, yet High-Quality Data?', *Perspectives on Psychological Science*, 6: 3–5.

Bunt, G. (2009), *iMuslims: Rewiring the House of Islam*, Chapel Hill: The University of North Carolina Press.

Burawoy, M. (2003), 'Revisits: An Outline of a Theory of Reflexive Ethnography', *American Sociological Review*, 68(5): 645–79.

Caillois, R. (1958), *Man, Play and Games*, Paris: Librairie Gallimard.

Caldas-Coulthard, C. and Coulthard, M.(1996), *Texts and Practices: Readings in Critical Discourse Analysis*, London: Taylor and Francis.

Calleja, G. (2007), 'Digital Game Involvement. A Conceptual Model', *Games and Culture*, 2(3): 236–60.

Cameron, L. and Maslen, R. (eds) (2010), *Metaphor Analysis: Research Practice in Applied Linguistics, Social Sciences and the Humanities*, London: Equinox.

Campbell, H. (2003), 'Congregation of the Disembodied', in M. Wolf (ed.), *Virtual Morality*, London: Peter Lang Publishing, pp. 179–99.

Campbell, H. (2005), *Exploring Religious Community Online, We Are One in the Network*, New York: Peter Lang Publishing.

Campbell, H. (2007), 'Who's Got the Power? Religious Authority and the Internet', *Journal of Computer-Mediated Communication*. Available online: http://onlinelibrary.wiley.com/doi/10.1111/j.1083-6101.2007.00362.x/full [accessed 26 June 2015].

Campbell, H. A. (2010), *When Religion Meets New Media*, London: Routledge.

Campbell, H. A. (2011), 'Internet and Religion', in M. Consalvo and C. Ess (eds), *The Handbook of Internet Studies*, Chichester: Wiley-Blackwell, pp. 232–50.

Campbell, H. A. (2012), 'Understanding the Relationship Between Religion Online and Offline in a Networked Society', *Journal of the American Academy of Religion*, 80(1): 64–93.

Campbell, H. (2013), *Digital Religion: Understanding Religious Practice in New Media Worlds*, London: Routledge.

Campbell, H. and DeLashmutt, M. (2013), 'Studying Technology & Ecclesiology in Online Multi-site Worship', *Journal of Contemporary Religion*, 29(2): 267–85.

Campbell, H. and Golan, O. (2011), 'Creating Digital Enclaves: Negotiation of the Internet Amongst Bounded Religious Community', *Media, Culture & Society*, 33(5): 709–24.

Campbell, H. and Grieve, P. (eds) (2014), Playing *with Religion in Digital Games*, Bloomington: Indiana University Press.

Campbell, H. A. and La Pastina, A. C. (2010), 'How the iPhone Became Divine: New Media, Religion and the Intertextual Circulation of Meaning', *New Media & Society*, 12(7): 1191–207.

Campbell, H. and Lövheim, M. (2011), 'Rethinking the Online-Offline Connection in Religion Online', *Information, Communication & Society*, 18(4): 1083–96.

Cantoni, L. and Tardini, S. (2003), *Internet*, New York: Routledge.

Cantoni, L. and Zyga, S. (2007), 'The Use of Internet Communication by Catholic Congregations: A Quantitative Study', *Journal of Media and Religion*, 6(4): 291–309.

Cantoni, L., Di Blas, N. and Bolchini, D. (2003), *Comunicazione, qualità, usabilità*, Milan: Apogeo.

Carrillo Masso, I. (2009), 'Developing a Methodology for Corpus-based Computer Game Studies', *Journal of Gaming & Virtual Worlds*, 1(2): 143–69.

Carrillo Masso, I. (2010), 'The Grips of Fantasy: Computer Games Characters in and Beyond Fictional Worlds', in A. Ensslin and E. Muse (eds), *Creating Second Lives: Reading and Writing Virtual Communities*, London: Routledge.

Carrillo Masso, I. (2015), *Towards a Unified Approach to the Study of PC Games* [PhD Thesis], Bangor: Bangor University.

Carrillo Masso, I. and Abrams, N. (2014), 'Locating the Pixelated Jew: A Multi-Modal Method for Exploring Judaism in *The Shivah*', in H. Campbell and P. Grieve (eds), *Playing with Religion in Digital Games*, Bloomington: Indiana University Press, pp. 47–65.

Castronova, E. (2005), *Play Between Worlds: The Business and Culture of Computer Games*, Chicago: Chicago University Press.

Central Intelligence Agency (2014), *The World Factbook*, https://www.cia.gov/library/publications/the-world-factbook/geos/in.html [accessed 18 May 2014].

Cesari, J. (2005), 'Mosques in French Cities: Towards the End of a Conflict?', *Journal of Ethnic and Migration Studies*, 31(6): 1025–43.

Chakraborti, N. and Zempi, I. (2013), 'Criminalising Oppression or Reinforcing Oppression? The Implications of Veil Ban Laws for Muslim Women in the West', *Northern Ireland Law Quarterly*, 62(1): 63–74.

Chama, J. (1996), 'Finding God on the Web', *Time Magazine*, 149(1), 16 December, 52–59. Available online: http://www.time.com/time/magazine/article/0,9171,985700,00.html [accessed 16 January 2015].

Chaput, M., Brummans, B. H. J. M. and Cooren, F. (2011), 'The Role of Organizational Identification in the Communicative Constitution of an Organization: A Study of Consubstantialization in a Young Political Party', *Management Communication Quarterly*, 25(2): 252–82.

Cheong, P. H. and Ess, C. (2012), 'Religion 2.0? Relational and Hybridizing Pathways in Religion, Social Media and Culture', in P. H. Cheong, P. Fischer-Nielsen, P. S. Gelfgren, and C. Ess (eds), *Digital Religion, Social Media and Culture: Perspectives, Practices, Futures*, New York: Peter Lang, pp. 1–24.

Cheong, P. H. and Poon, J. P. H. (2009), 'Weaving Webs of Faith: Examining Internet Use and Religious Communication among Chinese Protestant Transmigrants', *Journal of International and Intercultural Communication*, 2(3): 189–207.

Cheong, P. H., Huang, S. H. and Poon, J. P. H. (2011a), 'Religious Communication and Epistemic Authority of Leaders in Wired Faith Organizations', *Journal of Communication*, 61(5): 938–58.

Cheong, P. H., Huang, S. H. and Poon, J. P. H. (2011b), 'Cultivating Online and Offline Pathways to Enlightenment: Religious Authority in Wired Buddhist Organizations', *Information, Communication & Society*, 14(8): 1160–80.

Cheong, P. H., Hwang, J. M. and Brummans, B. H. J. M. (2014), 'Transnational Immanence: The Autopoietic Co-Constitution of a Chinese Spiritual Organization through Mediated Communication', *Information, Communication & Society*, 17(1): 7–25.

Cheong, P. H., Poon, J. P. H., Huang, S. H. and Casas, I. (2009), 'The Internet Highway and Religious Communities: Mapping and Contesting Spaces in Religion-Online', *The Information Society*, 25(5): 291–302.

Cheong, P. H., Fisher-Nielsen, P., Gelfren, S and Ess, Ch. (eds) (2012), *Digital Religion, Social Media and Culture. Perspectives, Practices and Futures*, New York: Peter Lang.

Cheruvallil-Contractor, S. (2012), *Muslim Women in Britain: De-mystifying the Muslimah*, London and New York: Routledge.

Cheruvallil-Contractor, S. (2013), 'Online Sufism – Young British Muslims, their Internet "Selves" and Virtual Reality', in T. Gabriel and R. Geaves (eds), *Sufism in Britain*, London: Continuum, pp. 161–76.

Cheruvallil-Contractor, S., Hooley, T., Moore, N., Purdam, K. and Weller, P. (2013), 'Researching the Non-Religious: Methods and Methodological Issues, Challenges and Controversies', in A. Day, G. Vincett and C. Cotter (eds), *Social Identities Between the Sacred and the Secular*, Aldershot: Ashgate, pp. 173–89.

Ciolek, M. T. (2004), 'Online Religion: The Internet and Religion', in H. Bidgoli (ed.), *The Internet Encyclopedia*, Hoboken, NJ: John Wiley & Sons, Inc., pp. 798–811.

Clarke, S. (2003), *Social Theory, Psychoanalysis and Racism*, London, UK: Palgrave.

Cobb, J. (1998), *Cybergrace, The Search for God in the Digital World*, New York: Crown Publishers.

Cobley, P. and Jansz, L. (1997), *Semiotics for Beginners*, London: Totem Books.

Commission on British Muslims & Islamophobia (1997), *Islamophobia: A Challenge for Us All; Report of the Runnymede Trust Commission on British Muslims and Islamophobia*, London, UK: Runnymede Trust.

Computer History Museum (n.d.), 'Complete Concordance of the Revised Standard Version Bible'. Available online: http://www.computerhistory.org/revolution/early-computer-companies/5/100/453 [accessed 15 February 2015].

Comte, A. (1883), *The Catechism of Positive Religion*, London: Trübner.

Connor, K. M., Davidson, J. R.T., and Lee, L.-C. (2003), 'Spirituality, Resilience, and Anger in Survivors of Violent Trauma: A Community Survey', *Journal of Traumatic Stress*, 16(5): 487–94.

Consalvo, M. and Ess, C. (2011), 'Introduction: "What is Internet Studies"?', in M. Consalvo and C. Ess (eds), *The Handbook of Internet Studies*, Chichester: John Wiley and Sons Ltd., pp. 1–8.

ConverJent (2013), *Jewish Time Jump*. New York: JTJNY.

Converse P. D., Wolfe E. W., Huang, X. and Oswald, F. L. (2008), 'Response Rates for Mixed-Mode Surveys Using Mail and E-mail/Web', *American Journal of Evaluation*, 29(1): 99–107.

Copsey, N., Dack, J., Littler, M. and Feldman, M. (2013), 'Anti-Muslim Hate Crime and the Far Right'. Centre for Fascist, Anti-Fascist and Post-Fascist Studies, Teeside University.

Corneliussen, H. G. and Rettberg, J. Walker (eds) (2008), *Digital Culture, Play and Identity: A World of Warcraft Reader*, Cambridge, MA: MIT Press.

Couldry, N. (2012), *Media, Society, World: Social Theory and Digital Media Practice*, London: Polity.

Couper, M. (2000), 'Review: Web Surveys: A Review of Issues and Approaches', *Public Opin Q*, 64(4): 464–94.

Couper, M. P. (2008), *Designing Effective Web Surveys*, Cambridge: Cambridge University Press.

Cowan, D. (2005), *Cyberhendge: Modern Pagans on the Internet*, New York: Routledge.

Craib, I. (1992), *Modern Social Theory – From Parsons to Habermas*, Hemel Hempstead: Harvester Wheatsheaf.

Culpeper, J. (2011), *Impoliteness*, Cambridge: Cambridge University Press.

Davidson, J. R. T. and Lee, L.-C. (2003), 'Spirituality, Resilience, and Anger in Survivors of Violent Trauma: A Community Survey', *Journal of Traumatic Stress*, 16(5): 487–94.

Dawkins, R. (2006), *The God Delusion*, Boston: Houghton Mifflin.

Dawson, L. and Cowan, D. (2004), *Religion Online: Finding Faith on the Internet*, London: Routledge.

Dawson, L. L. and Hennebry, J. (1999), 'New Religions and the Internet: Recruiting in a New Public Space', *Journal of Contemporary Religion*, 14(1): 17–39.

Deacy, C. and Arweck, E. (eds) (2009), *Exploring Religion and the Sacred in a Media Age*, Farnham: Ashgate.

Deakin, H. and Wakefield, K. (2014), 'Skype Interviewing: Reflections of Two PhD Researchers', *Qualitative Research*, 14(5): 603–16.

Dennett, D. C. (1995), *Darwin's Dangerous Idea*, New York: Simon and Schuster.

Denscombe, M. (2007), *The Good Research Guide: For Small-Scale Social Research Projects*, 3rd edn, Milton Keynes: Open University Press.

Denzin, N. (1997), *Interpretive Ethnography: Ethnographic Practices for the 21st Century*, Thousand Oaks, CA: Sage.

Dewey, J. (1958), *Experience and Nature*, Mineola: Dover Publications.

Diener, E. and Crandell, R. (1978), *Ethics in Social and Behavioural Research*, Chicago: University of Chicago Press.

Dillman, D. A., Tortora, R. D. and Bowker, D. (1998), *Principles for Constructing Web Surveys*, SESRC Technical Report.

Dillman, D. A., Phelps, G., Tortora, R., Swift, K., Kohrell, J., Berck, J. and Messer, B. L. (2009), 'Response Rate and Measurement Differences in Mixed-Mode Surveys Using Mail, Telephone, Interactive Voice Response (IVR) and the Internet', *Social Science Research*, 38(1): 1–18.

Dirksen, V., Huizing, A. and Smit, B. J. (2010), ' "Piling on Layers of Understanding": The Use of Connective Ethnography for the Study of (Online) Work Practices', *New Media & Society*, 12(7): 1045–63.

Dolnicar S., Laesser, C. and Matus, K. (2009), 'Online versus Paper', *Journal of Travel Research*, 47(3): 295–316.

Doniger, W. (2009), *The Hindus – An Alternative History*, New York: The Penguin Press.

Dovey, J. and Kennedy, H. W. (2006), *Game Cultures: Computer Games as New Media*, Maidenhead: Open University Press.

Ducheneaut, N., Yee, N., Nickell, E. and Moore, R. J. (2007), 'The Life and Death of Online Gaming Communities: A Look at Guilds in *World of Warcraft*', in *Proceedings of the SIGCHI Conference on Human Factors in Computing Systems*, New York: ACM, pp. 839–48.

Duhé, S (ed.) (2007), *New Media and Public Relations*, New York: Peter Lang.

Duncan, D. F., White, J. B. and Nicholson, T. (2003), 'Using Internet-based Surveys to Reach Hidden Populations: Case of Nonabusive Illicit Drug Users', *American Journal of Health Behavior*, 27(3): 208–18.

Economic and Social Research Council (ESRC) (2010), *Framework for Research Ethics (FRE)*, Swindon: ESRC.

Edwards, R. and Mauthner, M. (2002), 'Ethics and Feminist Research: Theory and Practice', in M. L. Mauthner, M. Birch, J. Jessop and T. Mille (eds), *Ethics in Qualitative Research*, London: Sage, pp. 14–31.

Elber, L. (1997, April 23). *Putting Faith in Film. Hollywood Takes Back-door Approach to Religion*. Online. Available at http://www.s-t.com/daily/04-97/04-23-97/c04ae124.htm, pp. 1-2.

Electronic Arts (2006–2007), *The Godfather*, Redwood City: Visceral Games.

Elm, M. S., Buchanan, E. A. and Stern, S. R.(2009), 'How do Various Notions of Privacy Influence Decisions in Qualitative Internet Research?' in Markham, A. N. and Nancy K. Baym (eds) *Internet Inquiry: Conversations About Method*, London: Sage, 70–98.

El-Nawawy, M. and Khamis, S. (2009), *Islam Dot Com: Contemporary Islamic Discourses in Cyberspace*, New York: Palgrave Macmillan, p. 3.

England, K. (1994), 'Getting Personal: Reflexivity, Positionality, and Feminist Research', *The Professional Geographer*, 46(1): 80–89.

Ensslin, A. (2010), 'Black and White: Language Ideologies in Computer Game Discourse', in S. Johnson and T. Milani (eds), *Language Ideologies and Media Discourse: Texts, Practices, Policies*, London: Continuum, pp. 205–22.

Ensslin, A. and Carrillo Masso, I. (2010), 'The Language of Gaming: Towards a Critical Discourse Analytical Approach', in *CADAAD 2010: Ideology, Identity and Interaction*, Lodz University, Poland, 13–15 September 2010.

Ess, C. (2004), 'Revolution? What Revolution? Successes and Limits of Computing Technologies in Philosophy and Religion', in S. Schreibman, R. Siemens and J. Unsworth (eds), *A Companion to Digital Humanities*, Oxford: Blackwell. Available online: http://www.digitalhumanities.org/companion/ [accessed 15 February 2015].

Ess & AoIR Ethics Working Committee (2002), 'Ethical Decision Making and Internet Research: Recommendations from the AoIR Ethics Working Committee. Available online: http://www.aoir.org/reports/ethics.pdf [accessed 14 July 2015].

Evans, J. R. and Mathur, A. (2005), 'The Value of Online Surveys', *Internet Research*, 15(2): 195–219.

Fairclough, N. (2003), *Analysing Discourse: Textual Analysis for Social Research*, London: Routledge.

Fairclough, N. (2004), *An Introduction to Critical Discourse Analysis in Education*, in R. Rogers (ed.), New Jersey: Lawrence Erlbaum, pp. 225–36 12p.

Fairclough, N. (2005), *A New Agenda in (Critical) Discourse Analysis*, in R. Wodak and P. Chilton (eds), 13 ed. Amsterdam: John Benjamins, pp. 53–70 18p.

Fairhurst, G. T. and Cooren, F. (2009), 'Charismatic Leadership and the Hybrid Production of Presence(s)', *Leadership*, 5: 1–22.

Fang, J., Shao, P. and Lan, G. (2009), 'Effects of Innovativeness and Trust on Web Survey Participation', *Computers in Human Behavior*, 25(1): 144–52.

Fernback, J. (2002), 'Internet Ritual: A Case of the Construction of Computer-Mediated Neopagan Religious Meaning', in S. Hoover and L. Scofield Clark (eds), *Practicing Religion in the Age of Media*, New York: Columbia University Press, pp. 254–75.

Ferrari, A. and Pastorelli, S. (eds) (2013), *Burqa Affair Across Europe: Between Public and Private Space*, London: Ashgate.

Finke, R. (1997), 'The Consequence of Religious Competition – Supply-Side Explanations for Religious Change', in Lawrence A. Young (ed.), *Rational Choice Theory and Religion – Summary and Assessment*, New York/London: Routledge, pp. 46–61.

Fleming, C. M. and Bowden, M. (2009), 'Web-based Surveys as an Alternative to Traditional Mail Methods', *Journal of Environmental Management*, 90(1): 284–92.

Fortes, M. (1961), 'Pietas in Ancestor Worship', *Journal of the Royal Anthropological Institute of Great Britain and Ireland*, 91(2): 166–91.

Fowler, F. J. (1995), *Improving Survey Questions: Design and Evaluation*, London: Sage.

Fowler, R. and Kress, G. (1979), 'Critical Linguistics', in R. Fowler et al (eds), *Language and Control*, London: Routledge and Kegan Paul, pp. 185–213.

Franks, M. (2001), *Women and Revivalism in the West: Choosing 'Fundamentalism' in a Liberal Democracy*, London: Palgrave Macmillan.

Frasca, G. (2003), 'Simulation Vs Narrative: Introduction to Ludology', in M. J. P. Wolf and B. Perron (eds), *The Video Game Theory Reader*, New York: Routledge.

Freud, Sigmund (1928), *The Future of an Illusion*, New York: H. Liveright.

Fuller, C. J. (1992), *The Camphor Flame – Popular Hinduism and Society in India*, Princeton: Princeton University Press.

Furseth, I. and Repstad, P. (2006), *An Introduction to the Sociology of Religion: Classical and Contemporary Perspectives*, Farnham: Ashgate.

G5 Sikh Media (n.d.), Shop [www]. Available at: http://g5sikhmedia.co.uk/index.php?option=com_virtuemart&Itemid=2&vmcchk=1&Itemid=2 [accessed 23 December 2011].

Gale, R. (2005), 'Representing the City: Mosques and the Planning Process in Birmingham', *Journal of Ethnic and Migration Studies*, 31(6): 1161–79.

Gatenby, B. and Humphries, M. (2000), 'Feminist Participatory Action Research: Methodological and Ethical Issues', *Women's Studies International Forum*, 23(1): 89–105.

Geyer, D. (1914), *The Pragmatic Theory of Truth as Developed by Peirce, James, and Dewey*, Illinois: University of Illinois.

Ghorashi, H. (2010), 'Culturalist Approach to Women's Emancipation in the Netherlands', in H. Moghissi and H. Ghorashi (eds), *Muslim Diaspora in the West: Negotiating Gender, Home and Belonging*, London: Ashgate, pp. 11–22.

Giddens, A. (1990), *The Consequences of Modernity*, Cambridge: Polity.

Giddings, S. (2008), 'Events and Collusions: A Glossary for the Microethnography of Video Game Play', *Games and Culture*, 4(2): 144–57.

Göle, N. (2011), 'The Public Visibility of Islam and European Politics of Resentment: The Minarets-Mosques Debate', *Philosophy & Social Criticism*, 37(4): 383–92.

Goodman, J. K., Cryder, C. E. and Cheema, A. (2012), 'Data Collection in a Flat World: The Strengths and Weaknesses of Mechanical Turk Samples', *Journal of Behavioral Decision Making*, 26: 213–24.

Google author (n.d.), 'How Search Works'. Available online: http://static.googleusercontent.com/external_content/untrusted_dlcp/www.google.com/en//intl/en/insidesearch/howsearchworks/assets/searchInfographic.pdf [accessed 24 September 2013].

Gorelick, S. (1991), 'Contradictions of Feminist Methodology', *Gender and Society*, 5(4): 459–77.

Gosling, S. D., Vazire, S., Srivastava, S. and John, O. P. (2004),' Should We Trust Web-Based Studies? A Comparative Analysis of Six Preconceptions about Internet Questionnaires', *The American Psychologist*, 59(2): 93–104.

Gottlieb, O. (2013), 'What was Isaac Thinking? What's Going Through Abraham's Head? What's Going On in the Great Mind of God?', in J. Johnson (ed.) *Is there a Jewish Identity in Video Games?* Available online: http://killscreendaily.com/articles/there-jewish-identity-videogames/ [accessed 5 May 2015].

Grieve, Gregory Price (2010), 'Virtually Embodying the Field – Silent Online Buddhist Meditation, Immersion, and the Cardean Ethnographic Method', *Online – Heidelberg Journal of Religions on the Internet*, 4(1): 35–62.

Grodal, T. (2003), 'Stories for Eye, Ear and Muscles: Video Games, Media and Embodied Experiences', in M. J. P. Wolf and B. Perron (eds), *The Video Game Theory Reader*, New York: Routledge, pp. 129–56.

Groves, R. M., Fowler, F. J., Couper, M. P., Lepkowski, J. M., Singer, E. and Tourangeau, R. (2009), *Survey Methodology*, 2nd edn, Hoboken, NJ: John Wiley and Sons.

Guest, K. J. (2003), *God in Chinatown: Religion and Survival in New York's Evolving Immigrant Community*, New York: New York University Press.

Gunter, B. (2009), 'Blogging – Private becomes Public and Public becomes Personalised', *Aslib Proceedings*, 61(2): 120–26.

Gurak, L. J. and Logie, J. (2003), 'Internet Protests, from Text to Web', in M. McCaughey and M. D. Ayers (eds), *Cyberactivism: Online Activism in Theory and Practice*, London, UK: Routledge, pp. 25–46.

Hadden, J. K. and Cowan, D. E. (eds) (2000), *Religion on the Internet, Research Prospects and Promises*, Amsterdam, London and New York: JAI Press.

Hafner, K. and Lyon, M. (1996), *Where Wizards Stay Up Late: Origins of the Internet*, New York: Simon and Schuster.

Hakken, D. (1999), *Cyborg@cyberspace: An Ethnographer Looks at the Future*, London: Routledge.

Halliday, M. A. K. (1989), *Spoken and Written Language*, Oxford: Oxford University Press.

Hammersley, M. and Atkinson, P. (2007), *Ethnography: Principles in Practice*, London: Taylor & Francis.

Hanna, P. (2012), 'Using Internet Technologies (such as Skype) as a Research Medium: A Research Note', *Qualitative Research*, 12(2): 239–42.

Haraway, D. (1988), 'Situated Knowledges: The Science Question in Feminism and Privilege of Partial Perspective', *Feminist Studies*, 14(3): 575–99.

Hardt-Mautner, G. (1995), 'Only Connect: Critical Discourse Analysis and Corpus Linguistics, in Papers of the English Language Institute, Wien: Austria' Available online: http://ucrel.lancs.uk/papers/techpaper/vol6.pdf [accessed 5 May 2015].

Hargittai, E. (2007), 'The Social, Political, Economic, and Cultural Dimensions of Search Engines: An Introduction', *Journal of Computer-Mediated Communication*, 12(3): 769–77.

Harré, R. and Van Langenhove, L. (1998), *Positioning Theory: Moral Contexts of Intentional Action*, London: Blackwell Publishers.

Harrison, J., MacGibbon, L., and Morton, M. (2001), 'Regimes of Trustworthiness in Qualitative Research: The Rigors of Reciprocity', *Qualitative Inquiry*, 7(3): 323–45.

Hart, T. (ed.) (2005), *Nonprofit Internet Strategies*, Hoboken, NJ: John Wiley & Sons.

Haughey, R. and Campbell, H. (2013), 'Modern-day Martyrs: Fans' Online Reconstruction of Celebrities as Divine', in D. Herbert, A. Greenhill and M. Gillespie (eds), *Social Media, Religion and Spirituality*, Berlin: De Gruyters, pp. 103–20.

Haw, K. (1996),'Exploring the Educational Experiences of Muslim Girls: Tales Told to Tourists–Should the White Researcher Stay at Home?' *British Educational Research Journal*, 22(3): 319–30.

Haw, K. (2009), 'From Hijab to Jilbab and the "Myth" of British Identity: Being Muslim in Contemporary Britain a Half-generation On', *Race Ethnicity and Education*, 12(3): 363–78.

Heckathorn, D. D. (1997), 'Respondent-Driven Sampling: A New Approach to the Study of Hidden Populations', *Social Problem*, 44(2).

Heidbrink, S., Knoll, T. and Wysocki, J. (2014), 'Theorizing Religion in Digital Games: Perspectives and Approaches', in S. Heidbrink and T. Knoll (eds), *Religion in Digital Games. Multiperspective and Interdisciplinary Approaches. Online – Heidelberg Journal of Religions on the Internet*, 5: 5–50. Available online: http://journals.ub.uni-heidelberg.de/index.php/religions/article/view/12156 [accessed 19 February 2015].

Heidbrink, S., Knoll, T. and Wysocki, J. (2015), ' "Venturing into the Unknown"(?) Method(olog)ical Reflections on Religion and Digital Games, Gamers and Gaming', in S. Heidbrink, T. Knoll and J. Wysocki (eds), *Religion in Digital Games Reloaded. Immersion into the Field. Online – Heidelberg Journal of Religions on the Internet*, 7: 61–84. Available online: http://journals.ub.uni-heidelberg.de/index.php/religions/article/view/18508 [accessed 19 February 2015].

Helland, C. (2000), 'Online-religion/Religion-online and Virtual Communitas', in J. K. Hadden and D. E. Cowan (eds), *Religion on the Internet: Research Prospects and Promises*, New York: JAI Press, pp. 205–33.

Helland, C. (2007), 'Diaspora on the Electronic Frontier: Developing Virtual Connections within Sacred Homelands', *Journal of Computer-Mediated Communication*, 12(3). Available online: http:onlinelibrary.wiley.com/doi/10.1111.j1083-6101.2007.00358.x/full (accessed 26 June 2015).

Helland, C. (2013), 'Ritual', in H. A. Campbell (ed.), *Digital Religion – Understanding Religious Practice in New Media Worlds*, Abingdon: Routledge, pp. 25–40.

Heller, M. (2009), 'Media, the State and Linguistic Authority', in S. Johnson and T. Milani (eds), *Language Ideologies and Media Discourse: Texts, Practices, Policies*, London: Continuum, pp. 277–82.

Helman, N. (2004), 'Yes, But Is It a Game?', in S. Compton (ed.), *Gamers: Writers, Critics and Programmers on the Pleasures of Pixels*, Brooklyn: Soft Skull Press, pp. 225–38.

Hendricks, J. (2006), *Neither Here Nor There: Identity Negotiation and Community Creation Among Qur'an only Muslims on the Internet*, Columbia, MO: University of Missouri Press.

Hercheui, M. D. (2011), 'A Literature Review of Virtual Communities: The Relevance of Understanding the Influence of Institutions on Online Collectives', *Information, Communication & Society*, 14(1): 1–13.

Herring, S. (2004), 'Slouching Toward the Ordinary: Current Trends in Computer-mediated Communication', *New Media and Society*, 6: 26–36.

Hewson, C., Yule, P., Laurent, D. and Vogel, C. (2003), *Internet Research Methods: A Practical Guide for the Behavioural and Social Sciences*, London, UK: Sage.

Hey, V. (1997), *The Company She Keeps: An Ethnography of Girls' Friendships*, Buckingham: Open University Press.

Hezbollah (2003), *Special Force (Hezbollah)*, Hezbollah.

Hine, C. (2007), 'Connective Ethnography for the Exploration of e-Science', *Journal of Computer-Mediated Communication*, 12: 618–34.

Hine, C. (2012), *The Internet. Understanding Qualitative Research*, Oxford: Oxford University Press.

Hine, C. (2015), *Ethnography for the Internet: Embedded, Embodied and Everyday*, London: Bloomsbury.

Ho, S. S., Lee, W. and Hameed, S. S. (2008), 'Muslim Surfers on the Internet: Using the Theory of Planned Behaviour to Examine the Factors Influencing Engagement in Online Religious Activities', *New Media and Society*, 10(1): 93–113.

Hock, R. (2005), *Yahoo! to the Max: An Extreme Searcher Guide*, New Jersey: Information Today, Inc.

Hojsgaard, M. and Warburg, M. (eds) (2005), *Religion and Cyberspace*, London: Routledge.

Hojsgaard, M. and Warburg, M. (2005), 'Introduction: Waves of Research', in M. Hojsgaard and M. Warburg (eds), *Religion and Cyberspace*, London: Routledge, pp. 1–11.

Holt, A. (2010), 'Using the Telephone for Narrative Interviewing: A Research Note', *Qualitative Research*, 10(1): 113–21.

Hooley, T., Marriott, J. and Wellens, J. (2012), *What is Online Research?* London: Bloomsbury.

Horton, J. J., Rand, D. G. and Zeckhauser, R. J. (2011), 'The Online Laboratory: Conducting Experiments in a Real Labor Market', *Experimental Economics*, 14: 399–425.

Housley, W. and Fitzgerald, R. (2002), 'The Reconsidered Model of Membership Categorization Analysis', *Qualitative Research*, 2: 59–83.

Houston, G. (1998), *Virtual Morality*, Leicester: Apollos.

Huang, C. J. (2009), *Charisma and Compassion: Cheng Yen and the Buddhist Tzu Chi Movement*, Cambridge, MA: Harvard University Press.

Huberman, M. A. and Miles, M. B. (1994), 'Data Management and Analysis Methods', in N. K. Denzin and Y. S. Lincoln (eds), *Handbook of Qualitative Research*, Thousand Oaks, CA: Sage, pp. 428–44.

Huberman, M. and Miles, M. (2002), *The Qualitative Researcher's Companion*, London: Sage.

Hunston, S. (2002), *Corpora in Applied Linguistics*, Cambridge: Cambridge University Press.

Hutchings, T. (2011), 'Contemporary Religious Community and the Online Church', *Information, Communication and Society*, 14(18): 1118–35.

Hutchings, T. (2012), 'I Am Second: Evangelicals and Digital Storytelling', *Australian Journal of Communication*, 39(1): 73–88.

Hutchings, T. (2014), 'Now the Bible is an App: Digital Media and Changing Patterns of Religious Authority', in K. Granholm, M. Moberg and Sofia Sjö (eds), *Religion, Media and Social Change*, Abingdon: Routledge, pp. 143–61.

Iannaccone, Laurence R. (1995), 'Voodoo Economics? Reviewing the Rational Choice Approach to Religion', *Journal for the Scientific Study of Religion*, 34(1): 76–89.

Illingworth, N. (2001), 'The Internet Matters: Exploring the Use of the Internet as a Research Tool', *Sociological Research Online*, 6(2). Available online: https://ideas.repec.org/a/sro/srosro/2001-24-2.html#biblio [accessed 16 July 2015].

INSTED (2007), *The Search for Common Ground Muslims, Non-Muslims and the UK Media*, London, UK: GLA.

Ipeirotis, P. (2009), Turker Demographics vs. Internet Demographics. Available online: http://www.behind-the-enemy-lines.com/2009/03/turker-demographics-vs-internet.html [accessed 26 June 2015].

Ipeirotis, P. (2010), Demographics of Mechanical Turk (CeDER Working Paper-10-01), New York University. Retrieved from http://hdl.handle.net/2451/29585 [last accessed 26 June 2015].

Irizarry, J. A. and Irizarry, I. T. (2014), 'The Lord is my Shepard: Confronting Religion in the Mass Effect Trilogy', in S. Heidbrink and T. Knoll (eds), *Religion in Digital Games. Multiperspective and Interdisciplinary Approaches. Online – Heidelberg Journal of Religions on the Internet*, 5: 207–26. Available online: http://journals.ub.uni-heidelberg.de/index.php/religions/article/view/12168 [accessed 19 February 2015].

Jacobs, S. (2010), *Hinduism Today*, London: Continuum.

Jakobsh, D. (2006), 'Authority in the Virtual Sangat: Sikhism, Ritual and Identity in the Twenty-First Century', *Online. Heidelberg Journal of Religions on the Internet*, 2(1): 24–40.

Jakobsh, D. (2012), ' "Sikhizing the Sikhs": The Role of "New Media" in Historical and Contemporary Identity Construction within Global Sikhism', in K. Myrvold and K. A. Jacobsen (eds), *Sikhs Across Borders: Transnational Practices of European Sikhs*, London: Continuum, pp. 141–63.

James, N. and Busher, H. (2009), *Online Interviewing*, London: Sage.

James, W. (1916), *Pragmatism: A New Name for Some Old Ways of Thinking*, New York: Longmans.

Jansen, B. J., Tapia, A. and Spink, A. (2010), 'Searching for Salvation: An Analysis of US Religious Searching on the World Wide Web', *Religion*, 40: 39–52.

Jeffery S., Fenn, C., Johnson, B., Smith, E. and Coumbe, J. (2009), 'A People's History of the Internet: From Arpanet in 1969 to Today', *The Guardian*. Available online: http://www.guardian.co.uk/technology/interactive/2009/oct/23/internet-arpanet [accessed 11 December 2011].

Jelen, T. G. (ed.) (2002), *Sacred Markets, Sacred Canopies*, Lanham, MD: Rowman and Littlefield.

Jenkins, H. (2004), 'Game Design as Narrative Architecture', in N. Wardrip-Fruin and P. Harrigan (eds), *First Person: New Media as Story, Performance, and Game*, Cambridge, MA: MIT Press, pp. 118–30.

Jenkins, H. (2006), *Convergence Culture. Where Old and New Media Collide*, New York, London: New York University Press.

Johns, M. D. (2013), 'Ethical Issues in the Study of Religion and New Media', in H. A. Campbell (ed.), *Digital Religion – Understanding Religious Practice in New Media Worlds*, Abingdon: Routledge, pp. 238–50.

Jones, S. (ed.) (1997), *Virtual Culture*, Thousand Oaks, CA: Sage Publications.

Jonker, G. (2005), 'The Mevlana Mosque in Berlin-Kreuzberg: An Unsolved Conflict', *Journal of Ethnic and Migration Studies*, 31(6): 1067–81.

Juul, J. (2002), 'The Open and the Closed: Game of Emergence and Games of Progression', in F. Mäyrä (ed.), *Computer Games and Digital Cultures Conference Proceedings*, Tampere: Tampere University Press, pp. 323–9. Available online: http://www.jesperjuul.net/text/openandtheclosed.html [accessed 19 February 2015].

Juul, J. (2003), *Half-Real: Video Games Between Real Rules and Fictional Worlds*, Cambridge, MA: MIT Press.

Kaveney, R. (2005), *From Alien to Matrix. Reading Science Fiction Film*, London, New York: I.B. Tauris.

Kellems, I. S., Hill, C. E., Crook-Lyon, R. E. and Freitas, G. (2010), 'Working with Clients who Have Religious/Spiritual Issues: A Survey of University Counseling Center Therapists', *Journal of College Student Psychotherapy*, 24(2): 139–55.

Kenny, D. (2001), *Lexis and Creativity in Translation: A Corpus-Based Study*, Manchester: St. Jerome.

Khabra, G. J. S. (2010), *Music of the Sikh Diaspora: Devotional Sounds, Musical Memory and Cultural Identity*. Unpublished M.A. thesis, Cardiff: University of Cardiff.

Khiabany, G. and Williamson, M. (2008), 'UK: The Veil and the Politics of Racism', *Race & Class*, 25(2): 85–96.

Kiesler, S., Siegel, J. and McGuire, T. W. (1984), 'Social Psychological Aspects of Computer-mediated Communication', *American Psychologist*, 39(10): 1123–34.

Kilde, J. H. (2011), 'The Park 51/Ground Zero Controversy and Sacred Sites as Contested Space', *Religions*, 2(3): 297–311.

Kiss, G. (2011), 'Facebook Began as a Geek's Hobby. Now it's More Popular than Google', *The Guardian*, 4 January. Available at: http://www.guardian.co.uk/technology/2011/jan/04/faceboook-mark-zuckerberg-google [accessed 9 December 2011].

Klostermaier, K. (1998), *A Concise Encyclopedia of Hinduism*, Oxford: Oneworld Publications.

Kluver, R. and Cheong, P. H. (2007), 'Technological Modernization, the Internet, and Religion in Singapore', *Journal of Computer-Mediated Communication*, 12(3): 1122–42.

Knoll, T. (2015), ' "Are Those the Only Two Solutions?" Dealing with Choice, Agency and Religion in Digital Games', in S. Heidbrink, T. Knoll and J. Wysocki (eds), *Religion in Digital Games Reloaded. Immersion into the Field. Online – Heidelberg Journal of Religions on the Internet*, 7: 207–26. Available online: http://journals.ub.uni-heidelberg.de/index.php/religions/article/view/18515 [accessed 19 February 2015].

Koch, N. S. and Emrey, J. A. (2001), 'The Internet and Opinion Measurement: Surveying Marginalized Populations', *Social Science Quarterly*, 82(1): 131–8.

Kozinets, R. V. (2006), 'Netnography 2.0', in R. W. Belk (ed.), *Handbook of Qualitative Research Methods in Marketing*, Cheltenham, UK and Northampton, MA: Edward Elgar Publishing, pp. 129–42.

Kress, G. and van Leeuwen, T. (1990), *Reading Images*, Victoria: Deakin University Press.

Kress, G. and van Leeuwen, T. (2006), *Reading Images: The Grammar of Visual Design*, London: Routledge.

Kruger, O. (2005), 'Discovering the Invisible Internet: Methodological Aspects of Searching Religion on the Internet', *Online: Heidelberg Journal of Religion on the Internet*, 1(1). Available online: http://archiv.ub.uni-heidelberg.de/volltextserver/5828/ [last accessed 16 July 2015].

Krzywinska, T. (2006), 'Blood Scythes, Festivals, Quests, and Backstories. World Creation and Rhetorics of Myth in World of Warcraft', *Games and Culture*, 1(4): 383–96. Available online: http://nideffer.net/classes/270-08/week_06_wow/rhetoricsofmyth.pdf [accessed 19 February 2015].

Krzywinska, T. (2008), 'World Creation and Lore: *World of Warcraft* as Rich Text', in H. G. Corneliussen and J. Walker Rettberg (eds), *Digital Culture, Play, and Identity. A World of Warcraft Reader*, Cambridge, MA and London: The MIT Press, pp. 123–41.

Kucklich, J. R. (2009), 'Virtual Worlds and Their Discontents: Precarious Sovereignty, Governmentality, and the Ideology of Play', *Games and Culture*, 4(4): 340–52.

Kurien, Prema A. (2007), *A Place at the Multicultural Table – The Development of an American Hinduism*, New Brunswick, NJ: Rutgers University Press.

Laban, R. (1975), *Laban's Principles of Dance and Movement Notation*, London. MacDonald and Evans.

Lahti, M. (2003), 'As We Become Machines: Corporealized Pleasures in Video Games', in M. J. P. Wolf and B. Perron (eds), *The Video Game Theory Reader*, New York: Routledge, pp. 157–70.

Lando, M. (2007), 'A Rabbi Superhero: The Wacky Premise of a Hit Videogame', *The Jerusalem Post*. Available online: http://www.jpost.com/Jewish-World/Jewish-Features/A-rabbi-as-superhero-the-wacky-premise-of-a-hit-video-game [accessed 1 February 2007].

La Porte, J. M. (ed.) (2009), *Introduzione alla Comunicazione Istituzionale della Chiesa*, Rome: Edusc.

Lastowka, G. (2006), 'Law and Games Studies', *Games and Culture*, 1(1): 25–8.

Lastowka, G. (2010), *Virtual Justice: The New Laws of Online Worlds*, New Haven, CT: Yale University Press.

Le Doeuff, M. (1989), *Hipparchia's Choice – An Essay Concerning Women, Philosophy, Etc.* translated by Trista Selous (1991), New York: Columbia University Press.

Le Doeuff, M. (1998), *The Sex of Knowing*, translated by Kathryn Hammer and Lorraine Code (2003), London: Routledge.

Lee, K. M., Park, N. and Jin, S. A. (2006), 'Narrative and Interactivity in Computer Games', in P. Vorderer and J. Bryant (eds), *Playing Video Games: Motives, Responses and Consequences*, Mahwah, NJ: Lawrence Erlbaum Associates, Inc, 304–22.

Lee, L. (2012), 'Research Note: Talking about a Revolution: Terminology for the New Field of Non-religion Studies', *Journal of Contemporary Religion*, 27(1): 129–39.

Lee, R. M. (2000), *Unobtrusive Methods in Social Research*. Buckingham, UK: Open University Press.

Lemke, J. (2001), 'Semantic Topography and Textual Meaning', in J. de Villiers and R. Stainton (eds), *Communication in Linguistics*, Toronto: Editions du GREF, pp. 237–60.

Lemke, J. (2002), 'Discursive Technologies and the Social Organization of Meaning', *Folia Linguistica*, 35(1–2): 79–96. [Special issue: 'Critical Discourse Analysis and Cognition', R. Wodak, issue editor], 2002.

Leonard, D. J. (2006), 'Not a Hater, Just Keepin' It Real: The Importance of Race-and Gender-Based Game Studies', *Games and Culture*, 1(1): 83–8.

Letherby, G. (2003), *Feminist Research In Theory And Practice*, Buckingham: Open University Press.

Lewis, R. (2007), 'Veils and Sales: Muslims and the Spaces of Postcolonial Fashion Retail', *Fashion Theory: The Journal of Dress, Body & Culture*, 11(4): 423–41.

Limerick, B., Burgess-Limerick, T. and Grace, M. (1996), 'The Politics of Interviewing: Power Relations and Accepting the Gift', *International Journal of Qualitative Studies in Education*, 9(4): 449–60.

Lincoln, Y. S. and Guba, E. G. (1985), *Naturalistic Inquiry*, Newbury Park, CA: Sage.

Lindlof, T. R. and Taylor, B. C. (2002), *Qualitative Communication Research Methods*, 2nd edn, Thousand Oaks, CA: Sage.

Lippert-Rasmussen, K. (2005), *Deontology, Responsibility, and Equality*, Copenhagen: University of Copenhagen Press.

Lövheim, M. (2005), 'Young People and the Use of the Internet as Transitional Space', *Online: Heidelberg Journal of Religions on the Internet*, 1(1). Available online: http://journals.ub. uni-heidelberg.de/index.php/religions/article/view/383 [accessed 26 June 2015].

Luft, Sh. (2014), 'Hardcore Christian Gamers: How Religion Shapes Evangelical Play', in H. Campbell and G. P. Grieve (eds), *Playing with Religion in Digital Games*, Bloomington, IN: Indiana University Press, pp. 154–79.

Lundby, K. (2011), 'Patterns of Belonging in Online/Offline Interfaces of Religion', *Information, Communication and Society*, 14(8): 1219–35.

Maccoby, H. (1988), *Early Rabbinic Writings* (Cambridge Commentaries on Writings of the Jewish and Christian World), Cambridge: Cambridge University Press.

Machin, D. (2007), *Introduction to Multimodal Analysis*, London: Bloomsbury.

Maclaran, P., Broderick, A., Takhar, A. and Parsons, E. (2008), 'The Computer as "Middle agent": Negotiating the Meanings of Marriage on a Sikh Online Dating Site', *European Advances in Consumer Research*, 8: 60–65.

Madge, C., O'Connor, H., Wellens, J., Hooley, T. and Shaw, R. (2006), 'Exploring Online Research Methods, Incorporating TRI–ORM: An Online Research Methods Training Programme for the Social Science Community'. Available online: http://www.restore.ac. uk/orm/ [accessed 28 February 2012].

Marcus, G. (1995), 'Ethnography in/of the World System: The Emergence of Multi-sited Ethnography', *Annual Review of Anthropology*, 24: 95–117.

Marcus, G. E. (1997), 'The Uses of Complicity in the Changing Mise-en-scène of Anthropological Fieldwork', *Representations*, 59: 85–108.

Marcus, G. E. (2001), 'From Rapport Under Erasure to Theaters of Complicit Reflexivity', *Qualitative Inquiry,* 7(4): 519–28.

Markham, A. (1998), *Life Online: Researching Real Experience in Virtual Space*, Plymouth: Altamira Press.

Markham, A. N. and Baym, N. K. (2009), 'Internet Inquiry: Conversations About Method', *Forum Qualitative Sozialforschung/Forum: Qualitative Social Research*, 11(3).

Markham, A. and Buchanan, E. (2012), *Ethical Decision-Making and Internet Research – Recommendations from the AoIR Ethics Working Committee (Version 2.0)*. Available online: http://www.aoir.org/reports/ethics2.pdf [accessed 19 February 2015].

Marriott, M. (1955), 'Little Communities in an Indigenous Civilization', in M. Marriott (ed.), *Village India – Studies in the Little Community*, Chicago: University of Chicago Press, pp. 171–222.

Marsh, J. (2009), *From Seasiders to Casuals United*, Barking, UK: Lulu Publishing.

Martini, P. J. and Springer, V. A. (2014), February. 'Finding Hidden Populations through Online Crowdsourcing Methods'. Poster presented at the Society for Personality and Social Psychology annual conference, Austin: TX.

Martini, P. J., Springer, V. A. and Richardson, J. T. (in press), 'Conducting Population Research Using Online Crowdsourcing: A Comparison of Amazon's Mechanical Turk to Representative National Surveys', *The Journal of Methods and Measurement in the Social Sciences*.

Marx, K. (1913), *The Eighteenth Brumaire of Louis Bonaparte*, Chicago: Charles H. Kerr.

Mason, J. (2002), *Qualitative Researching*, 2nd edn, London: Sage.

Mason, J. (2006), *Qualitative Researching*, London: Sage.

Mason, W. and Suri, S. (2012), 'Conducting Behavioral Research on Amazon's Mechanical Turk', *Behavioral Research Methods*, 44: 1–23.

Matthews, J. and Cramer, E. P. (2008), 'Using Technology Enhance Qualitative Research with Hidden Populations', *The Qualitative Report*, 13(2): 301–15.

Maussen, M. (2004), 'Policy Discourses on Mosques in the Netherlands 1980–2002: Contested Constructions', *Ethical Theory and Moral Practice*, 7(2): 147–62.

McKee, H. A. and Porter, J. E. (2009), *The Ethics of Internet Research: A Rhetorical, Case-based Process* (Vol. 59), New York: Peter Lang Publishing.

McLoughlin, S. (2005), 'Mosques and the Public Space: Conflict and Cooperation in Bradford', *Journal of Ethnic and Migration Studies*, 31(6): 1045–66.

McLuhan, M. (1964), *The Medium is the Message*, New York: Mentor.

McPhee, R. D. and Iverson, J. (2009), 'Agents of Constitution in Communidad', in L. L. Putnam and A. M. Nicotera (eds), *Building Theories of Organization: The Constitutive Role of Communication*, New York, NY: Routledge, pp. 48–87.

McPherson, M., Smith-Lovin, L. and Cook, J. M. (2001), 'Birds of a Feather: Homophily in Social Networks', *Annual Review of Sociology*, 27: 415–44.

Miczek, N. (2008), 'Online Rituals in Virtual Worlds: Christian Online Services between Dynamics and Stability', *Online: Heidelberg Journal of Religions on the Internet*, 3(1). Available online: http://www.journals.ub.uni-heidelberg.de/index.php/religions/article/view/392 [accessed 26 June 2015].

Miller, D. (2012), 'Social Networking Sites', in D. Miller and H. Horst (eds), *Digital Anthropology*, London: Berg, pp. 146–61.

Mishra, P. (17 August 2005), interview conducted at New Vishwanath temple (Mir Ghat), Varanasi, India.

Morey, P. and Yaqin, A. (2011), *Framing Muslims*, Harvard: Harvard University Press.

Mudie, M. (2010), 'Shock as Dudley Mosque Scheme Revived', *Express & Star*, 7 September 2010.

Murray, C. and Sixsmith, J. (1998), 'E-mail: A Qualitative Research Medium for Interviewing?', *International Journal of Social Research Methodology*, 1(2): 103–21.

Murray, J. H. (1997), *Hamlet on the Holodeck. The Future of Narrative in Cyberspace*, New York: Free Press.

Murray, J. H. (2005/2013), *The Last Word on Ludology v Narratology in Game Studies*. Available online: http://inventingthemedium.com/2013/06/28/the-last-word-on-ludology-v-narratology-2005/ [accessed 19 February 2015].

Muslim Defence League (2010) Facebook. Available online: http://www.facebook.com/pages/Muslim-Defence-League-MDL/108912969158686 [accessed 15 August 2010].

Muse, E. (2014), 'Requisite Chance: Requisite Variety as Rhetorical Principle in Procedural Fiction', Bangor: Bangor University.

Nagar, R. (2002), 'Footloose Researchers, "Traveling" Theories, and the Politics of Transnational Feminist Praxis', *Gender, Place and Culture*, 9(2): 179–86.

Narbona, J. (2011), *La comunicación institucional online de las organizaciones nonprofit*, Pontificia Università della Santa Croce, Rome.

Narbona, J. (2014), 'El online communication model: un marco teórico para analizar la comunicación institucional en internet', in A. Bailly-Bailliere and J. Milán (eds), *Church Communications: Faces, People, Stories* (Proceedings of the 8th Professional Seminar for Church Communications Offices), Rome: Edusc, pp. 275–84.

Nardi, B. A. (2010), *My Life as a Night Elf Priest: An Anthropological Account of World of Warcraft*, Ann Arbor, MI: University of Michigan Press.

Nardi, B. and Harris, J. (2006), 'Strangers and Friends: Collaborative Play in *World of Warcraft*', in *Proceedings of the 2006 20th Anniversary Conference on Computer Supported Cooperative Work*, New York: ACM, pp. 149–58.

Newby P. (2009), *Research Methods for Education*, London and New York: Routledge.

Newman, J. (2008), *Playing with Video Games*, London: Routledge.

Newon (2011, forthcoming), 'Semiotic Creativity in the Digital Ecology of an MMORPG Guild', in C. Thurlow and K. Mroczek (eds), *Digital Discourse: Language in the New Media*, New York: Oxford University Press.

Neyland, D. (2008), *Organizational Ethnography*, London, UK: Sage Publications.

Niedenthal, S. (2009), 'What We Talk About When We Talk About Game Aesthetics', in *Breaking New Ground: Innovations in Games, Play, Practice and Theory. Proceedings of DiGRA 2009*: 1–9. Available online: http://www.digra.org/wp-content/uploads/digital-library/09287.17350.pdf [accessed 19 February 2015].

Nielsen, J. and Landauer, T. K. (1993), 'A Mathematical Model of the Finding of Usability Problems'. Proceedings of ACM INTERCHI'93 Conference (Amsterdam, The Netherlands, 24–29 April 1993), pp. 206–13.

Nisa, E. (2013), 'The Internet Subculture of Indonesian Face-veiled Women', *International Journal of Cultural Studies*, 16(3): 241–55.

Noddings, N. (1984), *Caring: A Feminine Approach to Ethics and Moral Education*, Berkeley: University of California Press.

Norris, P. and Inglehart, R. (2004), *Sacred and Secular: Religion and Politics Worldwide*, Cambridge: Cambridge University Press.

Nosek, B. A., Banaji, M. R. and Greenwald, A. G. (2002), 'Eresearch: Ethics, Security, Design, and Control in Psychological Research on the Internet', *Journal of Social Issues*, 58(1): 161–76.

Oakley, A. (2003), 'Interviewing Women: A Contradiction in Terms', in Y. Lincoln and N. Denzin (eds), *Turning Points in Qualitative Research: Tying Knots in a Handkerchief*, Walnut Creek, CA: Altamira Press, pp. 243–64.

O'Donnell, J. (2015), 'A Digital Devil's Saga. Representation(s) of the Demon in Recent Videogames', in S. Heidbrink, T. Knoll and J. Wysocki (eds), *Religion in Digital Games Reloaded. Immersion into the Field. Online – Heidelberg Journal of Religions on the Internet*, 7: 139–60. Available online: http://journals.ub.uni-heidelberg.de/index.php/religions/article/view/18511 [accessed 19 February 2015].

Office for National Statistics (2014), *Internet access – Households and individuals 2014. Statistical Bulletin*. Available online: http://www.ons.gov.uk/ons/dcp171778_373584.pdf [accessed 18 January 2015].

O'Lear, S. R. M. (1996), 'Using Electronic Mail (E-mail) Surveys for Geographic Research: Lessons from a Survey of Russian Environmentalists'. *The Professional Geographer*, 48(2): 209–17.

O'Leary, A. (2012), 'Christian Leaders are Powerhouses on Twitter', *The New York Times*, 2 June: A1. Available online: http://www.nytimes.com/2012/06/02/technology/christian-leaders-are-powerhouses-on-twitter.html/ [accessed 15 February 2015].

O'Leary, S. (1996), 'Cyberspace as Sacred Space: Communicating Religion on Computer Networks', *Journal of the American Academy of Religion*, 64: 781–808.

O'Neill, M. (2010), *Tzu Chi: Serving with Compassion*, Singapore: John Wiley & Sons.

Opinionator (2010a) 'Riots in Dudley, England. Reports of Muslim Gangs Attacking People'. Available online: http://theopinionator.typepad.com/my_weblog/2010/07/riots-in-dudley-uk-reports-of-muslim-gangs-attacking-people.html [accessed on 2 August 2010].

Opinionator (2010b) ' "Unusual" Violent Riots Break out in Dudley, England'. Available online: http://theopinionator.typepad.com/my_weblog/2010/07/unusual-riots-break-out-in-dudley-england.html [accessed on 2 August 2010].

Orpin, D. (2005), 'Corpus Linguistics and Critical Discourse Analysis: Examining the Ideology of Sleaze', *International Journal of Corpus Linguistics*, 10(1): 37–61.

Palgi, P. and Abramovitch, H. (1984), 'Death: A Cross-Cultural Perspective', *Annual Review of Anthropology*, 13: 385–417.

Pan, B., Hembrooke, H., Joachims, T., Lorigo, L., Gay, G. and Granka, L. (2007), 'In Google We Trust: Users' Decisions on Rank, Position, and Relevance', *Journal of Computer-Mediated Communication*, 12(3): 801–23.

Paolacci, G., Chandler, J. and Ipeirotis, P. G. (2010), 'Running Experiments on Amazon Mechanical Turk', *Judgment and Decision Making*, 5: 411–19.

Park, A., Curtice, J., Thomson, K., Phillips, M., Clery, E. and Butt, S. (2010), *British Social Attitudes: The 26th Report*, London, UK: Sage.

Pateman, C. (1989), *The Disorder of Women: Democracy, Feminism, and Political Theory*, Stanford, CA: Stanford University Press.

Pearce, C. and Artemesia (2009), *Communities of Play: Emergent Cultures in Multiplayer Games and Virtual Worlds*, Cambridge, MA: MIT Press.

Pearrow, M. (2000), *Web Site Usability Handbook*, Independence: Charles River Media.

Pêcheux, M. (1982), *Language, Semantics and Ideology*, London: MacMillan.

Pew Research Center (2011), *Muslim Americans: No Signs of Growth in Alienation or Support for Extremism*. The Pew Research Center.

Pew Research Center (2013), *The World's Muslims: Religion, Politics and Society*, The Pew Research Center. Available online: http://www.pewforum.org/files/2013/04/worlds-muslims-religion-politics-society-full-report.pdf [accessed 15 January 2015].

Piela, A. (2011), *Muslim Women Online: Faith and Identity in Virtual World*, London: Routledge.

Piela, A. (2013), 'I am Just Doing My Bit to Promote Modesty: Niqabis' Self-portraits on Photo-sharing Websites', *Feminist Media Studies*, 13(5): 781–90.

Piela, A. (2014a), 'You've Been Framed! Niqabis in the British Mass-media', *Public Spirit*, 22 January. Available online: http://www.publicspirit.org.uk/niqabis-in-the-british-mass-media/ [accessed 1 February 2015].

Piela, A. (2014b), 'British Niqabis' Identities in the Context of Policy and Media Discourses on Islam', MSc diss, Open University, Milton Keynes.

Piela, A. (forthcoming), *Wearing the Niqab*: *Fashioning Identities Among Muslim Women in the UK*, London: IB Tauris.

Pihlaja, S. (2011), 'Cops, Popes, Kings, and Garbagemen: A Case Study of Dynamic Metaphor Use in Asynchronous Internet Communication', *Language@Internet* [Online], 8. Available online: http://www.languageatinternet.org/articles/2011/Pihlaja/ [accessed 6 June 2013].

Pihlaja, S. (2014), *Antagonism on YouTube: Metaphor in Online Discourse*, London: Bloomsbury.

Pinker, S. (1997), *How the Mind Works*, New York: Norton.

Pontifical Council for Social Communications (22 Feb 2002), *Ethics in Internet, at the Vatican website*. Available online: www.vatican.va/roman_curia/pontifical_councils/pccs/documents/rc_pccs_doc_20020228_ethics-internet_en.html [accessed 12 September 2011].

Raessens, J. (2006), 'Playful Identities, or the Ludification of Culture', *Games and Culture*, 1(1): 52–7.

Ramazanoğlu, C. and Holland, J. (2002), *Feminist Methodology – Challenges and Choices*, London: Sage Publications.

Rand, D. G. (2012), 'The Promise of Mechanical Turk: How Online Labor Markets Can Help Theorists Run Behavioral Experiments', *Journal of Theoretical Biology*, 299: 172–9.

Rantakallio, I. (2011), 'Making Music, Making Muslims: A Case Study of Islamic Hip Hop and the Discursive Construction of Muslim Identities on the Internet', *Unpublished Masters Dissertation*, University of Helsinki. Available online: http://home.zcu.cz/~dkrizek/BVMV/SEM3/Islamic%20HipHop.pdf [accessed 17 July 2015].

Rao, U. (2009), 'Caste and the Desire for Belonging', *Asian Studies Review*, 33: 483–99.

Reeves, F. (2008), *Muslims and non-Muslims in the Black Country: Relations post-9/11*, Birmingham, UK: Waterhouse.

Reeves, F., Abbas, T. and Pedroso, D. (2009), 'The "Dudley Mosque Project": A Case of Islamophobia and Local Politics', *The Political Quarterly*, 80(4): 502–16.

Riley, John W., Jr. (1983), 'Dying and the Meaning of Death: Sociological Inquiries', *Annual Review of Sociology*, 9: 191–216.

Rodriguez, H. (2006), 'The Playful and the Serious: An approximation to Huizinga's *Homo Ludens*', *Game Studies*, 6(1). Available online: http://gamestudies.org/0601/articles/rodriges [accessed 19 February 2015].

Rosenberg, J. (2012), 'Jewish Experience on Film—An American Overview'. *American Jewish Year Book* 3: 50.

Rosenthal, S. (2008), *Jewish Healing Programs: Best Practices Sampler*, New York, NY: National Center for Jewish Healing.

Ross, J., Irani, I., Silberman, M., Six, M., Zaldivar, A. and Tomlinson, B. (2010), 'Who are the Crowdworkers?: Shifting Demographics in Amazon Mechanical Turk'. In *CHI EA 2010*. (2863–72).

Rothenberg, J. (1981), Demythologizing the Shtetl, in *Midstream* (March 1981): pp. 25–31.

Royle, M. H. and Shellhammer, D. (2007), 'Potential Response Bias in Internet Use for Survey Religious Research', *Review of Religious Research*, 49: 54–68.

Ruppert, E., Law, J. and Savage, M. (eds) (2013), 'Special Issue on the Social Life of Methods', *Theory, Culture & Society*, 30(4).

Ryan, M.-L. (2006), *Avatars of Story*, Minneapolis: University of Minnesota Press.

Saha, L. (1997) (ed.), *International Encyclopaedia of the Sociology of Education*, New York: Pergamon.

Saint-Blancat, C. and Schmidt di Friedberg, O. (2005), 'Why are Mosques a Problem? Local Politics and Fear of Islam in Northern Italy', *Journal of Ethnic and Migration Studies*, 31(6): 1083–104.

Salganik, M. J. and Heckathorn, D. D. (2004), 'Sampling and Estimation in Hidden Populations Using Respondent-driven Sampling', *Sociological Methodology*, 34(1): 193–240.

Salmon, G. (2010), 'Learning Innovation for the Twenty-First Century', in U. D. Ehlers and D. Schneckenberg (eds), *Changing Cultures in Higher Education*, Berlin: Springer, pp. 27–41.

Sandhu, H. S. (1990), *First Sikh history in English* [Google groups]. Available online: http://groups.google.com/group/soc.culture.indian/browse_thread/thread/1af815c08b7f74c7# [accessed 23 October 2011].

Sangera, G. and Thapar-Bjökert, S. (2008), 'Methodological Dilemmas: Gatekeepers and Positionality in Bradford', *Ethnic and Racial Studies*, 31(3): 543–62.

Savicki, V., Lingenfelter, D. and Kelley, M. (1996), 'Gender Language Style and Group Composition in Internet Discussion Groups', *Journal of Computer-Mediated Communication*, 2(3).

Sax, L. J., Gilmartin, S. K. and Bryant, A. N. (2003), 'Assessing Response Rates and Nonresponse Bias in Web and Paper Surveys', *Research in Higher Education*, 44(4): 409–32.

Sayyid, S. and AbdoolKarim, V. (2011), *Thinking Through Islamaphobia: Global Perspectives*, London: Hurst.

Scheifinger, H. (2008a), 'Researching Religion on the WWW: Identifying an Object of Study for Hinduism', *Methodological Innovations Online*, 2(3): 30–49.

Scheifinger, H. (2008b), 'Hinduism and Cyberspace', *Religion*, 38(3): 233–49.

Scheifinger, H. (2009), 'The Jagannath Temple and Online Darshan', *Journal of Contemporary Religion*, 24(3): 277–90.

Scheifinger, H. (2010), 'Om-line Hinduism: World Wide Gods on the Web', *Australian Religion Studies Review*, 23(3): 325–45.

Scheifinger, H. (2012), 'Internet', in Knut A. Jacobsen (ed.), *Brill's Encyclopedia of Hinduism* (Volume IV), Leiden: Brill, pp. 700–706.

Schofield, J. W. (2002), 'Increasing the Generalizability of Qualitative Research', in M. Hammersley (ed.), *The Qualitative Researcher's Companion*, Milton Keynes, UK: The Open University.

Schut, K. (2007), 'Strategic Simulations and Our Past: The Bias of Computer Games in the Presentation of History', *Games and Culture*, 2(3): 213–35.

Schut, K. (2014), 'They Kill Mystery: The Mechanistic Bias of Video Game Representations of Religion and Spirituality', in H. Campbell and G. P. Grieve (eds), *Playing with Religion in Digital Games*, Bloomington, IN: Indiana University Press, pp. 255–76.

Sehgal, M. (2007), 'The Veiled Feminist Ethnographer: Fieldwork Among Women of India's Hindu Right', in M. K. Huggins and M.-L. Glebbeek (eds), *Women Fielding Danger: Negotiating Ethnographic Identities in Field Research*, Plymouth: Rowman and Littlefield Publishers, pp. 325–52.

Sellers, M. (2006), 'Designing the Experience of Interactive Play', in P. Vorderer and J. Bryant (eds), *Playing Video Games: Motives, Responses and Consequences*, Mahwah, NJ: Lawrence Erlbaum Associates, Inc.

Shaghaghi, A., Bhopal, R. S. and Sheikh, A. (2011), 'Approaches to Recruiting "Hard to Reach" Populations into Research: A Review of the Literature', *Health Promotion Perspectives*, 1(2): 86–94.

Shah, I. (1980), *The Way of the Sufi*, London: Octagon Press.

Shattuck, C. (2003), *Hinduism*, London: Routledge.

Shaw, A. (2010), 'What is Video Game Culture? Cultural Studies and Game Studies': *Games and Culture*, 5(4): 403–24.

Shih, T.-H. and Fan, X. (2008), 'Comparing Response Rates from Web and Mail Surveys: A Meta-Analysis', *Field Methods*, 20(3): 249–71.

Shirky, C. (2009), *Here Comes Everybody: How Change Happens When People Come Together*, London: Penguin.

Shirky, C. (2009), *Here Comes Everybody: The Power of Organizing Without Organizations*, London: Penguin.

Sicart, M. (2009), *The Ethics of Computer Games*, Cambridge, MA and London: MIT Press.

Sikhiwiki.Org (n.d.), 'Encyclomedia of the Sikhs' [www]. Available online: http://www.sikhiwiki.org/index.php/Main_Page [accessed 4 November 2011].

Sikhs.org (n.d.), 'Whats new on the Sikhism home page' [www]. Available online: http://www.sikhs.org/whatnew.htm [accessed 4 February 2009].

Simkins, D. W. and Steinkuehler, C. (2008), 'Critical Ethical Reasoning and Role-Play', *Games and Culture*, 3(3–4): 333–55.

Singh, J. (2014), 'Sikh-ing Online: The Role of the Internet in the Religious Lives of Young British Sikhs'. *Contemporary South Asia* 22: 82–97. doi: 10.1080/09584935.2013.870974.

Singh, S. (2012), 'Attending the Cyber Sangat: The Use of Online Discussion Boards among European Sikhs', in K. Myrvold and K. A. Jacobsen (eds), *Sikhs Across Borders: Transnational Practices of European Sikhs*, London: Continuum, pp. 119–40.

Šisler, Vít (2014), 'From Kuma\War to Quraish: Representation of Islam in Arab and American Video Games', in: H. A. Campbell and G. P. Grieve (eds), *Playing with Religion in Digital Games*, Bloomington: Indiana University Press, pp. 109–33.

Smith, B. P. (2006), 'The (Computer) Games People Play: An Overview of Popular Game Content', in P. Vorderer and J. Bryant (eds), *Playing Video Games: Motives, Responses and Consequences*, Mahwah, NJ: Lawrence Erlbaum Associates, Inc, pp. 48–63.

Soc.Religion.Sikhism (1995), *Discussions* [Google groups]. Available online: http://groups.google.com/group/soc.religion.sikhism/topics?start=2010&sa– [accessed 13 November 2011].

Sokol, D. (2007) 'Sikh Diaspora in Cyberspace: The Representation of Khalistan on the World Wide Web and Its Legal Context', *Masaryk University Journal of Law and Technology*, 1(2): 219–30.

Sooryamoorthy, R. (2008), 'Untouchability in Modern India', *International Sociology*, 23: 283–93.

Spector, W. (2014), Interview (Online), in J. Johnson (2014), 'Is There a Jewish Identity in Video Games?'. Available online at http://killscreendaily.com/articles/there-jewish-identity-videogames/ [accessed 5 May 2015].

Spence, L. (2014), 'Between Institutional Oppression and Spiritual Liberation: The Female Ordination Movement in the Catholic Church and its Utilisation of Social Media.' Paper presented to the 18th ISA World Congress of Sociology, 13–19 July 2014, Yokohama, Japan.

Spivak, G. C. (1993), 'Can the Subaltern Speak?', in P. Williams and L. Chrisman (eds), *Colonial Discourse and Post-Colonial Theory: A Reader*, Hemel Hempstead: Harvester Wheatsheaf, pp. 90–105.

Squire, K. (2008), 'Open-Ended Video Games: A Model for Developing Learning for the Interactive Age', in K. Salen (ed.), *The Ecology of Games: Connecting Youth, Games, and Learning*, The John D. and Catherine T. MacArthur Foundation Series on Digital Media and Learning, Cambridge, MA: The MIT Press, pp. 67–88.

Srinivas, M. N. (1962), 'A Note on Sanskritization and Westernization', in Mysore N. Srinivas, *Caste in Modern India and Other Essays*, London: J.K. Publishers, pp. 42–62.

Stacey, J. (1991), 'Can There be a Feminist Ethnography?', in S. B. Gluck and D. Patai (eds), *Women's Words: The Feminist Practice of Oral History*, London: Routledge, pp. 111–20.

Stark, R. and Bainbridge, W. S. (1985), *The Future of Religion*, Berkeley, CA: University of California Press.

Stark, R. and Bainbridge, W. S. (1987), *A Theory of Religion*, New York: Lang.

Steinkuehler, C. A. (2006), 'Why Game (Culture) Studies Now?' *Games and Culture*, 1(1): 97–102.

Stussi, M. (2008), 'Banning of Minarets: Addressing the Validity of a Controversial Swiss Popular Initiative', *Religion and Human Rights*, 3(2): 135–53.

Sudman, S., Sirken, M. G. and Cowan, C. D. (1988), 'Sampling Rare and Elusive Populations', *Science*, 240: 991–6.

Sultana, F. (2007), 'Reflexivity, Positionality and Participatory Ethics: Negotiating Fieldwork Dilemmas in International Research', *ACME Journal*, 6. Available online: http://www.acme-journal.org/vol6/FS.pdf [accessed 1 February 2015].

Suri, S. and Watts, D. J. (2011), 'Cooperation and Contagion in Web-based, Networked Public Goods Experiments', *PloS One*, 6(3): doi:10.1371/journal.pone.0016836

Sutherland, G. H. (2003), 'The Wedding Pavilion: Performing, Recreating, and Regendering Hindu Identity in Houston', *International Journal of Hindu Studies*, 1–3: 117–46.

Tapoban.Org (n.d.), 'About: Gurdwara Tapoban Sahib' [www]. Available online: http://www.tapoban.org/about.php [accessed 23 December 2011].

Taras, R. (2012), *Xenophobia and Islamophobia in Europe*, Columbia, USA: Columbia University Press.

Tarlo, E. (2007), 'Hidden Features of the Face Veil Controversy', *ISIM Review*, 19. Available online: https://openaccess.leidenuniv.nl/bitstream/handle/1887/17112/ISIM_19_Hidden_Features_of_the_Face_Veil_Controversy.pdf?sequence=1 [accessed 1 March 2014].

Taylor, J. R. (2011), 'Organization as an (Imbricated) Configuring of Transactions', *Organization Studies*, 32: 1273–94.

Temko, N. (2006), 'BNP Targets Heart of England', *The Observer*, 23 April 2006.

Tétreault, M. A. (2001), 'Frontier Politics: Sex, Gender, and the Deconstruction of the Public Sphere', *Alternatives: Global, Local, Political*, 26(1): 53–72.

Thompson, J. B. (1990), *Ideology and Modern Culture: Critical Social Theory in the Era of Mass Communication*, Stanford, USA: Stanford University Press.

Thompson, P. (2007), 'Corpus, Concordance, Classification: Young Learners in the L1 Classroom', *Language Awareness*, 16(3): 208–16.

Tracey, P. (2012), 'Religion and Organization: A Critical Review of Current Trends and Future Directions', *Academy of Management Annals*, 6: 87–134.

Tsuria, R., Yadlin-Segal, A., Vitullo, A. and Campbell, H. A. (2015), Approaches to Digital Methods in Studies of Digital Religion. Unpublished Paper.

Turkle, S. (1985), *The Second Self: Computers and the Human Spirit*, London: Granada Publishing.

Turkle, S. (1997), *Life on the Screen: Identity in the Age of the Internet*, New York: Touchstone.

Twitchell, J. B. (2004), *Branded Nation. The Marketing of Megachurch, College Inc., and Museumworld*, New York: Simon & Schuster.

Tzu Chi Foundation (2011), *Tzu Chi Missions*. Available online: http://tw.TzuChi.org/en/index.php?option=com_content&view=article&id=293%3Atzu-chi-missions&catid=58%3Atzuchi&Item id=283&lang=en [accessed 8 January 2012].

van Dijk, T. A. (1998), *Ideology*, London: Sage.

Van Laar, C., Derks, B. and Ellemers, N. (2013), 'Motivation for Education and Work in Young Muslim Women: The Importance of Value for Ingroup Domains', *Basic and Applied Social Psychology*, 35(1): 64–74.

Vertovec, S. (1997), 'Hinduism in Diaspora: The Transformation of Tradition in Trinidad', in Günther-Dietz Sontheimer and Hermann Kulke (eds), *Hinduism Reconsidered*, New Delhi: Manohar, pp. 265–93.

Vis, F., van Zoonen, L. and Mihelj, S. (2011), 'Women Responding to the Anti-Islam Film *Fitna*: Voices and Acts of Citizenship on YouTube', *Feminist Review*, 97(1): 110–29.

Voas, D. (2009), 'The Rise and Fall of Fuzzy Fidelity in Europe', *European Sociological Review*, 25(2): 155–68.

Wadjet Eye Games (2006), *The Shivah: A Rabbinical Adventure*, Los Altos: Wadjet Eye.

Wagner, R. (2012), 'You Are What You Install: Religious Authenticity and Identity in Mobile Apps', in H. Campbell (ed.), *Digital Religion: Understanding Religious Practice in New Media Worlds*, Abingdon: Routledge, pp. 199–206.

Warf, B. and Winsberg, M. (2010), 'Geographies of Megachurches in the United States', *Journal of Cultural Geography*, 27(1): 33–51.

Warner, R. S. (1993), 'Work in Progress toward a New Paradigm for the Sociological Study of Religion in the United States', *American Journal of Sociology*, 98: 1044–93.

Warren, M. (2007), 'Online Surveys and Qualitative Analysis: A Contradiction in Terms?' Available online: http://www.research.plymouth.ac.uk/methodologicalinnovations/Methods07/Presentations/warren.pps [accessed 21 March 2011].

Warwick, K. (2004), *I, Cyborg* (2nd edn), Urbana: University of Illinois Press.

web.archive.org [consulted on several occasions between October 2012 and June 2014]

Webb, S. (2000), 'Feminist Methodologies for Social Researching', in Dawn Burton (ed.), *Research Training for Social Scientists*, London: Sage Publications, pp. 33–48.

Weick, K. E. (1979), *The Social Psychology of Organizing*, 2nd edn, New York, NY: McGraw-Hill.

Weller, P. (ed.) (1997), *Religions in the UK: A Multi-Faith Directory*, Derby: University of Derby in association with the Inter Faith Network for the UK.

Weller, P. (1998a), 'MultiFaithNet: Religionen on Line', in R. Kirste and U. Tworushka (eds), *Religionen in Gespräch, Band 5, Die Dialogische Kraft des Mystischen*, Balve: Zimmerman Druck und Verlag GMbh, Germany, pp. 513–19.

Weller, P. (1998b), 'Multi-Faith Information Resources: Religions in the UK and MultiFaithNet', *Bulletin of the Association of British Theological and Philosophical Libraries*, 5 (2): 19–33.

Weller, P. (ed.) (2007), *Religions in the UK: Directory, 2007–2010*, Derby: Multi-Faith Centre at the University of Derby in association with the Inter Faith Network for the UK.

Weller, P. and Contractor, S. (2012a), *Learning from Experience, Leading to Engagement: Belieforama Policy Brief Research for European Institutions and Civil Societies*, Brussels: Belieforama. Available online: http://www.belieforama.eu/sites/default/files/documents/Belieforama-full-policy-brief_0.pdf [accessed 16 January 2015].

Weller P. and Contractor S. (2012b), *Learning from Experience, Leading to Engagement: Belieforama Policy Brief Research for European Institutions and Civil Societies: Executive Summary* (in seven languages), Brussels: Belieforama. Available online: http://www.belieforama.eu/sites/default/files/documents/2012-10%2520EXE%2520SUM%2520PB%2520PRINT.pdf [accessed 16 January 2015].

Weller, P., Feldman, A. and Purdam, K. et al. (2001), *Religious Discrimination in England and Wales. Home Office Research Report 220*. London: Research, Development and Statistics Directorate, The Home Office. Available online: http://webarchive.nationalarchives.gov.uk/20070507055347/http://communities.gov.uk/pub/945/ReligiousdiscriminationinEnglandandWales_id1504945.pdf. [accessed 16 January 2015].

Weller, P., Hooley, T. and Moore, N. (2011), *Religion and Belief in Higher Education: The Experiences of Staff and Students*, London: Equality Challenge Unit.

Weller, P., Purdam, K., Ghanea, N. and Cheruvallil-Contractor, S. (2013a), *Religion and Belief, Discrimination and Equality: Britain in Global Contexts*, London: Bloomsbury.

Weller, P., Purdam, K., Ghanea, N. and Cheruvallil-Contractor, S. (2013b), *Religion and Belief, Discrimination and Equality in England and Wales: A Decade of Continuity and Change. A Research Informed Policy Brief, 2013*, June 2013. Derby: University of Derby. Available online: http://www.derby.ac.uk/media/derbyacuk/contentassets/documents/ehs/collegeofeducation/centreofsocietyreligionandbelief/tpp/Research-informed-policy-brief.pdf [accessed 16 January 2015].

Wellman, B. (1997), 'An Electronic Group is Virtually a Social Network', in S. Kielser (ed.), *Culture of the Internet*, Mahwah, NJ: Lawrence Erlbaum, pp. 179–205.

Werbner, P. and Basu, H. (eds) (1998), 'Introduction', in *Embodying Charisma: Modernity, Locality and the Performance of Emotion in Sufi Cults*, London and New York: Routledge.

Wertheim, M. (1999), *The Pearly Gates of Cyberspace*, London: Virago.

West, A., Lewis, J. and Currie, P. (2009), 'Students Facebook "friends": Public and Private Spheres', *Journal of Youth Studies*, 12(6): 615–27.

Whiteman, N. (2012), *Undoing Ethics: Rethinking Practice in Online Research*, New York, Heidelberg, London: Springer.

Williams, D., Duchenaut, N., Xiong, L., Yuanyuan Z., Yee, N. and Nickell, E. (2006), 'From Tree House to Barracks: The Social Life of Guilds in *World of Warcraft*', *Games and Culture*, 1: 338–61.

Williams, M. (2003), 'The Problem of Representation: Realism and Operationalism in Survey Research', *Sociological Research Online*, 8(1). Available online: http//www.socresonline. org.uk/8/1/williams.html [accessed 17 July 2015].

Williams, R. (1988), *Religions of Immigrants from India and Pakistan: New Threads in the American Tapestry*, Cambridge: Cambridge University Press.

Wodak, R. and Meyer, M. (2001), *Methods of Critical Discourse Analysis*, London: Sage.

Wolf, M. J. P. (ed.) (2003a), *Virtual Morality: Morals, Ethics and New Media*, London: Peter Lang Publishing.

Wolf, M. J. P. (2003b), 'Abstractions in the Video Game', in M. J. P. Wolf. and B. Perron (eds), *The Video Game Theory Reader*, New York: Routledge, pp. 47–66.

Wood, R. T. A., Griffiths, M. D. and Eatough, V. (2004), 'Online Data Collection from Video Game Players: Methodological Issues', *Cyberpsychology & Behaviour*, 7(5): 511–18.

Yee, N. (2014), *The Proteus Paradox*, New Haven, CT: Yale University Press.

Yianlios, P. (n.d.), 'The Franklin Bible', *PNYLabs.com*. Available online: http://pnylab.com/ pny/products/bible/main.html [accessed 15 February 2015].

Youngs, G. (2009), 'Blogging and Globalization: The Blurring of the Public/Private Spheres', *Aslib Proceedings*, 61(2): 127–38.

YouTube (2008), *YouTube Privacy Policy* [Online]. Available online: http://uk.youtube.com/t/ privacy [accessed 11 November 2008].

YouTube (2010) *Sant Jarnail Singh Bhindranwale speech* [Video online]. Available online: http://www.youtube.com/watch?v=57YuzG8oslw [accessed 9 October 2011].

YouTube (2011) *How To Tie A Turban (Pagh)* [Video online]. Available online: http://www. youtube.com/watch?v=i6gBwv4fjDU [accessed 29 July 2011].

YouVersion (2013a), 'Our Year with the Bible – Infographic', *YouVersion.com*. Available online: http://blog.youversion.com/2013/12/our-year-with-the-bible-infographic/ [accessed 15 February 2015].

YouVersion (2013b), 'How the Bible is Shared – Infographic', *YouVersion.com*. Available online: http://blog.youversion.com/2013/07/how-the-bible-is-shared-infographic/ [accessed 15 February 2015].

YouVersion (2014a), 'Introducing Bible App 5', *YouVersion.com*. Available online: http:// blog.youversion.com/2014/04/introducing-bible-app-5/ [accessed 15 February 2015].

YouVersion (2014b), 'Our Year with the Bible Infographic 2014', *YouVersion.com*. Available online: http://blog.youversion.com/2014/12/our-year-with-the-bible-infographic-2014/ [accessed 15 February 2015].

Zagal, J. P., Fernandez-Vara, C. and Mateas, M. (2008), 'Rounds, Levels, and Waves: The Early Evolution of Gameplay Segmentation', *Games and Culture*, 3(2): 175–98.

Zaleski, J. (1997), *The Soul of Cyberspace: How Technology is Changing our Spiritual Lives*, San Francisco: Harper San Francisco.

Zborowski, M. and Herzog, E. (1962), *Life is With People: The Culture of the Shtetl*, Toronto: Schocken.

Zimmerman, E. (2013), *Manifesto for a Ludic Century* [Online]. Available online: http:// ericzimmerman.com/files/texts/Manifesto_for_a_Ludic_Century.pdf [accessed 5 May 2015].

Index